D1527399

Without Foundations

Without Foundations

Justification in Political Theory

DON HERZOG

Cornell University Press

ITHACA AND LONDON

First published 1985 by Cornell University Press.
Published in the United Kingdom by
Cornell University Press Ltd., London.

International Standard Book Number 0-8014-1723-6
Library of Congress Catalog Card Number 84-21492
Printed in the United States of America
*Librarians: Library of Congress cataloging information
appears on the last page of the book.*

*The paper in this book is acid-free and meets the guidelines for
permanence and durability of the Committee on Production Guidelines
for Book Longevity of the Council on Library Resources.*

For my teachers

CONTENTS

PREFACE

This book is about justification: about how political theorists argue for their views, how they structure their theories, why they draw on some fields and neglect others. Though I've been immersed in the subject for several years, I still have a glimmering of awareness that justification is one of those more or less arcane topics generally left to professional philosophers. I got entangled (or entangled myself) in the questions pursued here in a perfectly straightforward way, however.

What interested me from the start in political theory was the unabashed concern of that discipline with so-called normative or prescriptive or evaluative matters. Unlike the fabled politician on the stump, political theorists do much more than announce how the world ought to be. They devote themselves to working out arguments on these matters, arguments designed to justify their conclusions. Like everyone else, I suppose, I was initially intrigued by the colorful variety of causes supported in the history of political theory. That very variety, though, provoked worries about the business of arguing. How could political theorists justify their views? Did they have to forge some spectacular bridge over an is/ought gap? Should they find eternal and immutable principles of morality, or could they confidently invoke our shared moral judgments? Could nature serve as a critical standard? Was there a first philosophy of politics that would yield axioms? Such questions motivated this study.

[9]

PREFACE

Readers not particularly interested in justification will, I hope, still find much of interest here. There is a large literature on justification, but most of it seems to me just too far away from any concrete issue to be of much use. The introduction and conclusion aside, then, I develop the argument by scrutinizing the works of Thomas Hobbes, John Locke, six utilitarians, David Hume, and Adam Smith. I have not restricted my attention to their major works, so my interpretations involve some shifts of emphasis and some outright departures from the secondary literature. And I have not used these theorists to mount a case for the ancients or against the bourgeoisie: I have not sought to show that their failures dictate reclaiming the conceptual or political world of Athens; nor have I indicted the corrupt cultural content of their works to reveal the limits of capitalism. Instead I have tried to take them simply as theorists advancing arguments. As a result, the interpretations I offer are, I hope, faithful to the texts.

Talk of faithful interpretations may summon up recondite issues in hermeneutics. So a word is in order on the method I adopt in dealing with the history of political theory. Much has been written recently on the importance of history and social context in interpreting texts, and indeed there are good reasons for denying that political theorists escape their times and write works we can interpret without any reference to their contexts. Their agendas are set partly by the burning issues of the day; there are certain things they need not mention explicitly to their audiences, who will take them for granted (as indeed the theorists may); words change their meanings over time; and since social structures change, there will be ways in which their worlds are quite different from ours. These rather banal premises suggest that the interpretation of an author's text must draw on contingent considerations about the author's time. Accordingly, I have been guided here by such considerations, though they are hardly prominent in my text. The text has its contexts, and these are in part historically defined.

I do not believe, however, that history is valuable because it enables us to recapture the author's intentions, to reconstruct the

[1 0]

ghostly mental life of Thomas Hobbes as he drafted *Leviathan*. Hobbes claimed it was:

> Though words be the signs we have of one another's opinions and intentions; yet, because the equivocation of them is so frequent according to the diversity of contexture, and of the company wherewith they go (which the presence of him that speaketh, our sight of his actions, and conjecture of his intentions, must help to discharge us of): it must be extreme hard to find out the opinions and meanings of those men that are gone from us long ago, and have left us with no other signification thereof but their books; which cannot possibly be understood without history enough to discover those aforementioned circumstances, and also without great prudence to observe them.[1]

But the meaning of a text is not bound up in the author's (mentalistically cast) intentions. There are technical reasons for resisting that view of interpretation; it must be extremely hard, even with history and prudence, to have any confidence in an estimation of an author's intentions. But the case against intentions hardly hinges on technical niceties. Divine authorship aside, texts regularly display more and less than the author's intentions: more in that the author may be surprised at some elements of his work; less in that some ideas may never quite make it onto the page.

Interpretation, I suggest, is more like solving a jigsaw puzzle than like conjuring up the ghost in a defunct machine. We want a reading that illuminates the text, that resolves puzzles and doubts, that orders what can be ordered and shows why the rest can't be. The author's own view of the work, in letters or prefaces, may be helpful but can never be authoritative. I can put the point polemically. Interpreting the works of John Locke would present just the same challenges if Locke were a robot, if half the volumes were dashed off by his friend Molyneux, or if they all descended from the starry skies. And if *Hamlet* is ever written by

[1]Thomas Hobbes, *The Elements of Law Natural and Politic*, ed. Ferdinand Tönnies, 2d ed. (New York: Barnes & Noble, 1969), p. 68 (*The English Works of Thomas Hobbes*, ed. William Molesworth, 11 vols. [London, 1839–1845], IV: 75).

the fabled monkeys hammering away at their typewriters or by a computer spewing out random letters, interpreting it will pose just the same problems as interpreting the *Hamlet* Shakespeare wrote.

I owe much to friends and teachers, and happily I have found that the two roles are not mutually exclusive. Isaac Kramnick and Richard Polenberg of Cornell University, still unfailingly helpful, refrain from reminding me what a callow undergraduate I was. Stephen Holmes, Judith Shklar, and Michael Walzer taught me, more than I noticed then, in graduate school at Harvard University. I spent 1982–83 at the Institute for Advanced Study as Walzer's assistant and there revised the manuscript. While I was in Princeton, Amy Gutmann and Bernie Yack of Princeton University provided searching comments; I profited too from talks with Patricia Smith Churchland, Paul Churchland, Michael Doyle, and Allan Silver, all spending the year at the Institute. At various stages, Bruce Fink, Carleton Montgomery, Stephen Newman, Michael Sandel, and Andy Stark have commented on different chapters. I have come to rely heavily on Shelley Burtt's painstaking comments.

I hope all these people realize that my more or less gruff reactions were and are accompanied by abiding gratitude.

D.H.

Ann Arbor, Michigan

Without Foundations

INTRODUCTION

How can political theorists justify accounts of how the world ought to be? of what obligations citizens of democratic states have? of whether the state is legitimate? of when disobedience might be permissible? of whether liberal societies should pursue egalitarian policies? of what sort of tolerance is due radicals and terrorists? of what interest the state should take in promoting morality?

These questions are my concern. I should emphasize at once, however, that I have nothing to say on any of the concrete issues, tantalizing though they are. This book is about methodology, about the strategies of justification that political theorists use. The blizzard of arguments on concrete issues can become confusing. We begin to wonder just what sort of enterprise political theory is. What are we doing? How can we justify the views we recommend? Here I deliberately step outside the first-order business of arguing for some political views. My aim is to shed some light on the second-order questions. What might be a viable justification in political theory? Such questions of method are hardly interesting in themselves. With a clearer sense of the issues they raise, though, we can perhaps pursue the intriguing political questions in more perspicuous ways.

Again, my focus is on justification itself. There are plenty of arguments to be found here on legitimacy, obligation, and disobedience; on the rule of law; on free markets and religious toleration. But I dwell on the structure of these arguments, not their content. Talk of justification and methodology is at least a trifle bewildering; we are more at home with issues of substance. Exactly what is justification? Perhaps the best way to begin explaining it is to borrow a vocabulary from a neighboring field. Consider a sketch of the different projects available in moral theory.

A theorist may seek to explicate our shared moral views. Though the identity of the relevant community may be doubtful, and though some views are more widely shared or more firmly held than others, we do find some shared views. Presumably most twentieth-century Americans would agree that torturing innocent people is wrong. We share many such judgments, but we are often at a loss to explain how they cohere. An explication of a moral view is a suggested structure for it, a set of basic principles that yields pretty much the same judgments we do. Given such an explication, we may surmise that we were unconsciously employing that structure all along. But even if we were not, the explication may be a good one.

There is then the business of developing an adequate genealogy for a set of views, an explanatory theory showing why we hold them. Such theories may focus on principles of psychology, arguing that people, constituted as they are, come to hold certain views. Or they may focus on history, investigating the impact of some important development. Doubtless there are mixtures of these, and still other possibilities.

A particularly puzzling field is moral psychology, puzzling perhaps because it investigates so many different questions. Can someone do something just because it is right? How? How is weakness of will possible? Or was Socrates right after all? How are the virtues and vices developed? How do they connect up with deliberation, intention, and purposive action? What relation has morality to guilt, integrity, resentment, and self-consciousness? And so on.

Moral theorists may seek to identify what is special about moral discourse. Certain maneuvers seem appropriate in moral argument ("but that would harm her"), others out of place ("better remember he's bigger than you are"), even changing the nature of the argument. Why is that? In more theoretical terms, what rules define the moral language-game? Furthermore, how do moral concepts work? What commitments are built into the language of morality as it stands?

Finally, there is a distinctive part of epistemology and metaphysics devoted to morality. What sort of entity is the good? Is morality subjective, objective, or neither? Is there knowledge of moral truths? How do we arrive at such knowledge? How do we recognize moral error? Such questions these days are generally called meta-ethical.

Justification is none of these projects. Regardless of what structure our views have, where they came from, or what psychology they connect up with, we want to know if they're the right views. We justify a set of views to satisfy ourselves that they are. Justification, then, is not only different from genealogy, explication, and the rest; at least at first blush, it seems independent of them. Yet these projects are often run together haphazardly. While there may be systematic connections among them, we must be clear about what given theorists are attempting. Only then will we know what evidence they should be adducing and what counter-evidence we may adduce in turn.

Suppose we are discussing some thorny political question. It could be a more or less concrete question, such as whether the United States should refuse to sell grain to the Soviet Union. It could be some broader policy question, such as whether Medicaid should fund abortions on demand for the poor. It could even be some sweepingly general question, such as whether secular liberal society is a depraved mess, as critics on the right and left have claimed.

We might disagree emphatically on any of these questions. I might balk at your stubborn refusal to recognize manifest good sense, and I might find myself horrified to discover your belief that all the manifest good sense lies on your side of the issue. We might be inclined to disagree, but find ourselves unsure of just what the right position is. We might have no particular inclinations at all. Perhaps each of us has always been puzzled by the case against modernity.

Regardless of the issue and regardless of our initial attitudes, we are likely to find ourselves seeking intelligent arguments on these matters, for we want more than the fact of agreement. After all, we might be challenged as soon as we left our familiar surroundings. Or we might suspect that, though "everyone" agrees, we happen to agree on the wrong position. Should we hold one view instead of another?

Disagreement and doubt thus create the demand for justification. Unless we are willing to let political debate collapse into posturing and invective, we want to be able to provide reasons for our views, good reasons, terrific reasons if we can. We may even want to prove that our views are correct. We want, in a word, to be able to justify our views.

But how can we justify them? There are no recipes on file for accomplishing the trick, no algorithms, no consultants who will justify any view for a fee: Plato detested the Sophists at least partly for their purporting to do just that. Nor is it clear what sort of argument should count as a justification. Justification, it turns out, is an essentially contestable concept. Must we prove that our view is right? Must we show its deep connections with the fabric of the universe? Can we provide a preponderance of good reasons for it? Will it suffice to show that our considered intuitions yield the view?

There is an especially attractive example of justification, one that has haunted discussion of these matters since Euclid and that has left theorists such as Hobbes enchanted.[1] That example is the geometric proof, an argument commencing from self-evident axioms and proceeding by rigid deduction to its conclusions. The image remains attractive even when we concede that geometry doesn't really work that way, any more than our em-

---

[1] *Aubrey's Brief Lives*, ed. Oliver Lawson Dick (London: Secker and Warburg, 1950), p. 150: "He was 40 yeares old before he looked on Geometry; which happened accidentally. Being in a Gentleman's Library, Euclid's Elements lay open, and 'twas the 47 *El. libri* I. He read the Proposition. *By G—*, sayd he (he would now and then sweare an emphaticall Oath by way of emphasis) *this is impossible*! So he reads the Demonstration of it, which referred him back to such a Proposition; which proposition he read. That referred him back to another, which he also read. *Et sic deinceps* [and so on] that at last he was demonstratively convinced of that trueth. This made him in love with Geometry."

pirical knowledge does. It is difficult to imagine a more compelling justification: one must grant the premises, and, unless one is willing to dispute the laws of logic, one must grant what follows deductively.

Return for a moment to Medicaid and abortion. Suppose I suggest that the poor ought not to be deprived of Medicaid funding for abortion on demand. On being challenged to justify my view, I might offer a syllogism. I might argue that the poor ought not to be denied basic opportunities enjoyed by the rich, that denying the poor funding for abortion does deny them a basic opportunity enjoyed by the rich, and so presto! my view follows deductively.

But the conclusion is no better than its premises. Any view, whether true or false, appealing or outrageous, can be supported by some syllogism. As I may be crestfallen to discover, then, my syllogism settles nothing. Anyone reasonably adept in these matters will instantly challenge my major premise. What is wrong with denying the poor basic opportunities enjoyed by the rich? Now I urge that we ought not to be unjust, and I unveil a new syllogism, one with a more abstract major premise: it is unjust to deny the poor equality of opportunity; denying the poor basic opportunities enjoyed by the rich denies them equality of opportunity; therefore it is unjust to deny the poor basic opportunities enjoyed by the rich. Presumably I need not wait long for another challenge.

How might this argument end? There are several familiar possibilities. First is the infinite regress: it never ends at all. However abstract the major premise, it can be questioned, and a new syllogism can always be yanked out of the hat. Second is a collision with some brute fact: eventually some major premise will be true, but there will be no explanation of why. Other possibilities can be left aside: a loop in the chain of syllogisms, so that the thirty-ninth leads back to the fourteenth, or Nozick's self-subsumption, by which a premise explains itself.[2] The most enticing possibility is that of finding a self-evident major premise.

[2]Robert Nozick, *Philosophical Explanations* (Cambridge, Mass.: Harvard University Press, Belknap Press, 1981), pp. 119–121, 131–137.

Should I find such a premise, I may congratulate myself on having finished the argument decisively. I may believe I have produced a classically geometric justification. No one can deny the premise; no one subscribing to the meager principles of formal logic can quibble with what follows deductively.

There are, though, already some notable differences between a geometric proof and my imagined political argument, for the minor premises of my argument may be controversial. Its concepts may be fuzzy around the edges in politically crucial ways. A conservative might well suggest that denying the poor basic opportunities enjoyed by the rich is not the same as denying them equality of opportunity. She might urge that if the poor have the chance to be rich, if there have been no important legal barriers to their ascending the ladder of income distribution, they do enjoy equality of opportunity. Then we might spar over the relevant understanding of equality of opportunity. Here I want only to note that it will come as no surprise to find such champions of geometry as Hobbes insisting on rigorous definitions.

Now we can abandon Medicaid and abortion. The conception of justification this imagined argument summons up should be clear: one finds axiomatic premises and then deduces the position to be justified. Philosophers have traditionally called this a foundationalist view of justification, and I will adopt their coinage here. But I do not wish to treat the geometric model as the sum and substance of foundationalism. Instead I take it as an especially vivid member of a broader class of arguments. That broader class is what I call foundationalist. One way to characterize its salient features is this: any political justification worthy of the name must be grounded on principles that are (1) undeniable and immune to revision and (2) located outside society and politics. The first proviso allows for alternatives to self-evidence: perhaps no rational agent would deny the principles, or experience would be impossible without them, or we can show that God has promulgated them. The second proviso is deliberately open-ended: the foundationalists I discuss in this volume appeal to unalterable facts of human nature, to language, to theology and principles of rationality, and more.

This characterization of foundationalism is more suggestive than sharply defined. One might well desire a much crisper account. In what sense must the premises be undeniable? Must they be immune to revision from any and all quarters, or just from some quarters? Language is as thoroughly a social creation as anything else; just what does it mean to say language is outside society and politics? But I will not offer any further abstract account of foundationalism. Indeed I believe the demand for one should be resisted. For many theoretical concepts, definitions are either unavailable or unhelpful; foundationalism is one such concept. Yet definition is not the only way to gain an understanding of a concept. One alternative—a decidedly better one here—is to get a rough sense of what the concept is about and then to examine some instantiations of it. A suggestive characterization is enough to alert us to family resemblances without blinding us to interesting differences among members of the family. Besides, as I will note shortly, foundationalism is in part incurably metaphorical.

In any case, the general idea of a foundational argument is familiar enough to begin. Foundationalism often seems the very model of justification. Only a foundational argument, we want to say, could possibly provide a justification. Indeed there are good reasons for finding such arguments attractive; they have a number of genuine virtues I am happy to concede. Typically they are masterpieces of clarity and rigor. They derive enormous critical power by applying a set of extrapolitical standards to politics. They move far more briskly and decisively than our everyday political arguments. They boast immutable first principles that would give political theorists a fair claim to the timelessness they often seek. If they worked, they would resolve all our doubts and disagreements—even the kind of doubts generated by skeptics, the sort who will question any view, any premise, however sensible it seems.

But they do not work. That is a historical claim: I know of no successful foundationalist argument in political theory, or, for that matter, in any other field. However attractive it may seem, then, foundationalism is the view I mean to attack. I have no airtight metatheoretical case to offer, no way of showing that foundational arguments are doomed to fail; the issues at stake are forbiddingly abstruse. I can suggest immediately, though, that if Plato, Hobbes, Kant, Sidgwick, and countless brilliant others all failed, the reasonable hypothesis is that they were trying to square a circle. In the course of the discussion I will offer some other observations on the flaws of foundationalism.

Since we learn more by doggedly sticking with concrete contexts, though, I examine some actual political theories—those of Hobbes, Locke, some classical and contemporary utilitarians, and finally Hume and Smith. These writers are not quite liberals one and all, but they are a representative collection of the varied facets of the liberal tradition. And I will have much that is critical to say about their theories. Let me then again emphasize the methodological focus of this study. The study is not another exercise in liberal-bashing, now and then a fashionable sport. Nor for that matter does my qualified endorsement of Hume and Smith comprise an endorsement of liberalism. Lest my concern with justification vanish as I work through the theories, I offer here an overview of what I will say.

The chapter on Hobbes might be situated squarely in the literature on the obligation controversy. There, however, the attempt often seems to be to compile a dictionary entry under "Hobbes, obligation in." We find Oakeshott, for example, carefully distinguishing what he takes to be genuine obligations from pretender candidates in Hobbes.[3] I wish here to redefine the question a bit and pursue an explanatory puzzle: given his skeptical views on evaluative discourse, how can Hobbes draw so freely on the moral concepts? Neither of the major readings worked out in the literature—that Hobbes's argument is purely prudential, or that it includes moral considerations stemming from God—seems satisfactory. I argue that Hobbes tries to develop, side by side with his prudential argument, a wholly secular moral argument. He wants to show that his conclusions are built into the moral and political concepts. But the substantial questions of morals and politics can hardly be settled by defini-

[3]Michael Oakeshott, "Introduction to *Leviathan*," in his *Hobbes on Civil Association* (Berkeley: University of California Press, 1975), pp. 64–69.

tional maneuvers, however skilfully executed. Nor does the prudential argument, while promising, suffice to justify its conclusions. I argue that the generality of the argument, its ahistorical appearance, vitiates it. I argue too that Hobbes's appeals to necessity have no force.

The chapter on Locke falls into three parts. First I turn my attention to the *Second Treatise*, which seems to me best understood as three independent social-contract arguments conducted together. The text of course is not so clear: the three-contract reading is idealized, a rational reconstruction rather than mere repetition. I offer it neither to recapture Locke's inchoate thoughts nor to outline his "teaching," but rather to impose order on the text without mangling it. Locke's three uses of the social contract leave him with a historical case against Filmer, a theory of political obligation hanging on consent, and a theory of legitimacy hanging on the hypothetical choices of rational agents. Nowhere in the *Treatises*, however, does Locke try to explain the force of appealing to consent or rational choice. Second, then, I survey his other writings for a theory that will do the necessary work. Again with a bit of idealizing, I find a striking moral theory centering on God and pleasure. Rational agents, Locke holds, will maximize their pleasure by responding to the allure of heaven and the threat of hell. They will live the moral life God demands of us. Third, I ask whether the moral theory, even if it did work, would prop up the political theory. I conclude it would not.

I treat utilitarianism as one doctrine. While there are of course differences among the theories of Bentham, Mill, Sidgwick, Harsanyi, Hare, and Brandt, differences to which I pay some attention, the similarities warrant grouping them together. It might seem that this chapter has little to do with political theory, since it neglects politics. Quite simply, I wish to suggest that utilitarianism has nothing to do with politics or morality or anything else in the world. The utilitarian calculus is radically incomplete. I do not mean that it diverges from our convictions about fairness or justice. Since explication is different from justification, a utilitarian can dismiss such convictions as misguided. (The literature arguing that utilitarianism doesn't match our "moral intuitions" thus seems irrelevant or at least not decisive.)

I argue that utilitarianism has zany implications, but only to emphasize that accepting it would be far more than systematizing what Sidgwick calls the morality of common sense. I mean rather that utilitarianism, for all its vaunted rigor and precision, fails to set out a procedure for making choices. Handed a utilitarian handbook and all the desired information about possible worlds and mental states, a dedicated genius would find that the handbook lacked sufficient instructions to make recommendations. Should that be so, the literature on utilitarianism would take on a comic tone. For the debate over whether we should make utilitarian choices would have to collapse into a debate over what a utilitarian choice would be. Nor, as I argue, do utilitarians give us any reason to adopt their standard.

I argue, then, that Hobbes, Locke, and the utilitarians fail to justify their conclusions. I do so not because I love to shred theories, but because I want to clear the ground for a different way of conceiving justification. For all the differences in their theories, Hobbes, Locke, and the utilitarians try to justify their conclusions by digging into increasingly remote and abstract terrain. Hobbes may turn to language, Locke to divine command, and the utilitarians to the principle of utility, but in each case the motivation is the same: to try to find foundations that will support their conclusions. It is possible that they fail just because they don't find the right foundation, but I wish instead to suggest that there is something strange about the quest for foundations.

So I turn to the theories of Hume, not properly a utilitarian at all, and Smith. Their theories have no foundations, and that is why they succeed as much as they do. Neither man's works are canonized in the traditional line of classics of political theory. Today Hume is a philosopher first and foremost and, with grumbling concessions, a historian on the side; Smith is an economist, an analyst of the market, and secondarily the author of a minor work in ethics. Both writers do argue about politics, however, and the strategy of justification they employ seems appealing. Briefly, they justify an institution by showing that it is better than the available alternatives. I call this approach contextual justification. A political theory of this sort, instead of fleeing the profane world of facts into the sacred realm of value, will necessarily bring in historical considerations, sometimes extensively. It will draw on our moral and political beliefs to help rank what is better, but it will force them to collide with history and society, and so will criticize them. It will also have to rely on social theory to buttress its claims about counterfactual worlds. Finally, Hume and Smith will be unable to offer a timeless teaching, a set of political principles supposed to hold transhistorically. These points may seem to militate against taking their approach as a model. Yet that, I wish to urge, is just how we should take it.

There is a touch of irony in nominating Hume as a model in these matters. For the problem of justification, as it is often cast, is inextricably bound up with the celebrated is/ought gap bequeathed by Hume:

> I cannot forbear adding to these reasonings an observation, which may, perhaps, be found of some importance. In every system of morality, which I have hitherto met with, I have always remark'd, that the author proceeds for some time in the ordinary way of reasoning, and establishes the being of a God, or makes observations concerning human affairs; when of a sudden I am surpriz'd to find, that instead of the usual copulations of propositions, *is*, and *is not*, I meet with no proposition that is not connected with an *ought*, or *ought not*. This change is imperceptible; but is, however, of the last consequence. For as this *ought*, or *ought not*, expresses some new relation or affirmation, 'tis necessary that it shou'd be observ'd and explain'd; and at the same time that a reason should be given, for what seems altogether inconceivable, how this new relation can be a deduction from others, which are entirely different from it.[4]

Worries about the is/ought gap have made justifying a prescriptive view seem perfectly intractable, our options unutterably bleak. If our grounding principles lie in the realm of fact, how can we ever cross over into the realm of value? But how can we find normative grounding principles with the right sort of solidity? Some philosophers have sought to show that Hume was

[4]David Hume, *A Treatise of Human Nature*, ed. L. A. Selby-Bigge, 2d ed. rev. by P. H. Nidditch (Oxford: Clarendon, 1980), pp. 469–470. Hume's italics.

ironic or simply mistaken, that there are valid deductive arguments from is to ought, fact to value. I will take a different tack. For what it's worth, I think that Hume did hold that we cannot deduce ought from is and that he was right to say so. In the quoted paragraph Hume even provides a shrewd hint on how to demolish arguments that purport to do so. But when it comes to justifying a political theory, the is/ought gap is irrelevant—provided we scrap the foundationalist program. I return to these matters in the conclusion, where I will be better equipped to discuss them.

For now, I can simply summarize the strategy of the book. I mean to criticize foundationalism by examining Hobbes, Locke, and utilitarianism, and to defend contextualism by examining Hume and Smith. That strategy, of course, is excessively neat and tidy, and will provoke doubts. Perhaps I can avert needless criticism by emphasizing two aims I am not pursuing in this book, and by saying a bit about the point of what I am pursuing.

First, I develop no account in intellectual history of why foundationalism seemed attractive to these writers. No doubt there is a complicated and interesting tale of the quest for certainty to be spun here, partly a sweeping story about the basic dynamic of Western philosophy, partly a more fine-grained sketch of the impact of modern science, partly the normal congeries of far-flung events combining in quirky ways, partly the tactical exigencies of the moment. But I don't even begin to spin that tale. Accordingly, I am in no position to blame my foundationalists for not arguing differently, and in any event I do not wish to do so. Instead, my argument is directed to today's debates. I want to suggest that we ought not to emulate their foundationalism.

Second, casting one set of authors as foundationalists and another as contextualists is in fact partial or one-sided. I readily concede that one can find extraordinarily shrewd contextual arguments in my foundationalists. Hobbes, for example, explores the devastating effects of the ethics of honor and glory. He can easily be read as defending the "bourgeois" life by showing its preferability to the life of nobles savaging each other and religious fanatics running amok. But those arguments are not the center of his political theory. My interpretations bring out what

I take to be essential in each theory as far as justification goes. While I do, for example, discuss the foundational elements in Hume and Smith, I do not dwell on them. Provided no undue distortion is introduced, such selective emphasis is after all what interpretation is about. We want more than a simple rehearsal of everything the author said, lest we end up in the dubious position of Borges and Bioy-Casares's critic, who set out to write the definitive work on the *Divine Comedy* and ended by reproducing it in its entirety.[5]

Finally, why attack foundationalism now? Haven't Quine and his followers effectively demolished the claim that knowledge needs foundations? Haven't political theorists long ago stopped searching for foundations? Three points are worth making.

First, foundationalism, in all its purity, still regularly appears in moral and political theory. To take just one example, Robert Nozick's search for "the truth about ethics and political philosophy" leads him to seek the "Foundations of Ethics."[6] Foundationalism seems to occupy some otherwise empty theoretical space; it is like a research program remarkably impervious to criticism. If nothing else, we want to understand what is distinctive about it and see why it so regularly resurfaces in the literature.

Second, this book is not an exercise in skepticism for its own sake. There are two constructive goals to my criticism. Probing a theory, instead of "barely comprehending what is affirmed or denied in each proposition," is in fact the best way to understand it.[7] The point holds whether we are exploring a theory of justification or a given political theory. I am then critical, sometimes tenaciously so, of the theories I examine. The second point is true perhaps of most skeptical rhetoric. I want to clear the ground in order to make room for a less prominent view. Criti-

[5]Jorge Luis Borges and Adolfo Bioy-Casares, *Chronicles of Bustos Domecq*, trans. Norman Thomas di Giovanni (New York: Dutton, 1976), pp. 43–44. This volume, a barbed exploration of creativity, plagiarism, and criticism, is not without theoretical interest.
[6]Robert Nozick, *Anarchy, State, and Utopia* (New York: Basic Books, 1974), p. x; Nozick, *Philosophical Explanations*, pp. 399–570.
[7]John Locke, "Of the Conduct of the Understanding," in *The Works of John Locke*, 10 vols. (London, 1823), III:250.

cizing foundationalism is an effective way to illuminate the merits of contextual arguments, merits I believe are insufficiently appreciated.

Third, we can think of foundationalism as an ideal type. Different enterprises in political theory may be more or less foundationalist; the ideal type can sensitize us to the structure of these enterprises and the problems they face. Generally, the logic of ideal types in historical studies also serves well in the history of political thought. Studies of concrete instances unguided by theoretical concerns are unsatisfactory; so are meandering theoretical ruminations not grounded in any concrete instances. The two must be combined. We want to shuttle back and forth, refining the theory with findings from the cases, deepening our grasp of the cases with a theoretically informed agenda. This approach provides a way of linking the history of political thought to our own theoretical concerns, without subscribing to the view that one reads the classics because they might be simply true. Here, I intend my argument about justification to illuminate the political theories I discuss, and I intend the chapters to lend support to the general argument.

Still, foundationalism is an odd ideal type. Instead of being a rigorously structured concept, it is an elusive metaphor. Theories are not buildings. Theories without undeniable first premises do not hover mysteriously in thin air; nor do they inevitably plummet to crashing defeat. But playing with imagery will not do; nor will sticking with metatheoretical considerations. I have taken Locke's complaint to heart: "Unmaskers, when they turn disputants, think it the best way to talk at large, and charge home in generals: but do not often find it convenient to quote pages, set down work, and come to particulars."[8] So I do quote pages, set down work, and come to particulars, as precisely as I can, in the chapters that follow.

---

[8]John Locke, *A Second Vindication of the Reasonableness of Christianity*, in *Works* VII:211.

CHAPTER ONE

HOBBES'S PRESCRIPTIVE ARGUMENTS

In 1705, Samuel Clarke undertook a demonstration of the fitness of morality. Clarke thought his task so easy—"These things," he declared, "are so notoriously plain and self-evident, that nothing but the extremest stupidity of Mind, corruption of Manners, or perverseness of Spirit, can possibly make any Man entertain the least doubt concerning them"—that his readers may well have wondered why he found it necessary to argue the point. Anticipating just this rejoinder, Clarke noted, "Indeed it might justly seem altogether a needless undertaking, to attempt to prove and establish the eternal difference of Good and Evil; had there not appeared certain Men, as Mr Hobbes and some few others, who have presumed, contrary to the plainest and most obvious reason of mankind, to assert, and not without some

Throughout the chapter, I cite from Thomas Hobbes, *Leviathan*, ed. C. B. Macpherson (Harmondsworth: Penguin, 1968); the Anchor *De Homine* and *Philosophical Rudiments Concerning Government* (*Man and Citizen*, ed. Bernard Gert [New York: Doubleday, 1972]); Tönnies's *Elements* (*The Elements of Law Natural and Politic*, ed. Ferdinand Tönnies, 2d ed. [New York: Barnes & Noble, 1969]); and Joseph Cropsey's *Dialogue* (*A Dialogue between a Philosopher and a Student of the Common Laws of England*, ed. Joseph Cropsey [Chicago: University of Chicago Press, 1971]). For all the rest of Hobbes's works, and additionally for these (except for *De Homine*, tranlated from Hobbes's Latin), I cite from *The English Works of Thomas Hobbes*, ed. William Molesworth, 11 vols. (London, 1839–1845), as *EW*. Finally, italics throughout are Hobbes's own, unless otherwise noted.

Subtilty indeavoured to prove, that there is no such real Difference originally, necessarily, and absolutely in the Nature of Things." Clarke then went on at some length to argue against one "notorious Absurdity and Inconsistency in Mr Hobbes' Scheme" after another.[1]

Hobbes incurred Clarke's wrath (and, for that matter, that of Ralph Cudworth, Henry More, and countless others[2]) by denying the objectivity of values: "Whatsoever is the object of any mans Appetite or Desire; that is it, which he for his part calleth *Good*: and the object of his Hate, and Aversion, *Evill*; And of his Contempt, *Vile* and *Inconsiderable*. For these words of Good, Evill, and Contemptible, are ever used with relation to the person that useth them: There being nothing simply and absolutely so; nor any common Rule of Good and Evill, to be taken from the nature of the objects themselves."[3] Nor has the vitriol launched at Hobbes been exclusively of seventeenth- and eighteenth-century vintage. In this century, one scholar labeled Hobbes a "moral defective"; another, after quoting some of Hobbes's skeptical statements, commented, "It is idle to qualify or defend such a political philosophy: it is rotten at the core."[4]

Hobbes may be a dauntless skeptic, but he hardly abstains from the suspect vocabulary of evaluation. Talk of just and unjust, right and wrong, duty and obligation, natural right and nat-

---

[1]Samuel Clarke, *Discourse upon Natural Religion*, excerpted in *British Moralists*, ed. L. A. Selby-Bigge, 2 vols. (Oxford, 1897), II:6, 40; also in D. D. Raphael's edition of the *Moralists*, 2 vols. (Oxford: Clarendon, 1969), I:194, 219.

[2]Samuel Mintz's *The Hunting of Leviathan* (Cambridge: Cambridge University Press, 1962), a fascinating study of contemporary reactions to Hobbes, contains virtually no discussion of the reaction to Hobbes's skepticism (see pp. 153–154).

[3]*Leviathan*, p. 120 (*EW* III:41). Hobbes here denies that values are objective and affirms that evaluative discourse is emotive. The two theses are independent. See too the skeptical claims in his early tract on first principles in *Elements*, p. 208; also *Elements*, pp. 29, 93–94 (*EW* IV:32, 109); *Rudiments*, pp. 150, 282–283 (*EW* II:47, 196); *Leviathan*, pp. 120, 216 (*EW* III:41, 146); *De Homine*, p. 47; *EW* V:192; *EW* VI:220.

[4]George Catlin, *Thomas Hobbes as Philosopher, Publicist, and Man of Letters* (Oxford: Basil Blackwell, 1922), p. 14; W. G. Pogson Smith, in a posthumous essay prefacing the Oxford edition of *Hobbes's Leviathan* (Oxford: Clarendon, 1967), p. xvii. I owe the Catlin reference to Mintz, p. 155.

ural law, good and bad, merit and due, flows freely from his pen. He carefully distinguishes between just men and just actions,[5] insists that *"the laws of nature are immutable and eternal,"*[6] and discourses at length on the duties and obligations of sovereigns.[7] His moral claims may often strike us as idiosyncratic, made of the same stuff as the careening world of *The Mikado*, where "I am right, and you are right, and all is right as right can be!" Nonetheless, they do seem genuinely moral, so much so that a sizable literature is devoted to vindicating Hobbes from charges of outrageous skepticism and moral defectiveness.[8] Yet on Hobbes's own account, we seem bound to take his putatively moral talk as a curiously disguised version of his personal preferences, to take *Leviathan* in turn as the confessions of his particular aversions and desires.

So Hobbes appears badly inconsistent on the fundaments of ethics. He often makes out apparently moral arguments, yet he also casts the whole business of moral argument in a radically skeptical light. This puzzle, I think, has given rise to the obligation controversy in the literature on Hobbes. I intend to offer a reading of Hobbes that will resolve at least some of that controversy. Yet my interest is not purely explicative: I want to assess

[5]*Elements*, pp. 83–84 (*EW* IV:97–98); *Rudiments*, pp. 138–139 (*EW* II:32–33); *Leviathan*, pp. 206–208 (*EW* III:135–137); *De Homine*, pp. 74–75.

[6]*Rudiments*, p. 140 (*EW* II:46); the same without the italics in *Leviathan*, p. 215 (*EW* III:145); the lawyer and the philosopher, *Dialogue*, pp. 55–56, 140 (*EW* VI:6, 122), agree here.

[7]*Elements*, pp. 178–184 (*EW* IV:213–220); *Rudiments*, pp. 257–270 (*EW* II:165–181); *Leviathan*, pp. 376–394 (*EW* III:322–343); see too *EW* V:177–178.

[8]A. E. Taylor, "The Ethical Doctrine of Hobbes," *Philosophy* 13 (October 1938): 406–424, reprinted in K. C. Brown, ed., *Hobbes Studies* (Oxford: Basil Blackwell, 1965); Howard Warrender, *The Political Philosophy of Hobbes* (Oxford: Clarendon, 1957); Harvey C. Mansfield, Jr., "Hobbes and the Science of Indirect Government," *American Political Science Review* 65 (March 1971): 97–110; Gert's introduction to *Man and Citizen*; David Gauthier, "Thomas Hobbes: Moral Theorist," *Journal of Philosophy* 76 (October 1979): 547–559. The position here is different from that of Gauthier's earlier *The Logic of Leviathan* (Oxford: Clarendon, 1969). I suspect that Michael Oakeshott, *Hobbes on Civil Association* (Berkeley: University of California Press, 1975), intends a moral reading. C. B. Macpherson, *The Political Theory of Possessive Individualism* (Oxford: Clarendon, 1962), pp. 71–78, argues that Hobbes successfully bridges the is/ought gap.

Hobbes's prescriptive arguments, and I want to provoke doubts about moral arguments and the state. I am concerned only indirectly with the content of Hobbes's prescriptive arguments. My real concern is with their structure. I will not, for example, argue at any length for any account of what Hobbes believes we are obliged to do; I will argue at some length for an account of Hobbes's theory of how one goes about demonstrating an obligation.

I begin with a presentation of Hobbes's *prudential argument*, along with a rebuttal to the claim that that is all Hobbes has to offer. I move on to puzzle over an argument Hobbes uses again and again, one I call the *argument from necessity*. More confidently, I present Hobbes's views on science and truth and argue that they provide Hobbes with what I call an *argument from ordinary language* for morality. That argument seems empty, so finally I examine Hobbes's faltering attempts to inject some substance into his moral argument.

The Prudential Argument

Hobbes is best known for his prudential argument, ideally showing that obedience to an absolute sovereign is in everyone's interest. Whether that argument is all Hobbes employs I set aside for the moment; first I want to sketch the argument itself.

Hobbes invites us to "consider men as if but even now sprung out of the earth, and suddenly, like mushrooms, come to full maturity, without all kind of engagement to each other"⁹—men, most notably, not under any authority. Hobbes argues first that those so situated would be equal in decisive respects: "as to the strength of body, the weakest has strength enough to kill the strongest"; as to mental ability, "they will hardly believe there be many so wise as themselves," and, he adds ironically, "this proveth rather that men are in that point equall, than unequall. For there is not ordinarily a greater signe of the equall distribu-

⁹*Rudiments*, p. 205 (EW II:109).

tion of any thing, than that every man is contented with his share."[10]

The next premise of the argument is that "every man is desirous of what is good to him, and shuns what is evil . . . by a certain impulsion of nature, no less than that whereby a stone moves downward."[11] So arises the vexing question of whether, or in what sense, Hobbes was a psychological egoist, a question in which I do not wish to become embroiled.[12] Hobbes does not consistently maintain that all voluntary actions arise from the actor's concern with his or her own welfare; he tells us, for example, that people will violate the social contract and so risk punishment when "either themselves or their near friends are to suffer."[13] Nor is his egoism merely "tautological," "based upon the statement stipulating the use for 'good.'"[14] Hobbes's claim that "no man can be ignorant that the voluntary actions of men, by a natural necessity, do follow those opinions which they have concerning good and evil, reward and punishment"[15] is apparently not a claim about the use of the words *good, evil, reward,* and *punishment*. Hobbes thinks that whenever we believe something to be good (or the best), we pursue it. He does not allow for

[10]*Leviathan*, p. 184 (*EW* III:111). The separate attention to mental equality is new in *Leviathan*; in *Elements*, p. 70 (*EW* IV:81–82), and *Rudiments*, p. 114 (*EW* II:6–7), Hobbes contents himself with the grim equality of the ability to kill.
[11]*Rudiments*, p. 205 (*EW* II:109).
[12]Hobbes seems to maintain psychological egoism in *Elements*, pp. 71, 73, 74, 84, 99–100 (*EW* IV:83, 85, 86, 98–99, 117); *Rudiments*, pp. 118, 125, 131, 146, 176, 212, 283, 365 (*EW* II:12, 19, 26, 42, 75, 116, 196, 293); *Leviathan*, pp. 192, 209, 213, 244, 303, 310–311, 339, 567 (*EW* III:120, 138, 143, 176–177, 241, 250, 281, 537); *De Homine*, p. 48; *EW* VI:200. Especially compelling is the psychology in *Elements*, pp. 31–48 (*EW* IV:34–53), partly reprinted in Raphael's *Moralists*, I:6–15, whose egoistic content is purged in *Leviathan*; note here F. S. McNeilly, *The Anatomy of Leviathan* (London: Macmillan, 1968), pp. 96–136, especially 106–117.
[13]*Rudiments*, pp. 176–177 (*EW* II:75). It could be claimed that one may feel personally threatened when one's close friends are attacked, but see too *Rudiments*, p. 183 (*EW* II:83); *Leviathan*, p. 180 (*EW* III:106–107); and *De Homine*, p. 60.
[14]Stuart M. Brown, Jr., "Hobbes: The Taylor Thesis," *Philosophical Review* 68 (July 1959): 322, reprinted in Brown, *Hobbes Studies*, p. 70. See too Gert's introduction to *Man and Citizen*, pp. 5–13.
[15]*Rudiments*, p. 365 (*EW* II:293).

variants of weakness of will or neurosis. People often do act against their own true good; they are misled by passion, or reason badly, or don't have the requisite information. But they do proceed, on Hobbes's account, always and necessarily to pursue what they think is good. This, I take it, is the meaning of Hobbes's dictum "To will an error, is impossible,"[16] as well as the upshot of his account of the will.

But back to our freshly ripened mushroom-men, who already are coming to blows. Since "many men's appetites carry them to one and the same end; which end sometimes can neither be enjoyed in common nor divided, it followeth that the stronger must enjoy it alone, and that it be decided by battle who is the stronger."[17] Put this way, the argument is too abrupt. Why can't they amicably agree that the stronger should prevail, or hit upon a fair solution?

Hobbes, however, offers a more subtle and compelling argument to the same end. He claims that human desire is necessarily insatiable, a claim he deftly derives from his materialism: "There is no such thing as perpetuall Tranquillity of mind, while we live here; because life it selfe is but Motion, and can never be without Desire, nor without Feare, no more than without Sense."[18] We can leave aside the quaintly scientistic trappings of Hobbes's physiological psychology. His belief that "ambition and greediness of honours cannot be rooted out of the minds of men"[19] leads to a more compelling line of argument. Honor is one of those curious positional goods, and scarcity is built into the logic of its social distribution: "Glory is like honour; if all men have it no man hath it, for they consist in comparison and precellence."[20]

Hobbes believes too that it is distinctively human to plan for the future. He tells us that "man is famished even by future hun-

[16]*Rudiments*, p. 358 (*EW* II:285); also *Dialogue*, p. 126 (*EW* VI:102).
[17]*Elements*, p. 71 (*EW* IV:82).
[18]*Leviathan*, pp. 129–130 (*EW* III:51); also pp. 139, 160–161 (*EW* III:62, 85).
[19]*Rudiments*, p. 265 (*EW* II:175); see too *Elements*, p. 102 (*EW* IV:120); *Rudiments*, pp. 168, 229, 252, 265 (*EW* II:66–67, 136, 160, 175); *Leviathan*, p. 225 (*EW* III:156).
[20]*Rudiments*, p. 113 (*EW* II:5).

ger."[21] On his theory of mental activity, "the Thoughts, are to the Desires, as Scouts, and Spies, to range abroad, and find the way to the things Desired."[22] Looking ahead, Hobbes's hypothetical men find that some will seek to satisfy all their desires.[23] The recklessness of these impetuous, vainglorious fellows precipitates a state of general insecurity. Even those who would be willing somehow to contain their own desires are forced to compete for scarce resources. So arises "a general inclination of all mankind, a perpetuall and restlesse desire of Power after power, that ceaseth only in Death."[24]

Briefly, the argument so far is that "masterlesse men"[25] are forced, whether they like it or not, into a mad scramble for scarce resources. In looking ahead, each sees that some men will always seek more, so each "cannot assure the power and means to live well, which he hath present, without the acquisition of more."[26] As far as the logic of the argument goes, all Hobbes needs to say is that it would be prudent to infer that someone might seek more. We might then look askance at his venturing the further claim that indeed some will seek more. That claim hardly seemed problematic, though, in a society all too familiar with a grasping nobility. In any case, the race is on, and its bleak outcome is recorded in Hobbes's celebrated litany of woes:

> In such condition, there is no place for Industry; because the fruit thereof is uncertain: and consequently no Culture of the Earth; no Navigation, nor use of the commodities that may be imported by Sea; no commodious Building; no Instruments of moving, and removing such things as require much force; no knowledge of the face of the Earth; no account of Time; no Arts; no Letters; no Society; and which is worst of all, continuall fear, and danger of vio-

[21]*De Homine*, p. 40.

[22]*Leviathan*, p. 139 (*EW* III:61); also *Rudiments*, p. 282 (*EW* II:195). Note too reason's devotion to low time preference in *De Homine*, p. 55.

[23]*Elements*, p. 71 (*EW* IV:82); *Rudiments*, p. 114 (*EW* II:7); *Leviathan*, pp. 161, 184–185 (*EW* III: 85–86, 111–112).

[24]*Leviathan*, p. 161 (*EW* III:85–86).

[25]*Leviathan*, pp. 238, 266 (*EW* III:170, 201).

[26]*Leviathan*, p. 161 (*EW* III:86). Hobbes offers a somewhat different summary of the argument in *Leviathan*, p. 185 (*EW* III:112).

lent death; And the life of man, solitary, poore, nasty, brutish, and short.[27]

No one likes "this warre of every man against every man,"[28] for, Hobbes tells us, "all men agree on this, that Peace is Good."[29] Hobbes offers two arguments to show why peace is good. He claims that we naturally "avoid that which is hurtful; but most of all that terrible enemy of nature, death, from whom we expect both the loss of all power, and also the greatest of bodily pains in the losing."[30] But fear of violent death is readily overemphasized. Hobbes has latched onto a far more powerful sociological argument, leaving the contentious realm of human nature aside. The key here is again the logic of insecurity. Trust is an essential ingredient in cooperation; without it, all sorts of enterprises founder. And there can be no trust without peace. Peace is not the end of human life: "There is no such *Finis ultimus*, (utmost ayme,) nor *Summum Bonum*, (greatest Good,) as is spoken of in the Books of the old Morall Philosophers."[31] Rather, peace is an essential requirement for realizing one's ends. Hobbes tends to portray what looks to jaundiced critics like a scandalously sedate bourgeois life, or living "delightfully,"[32] as the likely end. Yet the argument holds good for all kinds of life plans—including, for example, the pursuit of virtue. There is simply no reason to take Hobbes's emphasis on peace as the betrayal of a traditional concern with the good life.

The state of nature poses an unmistakably severe problem and so calls forth Hobbes's draconian solution: the erection of an ab-

[27]*Leviathan*, p. 186 (*EW* III:113).
[28]*Leviathan*, p. 188 (*EW* III:115); also *Rudiments*, p. 118 (*EW* II:12).
[29]*Leviathan*, p. 216 (*EW* III:146).
[30]*Elements*, p. 71 (*EW* IV:83).
[31]*Leviathan*, p. 160 (*EW* III:85).
[32]Hobbes's usual language is "commodious"; for delight and delectation, see *Rudiments*, p. 259 (*EW* II:167–168). Gert, in his introduction to *Man and Citizen*, p. 15, detects a categorical imperative in "reason declaring peace to be good" and similar constructions. See *Rudiments*, p. 151 (*EW* II:48) and p. 150 (*EW* II:47); *Elements*, p. 74 (*EW* IV:86). But a more modest gloss will do the trick: reason declares peace to be good, meaning simply that reason discovers that peace is necessary for satisfying desire.

solute sovereign. The lack of authority, remember, is one of the factors that get the mushroom-men into such a scrape. Under authority, the vainglorious will be deterred, by threat of punishment, from their inflammatory pursuit of power. When men look ahead, then, they will discover no incipient mischief. Just as peace is required for the goods offered by social cooperation, so, Hobbes suggests, the sovereign is required for peace. Once these men see the availability of a solution, they will "by a natural necessity" flock to it, provided each has some assurance the others are doing the same. So Hobbes solves the problem he poses his masterless men.

Why should we take any interest in such overtly hypothetical tales? Why should we take some hypothetical men's hypothetical willingness to establish and obey an absolute sovereign as indicating anything whatever about our doing so? Hobbes's answer would be that, should we choose to disobey our sovereign, we will find ourselves in the entirely unenviable position of those hypothetical creatures, anxiously praying for an absolute sovereign; so we might as well learn a lesson from them and obey our sovereign in all things (except when the sovereign threatens our life or salvation or has lost effective power). Both by introspection and by our experience of jealously locked doors, we can know that we are like them.[33] Here, then, is the prudential argument. Whatever our ends, we need peace to achieve them; peace can be enjoyed securely only under an absolute sovereign; so in a strictly prudential sense we ought to obey an absolute sovereign.

The argument is addressed to us, not to hypothetical men; it is designed to show us why we should obey our real sovereign, not to show them why they should have a hypothetical one. Two points follow. First, the accusation that Hobbes illicitly smuggles psychological and social facts about bourgeois men into his state of nature[34] is misplaced. If he is addressing bourgeois men,

[33]*Elements*, p. 1 (*EW* IV:1–2); *Rudiments*, pp. 99, 103 (*EW* II:xv, xx); *Leviathan*, pp. 83, 186–187 (*EW* III:xii, 113–114); *EW* I:74.

[34]At least intimated by Macpherson, *Political Theory of Possessive Individualism*, pp. 17–29, and surely urged by Rousseau in the second *Discourse*.

those facts belong in the state of nature,[35] for it is those bourgeois men who will find themselves in that state of nature if they overthrow their sovereign. We ought not to be misled by the word *nature* into thinking that Hobbes is painting some pristine portrait of human nature stripped of all the effects of social context. His state of nature is a curious melange of asocial anarchy, with neither arts nor letters, and psychological traits as quintessentially social as honor and vainglory. Hobbes flirts with no incoherence in blending the two: some of society would collapse without politics, he thinks, but not all.[36] Second, as far as the prudential argument goes, the social contract weakens Hobbes's position. Hard pressed as he is to tell a convincing story about how the gladiators of the war of all against all might manage to convoke a meeting and agree on a sovereign, Hobbes would perhaps do better to deny the very possibility of any escape from his state of nature. Though historically extravagant, such a denial would render even more horrible the consequences of disobeying and so toppling a sovereign: the life of man would then be solitary, poor, nasty, brutish, and short—forever.

Barring the accidents of chronology, the argument could have been formulated in terms of game theory as a large-scale prisoners' dilemma. The highest payoff to each player would attach to convergence on agreement to an absolute sovereign; but each player would know that if he renounces some powers and (enough) others don't, an awfully harsh payoff awaits. Limited knowledge, preplay communication, and commitment possibilities would be built into the game: each player would not be sure if others were willing to squelch their infinite desires in the interests of peace; each would be unable to communicate readily with

[35]Hobbes sometimes suggests that *Leviathan* was intended simply to calm down his frenzied contemporary England: *EW* VII:5, 335–336. Were that so, he could legitimately import into his state of nature any and all extrapolitical facts about England around 1650.

[36]But why does Hobbes call it the *natural* state of man, and what does he mean by suggesting that politics is conventional? He wishes to invert and so mock a characteristically Aristotelian view of politics. He wishes also to claim that a satisfactory account of political authority must focus on consent or other "positive" acts. But the claim that politics isn't natural doesn't explain that claim; rather, it repeats it.

the others; each would doubt promises the others made; threats would be at best somewhat effective. We need not build any moral strictures into this game. The prudential argument proceeds easily without them.

That is why I have omitted Hobbes's putatively moral terms: right of nature, law of nature, transfer of right in covenant, and so on. They obscure the argument. Most often, the moral language can be transformed readily into the language of self-interest. So Hobbes explicitly transforms the laws of nature, here "but Conclusions, or Theoremes concerning what conduceth to the conservation and defence of themselves."[37]

The question, though, is whether all of Hobbes's putatively moral claims must be understood as disguised prudential claims. Here the spectre of psychological egoism rears its worrisome head to support an affirmative answer. It might seem that automatons mechanically pursuing self-interest simply cannot respond to the claims of morality, that a theorist describing such automatons cannot invoke those claims. Thomas Nagel, for example, has argued that there is no room in Hobbes for moral obligation, since "nothing could be called a moral obligation which in principle never conflicted with self-interest."[38] Yet the view of Hobbes's psychological egoism I have offered allows us to exorcise this spectre. In my view Hobbes's egoism means only that we will unerringly submit to an absolute sovereign once we see that submission yields a state of affairs we deem good. But for the prudential argument, Hobbes needs to show only that peace is in everyone's interests, whether those interests are systematically pursued or not, whether they are egoistic or altruistic. He

---

[37]*Leviathan*, pp. 216–217 (*EW* III:147); note particularly *Rudiments*, p. 110 (*EW* II:2): "conditions of society, or of human peace, that is to say (changing the words only), what are the fundamental *laws of nature*." Hobbes also casts the law of nature as God's command. But I have nothing to contribute to the debate on the nature and sincerity of Hobbes's religious views. Hobbes discusses contemporary charges of atheism at *EW* IV:292–295, 425–429; *EW* VII:349–353.

[38]Thomas Nagel, "Hobbes's Concept of Obligation," *Philosophical Review* 68 (January 1959): 74. See too Blair Campbell, "Prescription and Description in Political Thought: The Case for Hobbes," *American Political Science Review* 65 (June 1971): 380n.18: "A doctrine which suggests that we are always obliged to the state is not a moral doctrine."

does not need to show that compliance with his proposals will in fact follow automatically. Egoism, then, however conceived, is simply not an essential part of the argument. In any case, we want to leave room both for ethical egoism, the view that each (morally) ought to pursue his or her own interests, and for arguments showing that, properly understood, morality and self-interest coincide. Nagel's dictum would eliminate that room.

There may be room in Hobbes for morality, but it is quite another matter to show that the room is not empty. We can start by noting that the almost magical transformation of laws of nature into rational theorems cannot always be duplicated. Consider Hobbes's assertion that "it is not therefore the Victory, that giveth the right of Dominion over the Vanquished, but his own Covenant."[39] A prudential reconstruction of "right of Dominion" would look something like: "X has a right over Y" means "Y can recognize X's superior strength and obey his commands or suffer the consequences, and Y is better off capitulating," along with riders about X. Why then is Covenant even relevant, let alone necessary? Why isn't sufficiently superior strength, or Victory, enough?

Consider too Hobbes's explanation of his claim that "*contracts oblige us*": "*To be obliged*, and *to be tied being obliged*, seem to some men to be one and the same thing; and that therefore here seems to be some distinction in words, but none indeed. More clearly therefore, I say this: that a man is obliged by his contracts, that is, that he ought to perform for his promise sake; but that the law tries him being obliged, that is to say, it compels him to make good his promise for fear of the punishment appointed by the law."[40] Here Hobbes goes out of his way to distinguish a moral reason arising from promising itself from a prudential reason arising from the unpleasant prospect of punishment. I suppose it could be argued that the apparently moral obligation to keep promises is in the end as prudential as the other. After all, Hobbes argues that it is always in our interest to keep promises, since we can never sensibly risk the exclusion from society that

[39]*Leviathan*, pp. 255–256 (*EW* III:189).
[40]*Rudiments*, p. 273n. (*EW* II:185n.).

should follow the discovery that we have broken them.[41] But I think this move fails to do justice to Hobbes ("he ought to perform for his promise sake," not his own sake). Perhaps my best reason for thinking so is Hobbes's independently grounded moral argument, which I discuss in the section on Science, Truth, and Morality.

I will argue, then, that the well-worn prudential argument is not an exhaustive account of Hobbes. Before pressing on, though, I want to make some critical remarks about that argument. I have discussed only sovereignty by institution, because I think Hobbes's use of sovereignty by acquisition gets him into trouble. He sometimes neatly joins the two: "If they fight, civil society ariseth from the victory; if they agree, from their agreement."[42] If the hypothetical state-of-nature account is addressed to real people, this will not do. Suppose someone—call him Cromwell—proudly fancies himself strong; he may then be perfectly willing to risk the state of war, counting on his own quick victory and subsequent emergence as sovereign. After all, we "naturally love Liberty, and Dominion over others," on Hobbes's account.[43] The argument can appeal to everyone's interests only if the state of war is bleak for everyone; Hobbes would do better to stick to his emphasis on equality and sovereignty by institution.

There are further tangles in the argument, tangles we can begin unraveling by focusing on peace. Hobbes's argument for the primacy of peace is an ingenious attempt to derive one good from the multiplicity of human goods, but it does not cut as deeply as he seems to think it does. He insists, for example, that "it is not possible there can be a greater" benefit than "the peace and preservation of every particular man."[44] Some of us, though, relish climbing sheer cliffs, fully aware of the risks; others relish war itself. Granted, these activities require some elements of cooperation and stability. Still, they can be pursued without the exten-

[41]*Leviathan*, pp. 203–205 (*EW* III:132–134), where Hobbes responds to the Foole.
[42]*Rudiments*, p. 113n. (*EW* II:6n.).
[43]*Leviathan*, p. 223 (*EW* III:153), also p. 598 (*EW* III:572); *EW* VI:404.
[44]*Elements*, p. 137 (*EW* IV:161).

sive social peace Hobbes defends. Peace may well be a good most of the time for most of us, but that fact is glaringly insufficient for the prudential argument.

Doubtless Hobbes wishes to push past a description of the peaceful man on to an encomium to him. He wishes to condemn competitive souls, nobles seeking glory, religious fanatics, and power-hungry clerics, not just because they do not see the consequences of their actions, but also because they have bad desires, the wrong ends; they *ought* to have ends that don't threaten peace. Hobbes therefore tries to undercut much religion, to expose it gleefully as a mass of delusions, to discard it summarily as madness. He tries further to minimize the occasions for disobedience prompted by religious scruples. He wishes too, as in *Behemoth*, to portray as vividly as he can the ravages of civil war. But we may suspect that these efforts will not certify peace as so extraordinarily important. Hobbes, of course, cannot think that all ends require peace. His saying so ignores the very nobles and religious fanatics whose eminently rational activities rip apart England and motivate his work. The apparent observation is then actually an idealization or a covert recommendation. Peace may not be a requisite for all ends, but think how much better off most of us would be if it were!

Note Hobbes's fifth law of nature:

> *That every man strive to accommodate himselfe to the rest.* For the understanding whereof, we may consider, that there is in mens aptnesse to Society; a diversity of Nature, rising from their diversity of Affections; not unlike to that we see in stones brought together for building of an Ædifice. For as that stone which by the asperity, and irregularity of Figure, takes more room from others, then it selfe fills; and for the hardnesse, cannot be easily made plain, and thereby hindereth the building, is by the builders cast away as unprofitable, and troublesome: So also, a man that by asperity of Nature, will strive to retain those things which to himselfe are superfluous, and to others necessary; and for the stubbornness of his Passions, cannot be corrected, is to be left, or cast out of Society, as cumbersome thereunto.[45]

[45]*Leviathan*, p. 209 (*EW* III:138–139). I owe the following point to Stephen Holmes, who persuaded me that the prudential argument isn't exactly prudential.

This passage invites a blandly prudential reading. Seeking peace will mean accommodating yourself, and since you want peace you had better do so. But again we can see a covert recommendation: since nobles and religious fanatics are useless stones that get in the way, throw them out. Their actions may be perfectly rational, given their ends. They will hardly be moved by Hobbes's argument. But because they interfere with the rest of us, our seeking peace will mean warring against them.

Note too the ninth law of nature:

> If Nature therefore have made men equall, that equalitie is to be acknowledged: or if Nature have made men unequall; yet because men that think themselves equall, will not enter into conditions of Peace, but upon Equall Termes, such equalitie must be admitted. And therefore for the ninth law of Nature, I put this, *That every man acknowledge other for his Equall by Nature.*[46]

It was because all men are equal that only capitulation to an absolute sovereign could do the trick. But now the argument is inverted: because capitulation is the end, all men had better think of themselves as equal. This puzzling move should at least give pause to those prone to thinking of conceptions of the self and the like as the heart of political theory, the base on which political conclusions are erected. As often as not, I suspect, revisions in such realms by political theorists are politically motivated.

These laws of nature disrupt the official claim that the laws of nature are "but Conclusions, or Theoremes," simple hypothetical imperatives. They also disrupt the claim that "all men agree on this, that Peace is Good." Not all men do agree that peace is good. The argument is not a simple prisoners' dilemma, since not all the players are aiming at peace. The players who do seek peace will simply have to throttle the others. Hobbes never even hints that the "true" self-interest of the latter group will thus be served. They will be tossed out of society, like irregular stones, and we will profit from their loss.

We can still wonder, however, whether Hobbes's prescriptions are good ones. Most objectionable is the linchpin of the argument, the claim that an absolute state is the means to peace.

---

[46]*Leviathan*, p. 211 (*EW* III:141).

Hobbes has both empirical and conceptual reasons for thinking the state must be absolute. He relies on slippery-slope arguments to show that any limited state soon collapses, and on the concept of sovereignty to show that all power must lie in the hands of an assignable set of people above the law. But to anyone outside a society as politically fragile as the England of Hobbes's *Behemoth*, the slippery-slope arguments are unpersuasive, as history attests. We have seen limited states survive quite handily. Sovereignty, on the other hand, is a good example of a theoretical concept that obfuscates the world instead of illuminating it. Divided sovereignty is a contradiction in terms. Political authority, however, can be divided and still exist: witness any federalist structure or division of powers. Similarly, political power can be limited by the rule of law.[47]

Arguably, the introduction of any state, absolute or not, as the solution of Hobbes's war of all against all is insufficiently motivated. Unless Hobbes entertains dubious beliefs about authority's moderating the passions of those in power, he should be worrying too about the (organized) war of some against the rest. The state, I would argue, emerges as the solution to Hobbes's problem only because he laboriously cloaks the state in the dreamy robes of mystification. It is striking that Hobbes bitterly condemns metaphor and himself develops an elaborate body-politic metaphor.[48] That body politic, a mechanical one with springs, strings, and wheels,[49] sardonically mocks contemporary organic conceptions of society. It also systematically misdescribes the state, even the absolute state, in a way that has a political payoff. If the Leviathan state is a colossally large actor, even a *"Mortall God,"*[50] we will certainly cringe before it. Hobbes's sovereign, like the Wizard of Oz, is an awe-inspiring figure. But is is, after all, only Hobbes behind the curtain, pulling the levers and creating that figure. We can play Dorothy, and demand that Hobbes unpack the metaphor and develop a

---

[47]See the penetrating discussion in H. L. A. Hart, *The Concept of Law* (Oxford: Clarendon, 1975), pp. 49–76.

[48]*Leviathan*, pp. 116–117, 81 (*EW* III:37, ix).

[49]*Leviathan*, p. 81 (*EW* III:ix).

[50]*Leviathan*, p. 277 (*EW* III:158).

more straightforward justification. If anarchism (for that is what the state of nature is) is to be dismissed, we want to hear cogent arguments.

In this respect, the ahistorical pretensions of Hobbes's argument are a disability, not a strength. It may be that only an absolute state could have put an end to English civil war. But it is impossible to make any claims about what the life of masterless men necessarily is, for the character of that life will vary with social context. Asked to choose between anarchism and political society, with no context provided, we can only shrug. Is anarchism Hobbes's state of nature or a pastoral paradise? Is political society our favorite constitutional system or some totalitarian horror? For the choice to be intelligible, we need to constrain the set of possible outcomes; and the relevant constraints are at hand, in social context. Some possibilities—perhaps some of those a political theorist might dream up—are unavailable in the world.

The prudential argument has, as it must, a social context. Hobbes's desire to legislate timelessly, to frame a doctrine suitable for teaching ever after in the universities,[51] prevents him from incorporating such contingent details of context. The argument takes on force and color, however, only when we make that context explicit, when we insert *Behemoth*'s perpetually obscure schoolmen and religious sects, its fractious nobles and insolent Parliament, into the political theory. Only then does the choice between anarchism and the state become definite enough to be meaningful.

"But then the argument is no longer timeless." That will depend on what we mean by timelessness. Surely we cannot simply slap Hobbes down on twentieth-century society as a justification for unquestioning obedience. We face not fragile governments on the verge of collapse, but overweening governments that themselves threaten peace. If they are gods, they are most assuredly Manichaean. If a timeless political theory

---

[51]Note *Leviathan*, pp. 384–385, 407–408, 727–728 (*EW* III:331–332, 357–358, 712–713); Thomas Hobbes, "The Life of Thomas Hobbes of Malmesbury," trans. J. E. Parsons, Jr., and Whitney Blair, *Interpretation* 10 (January 1982): 5.

is one that applies regardless of social context, timeless political theories will be thoroughly vacuous.

The Argument from Necessity

"God is King of all the Earth by his Power," Hobbes announces.[52] The claim seems innocent enough, but Hobbes spells it out in a sinister way. He appeals to necessity, and the argument from necessity covers more than God. The logic of the argument is bewildering and unsatisfactory. Here I start with Hobbes's views on God and then broaden my focus.

Hobbes wants to say not only that God does rule because of his infinite power, but also that "God in his natural kingdom hath a *right* to rule, and to punish those who break his laws, from his sole *irresistible power*."[53] Underlining the point, he goes on to declare that "the *obligation* of yielding him obedience lies on men by reason of their weakness."[54] Moreover, God's actions are self-justifying: "The *power* of God alone without other helps is sufficient *justification* of any action he doth."[55]

We can immediately note a peripheral problem with this argument, one that parallels Hobbes's claims for the laws of nature. Hobbes wants to say that we are obliged to obey the laws of nature, understood as God's commands; he also wants to say that there is "no Obligation on any man, which ariseth not from some Act of his own"; so he is led to the obtuse claim that "the law of nature is the assent itself that all men give to the means of their own preservation," even though he also wants to say that "it is manifest that the *divine laws* sprang not from the consent of men,

---

[52]*Leviathan*, p. 179 (*EW* III:105). And "we are Gods Slaves," *Leviathan*, p. 668 (*EW* III:648).

[53]*Rudiments*, p. 292 (*EW* II:206). I've changed Hobbes's italics.

[54]*Rudiments*, p. 294 (*EW* II:209).

[55]*EW* IV:249, discussed at *EW* V:115–117. Note that it isn't any special fact about God other than his power that gives rise to his right to rule; it isn't, for example, that God is essentially good and so gains the right to use his infinite power. Any irresistibly powerful agent has the right to rule: *Rudiments*, pp. 292–293 (*EW* II:206–207); *Leviathan*, p. 397 (*EW* III:345–346); *EW* V:146; *EW* IV:250, discussed at *EW* V:117–147.

nor yet the *laws of nature*. For if they had their original from the consent of men, they might also by the same consent be abrogated; but they are unchangeable."[56] As for God's right of ruling, Hobbes wants to say that it arises from God's irresistible power alone; but he says too "that the Right of all Soveraigns, is derived originally from the consent of every one of those that are to bee governed."[57] The contradictions are comprehensible if, as I believe, Hobbes employs independent prescriptive arguments with different requirements. For the prudential argument, consent is unnecessary, and in fact entirely beside the point; but for the argument from ordinary language, consent may well seem crucial. The methodological moral of the story is simple: we can take outright contradictions in texts as signs that the author is juggling competing demands; then we can ask what those demands might be.

There is something odd in Hobbes's claims for God's deriving right from power. They smack of might makes right—and indeed Hobbes decrees also that "irresistible might in the state of nature is right."[58] Some of the oddness fades away if we take these claims to be disguised prudential claims, and some of it fades away if we adopt a certain construction of justification.

Suppose we take "*X* has a right to rule *Y*" as meaning something like "*X* is powerful enough to enforce her will on *Y*, *X* is (possibly) inclined to do so, and *Y* will deem himself better off by submitting," along with riders about *Y*'s (possible) awareness of this state of affairs and ability to act purposively. Suppose further we take "*Y* is obliged to obey *X*" as meaning the same.[59] These would be translations, if gimmicky ones, of the apparently moral claims we started with; but we would have moved wholly into the worlds of power and self-interest. If God's right is rendered in this way, the mystery and horror of, say, Hobbes's pronouncement that "irresistible might in the state of

---

[56]*Leviathan*, p. 312 (*EW* III:251); *Rudiments*, p. 207 (*EW* II:110); *Leviathan*, p. 268 (*EW* III:203); *EW* V:180; *Rudiments*, p. 273 (*EW* II:184).
[57]*Leviathan*, p. 599 (*EW* III:573).
[58]*Elements*, p. 74 (*EW* IV:86).
[59]See John Plamenatz, "Mr. Warrender's Hobbes," *Political Studies* 5 (October 1957): 296–297, reprinted in Brown, *Hobbes Studies*, p. 75.

nature is right" dissolve. The point is simply that it is in every-one's interest to submit to one strong enough to be ruler when there is no ruler around already.

Brian Barry has made an apt suggestion for disposing of the troublesome claim that God is justified in whatever he does.[60] We take *justify* to mean "make just": "I said no more," writes Hobbes, in explaining the dictum that "power irresistible justi-fies," "but that the power, which is absolutely irresistible, makes him that hath it above all law, so that nothing he doth can be un-just."[61] We then connect up this account of justification with Hobbes's account of justice, which is keeping contracts and obeying laws.[62] Since the sovereign has made no contract with the rest of us and is above the laws, he cannot act unjustly: this is a matter of conceptual coherence, not a claim about the infallible wisdom or goodness of sovereigns.[63] God is justified in all he does; that is, God acts justly in all he does; that is, God never breaks a law or violates a convenant—for to whose law is God subject? With whom has he covenanted?[64] Here too lies a possi-ble explanation for Hobbes's qualification that only *"power irre-sistible justifies all actions, really and properly*, in whomsoever it be found; less power does not."[65] Very strong, even overwhelm-ingly strong, agents are actual or possible subjects of stronger agents, so we can conceive of their acting unjustly, that is, unjus-tifiedly. Only irresistibly strong agents are necessarily above the law.

[60]Brian Barry, "Warrender and His Critics," *Philosophy* 43 (April 1968): 133n.9, uses the quotation I'm about to cite, but the quotation is at *EW* V:146, not, as the article has it, *EW* IV:146.

[61]*EW* V:146; also *Elements*, p. 157 (*EW* IV:186); *Rudiments*, pp. 382–383 (*EW* II:314); *Leviathan*, p. 623 (*EW* III:599–600).

[62]*Leviathan*, pp. 103, 202 (*EW* III:21, 131).

[63]*Leviathan*, pp. 232, 367 (*EW* III:163, 312–313); though see too *EW* IV:333 ("an unjust judgment does not take away from any king his right of judica-ture"); *Rudiments*, p. 181n. (*EW* II:80n.); and perhaps *Leviathan*, p. 325 (*EW* III:266), the only places I've found where Hobbes speaks of a ruler acting unjustly.

[64]In Hobbes's rendition of Abraham's covenant with God in *Leviathan*, pp. 499–501 (*EW* III:461–463), God seems to commit himself to nothing; also *EW* V:117. But see *Leviathan*, pp. 443–444 (*EW* III:397–398), and *Rudiments*, pp. 311–312 (*EW* II:228–229), where God does guarantee Abraham the inheri-tance of Canaan.

[65]*EW* IV:250, discussed at *EW* V:116–117.

Yet Hobbes appeals to necessity to make statements that do not lend themselves so readily to these kinds of explanation. Take his passing reference to "the natural right of preservation, which we all receive from the uncontrollable dictates of necessity."[66] What might this mean? How do the dictates of necessity give rise to a right? Perhaps, as Hobbes sometimes maintains, we have to seek our own self-preservation. Perhaps we are built that way, out of genetic concrete. Mightn't that be wrong instead of right? Mightn't that be just another fact about human beings, and have no moral significance whatever? We might focus here on Hobbes's so-called naturalistic account of right and so take him to say only that we *can* try to preserve ourselves because we must.[67] But Hobbes often does use *right* in a putatively moral way; he has in mind here not just physical obstacles to motion, but also moral constraints.[68]

I will take the liberty of quoting extensively, not to spread my confusion, but to suggest that it is not only my own. Hobbes has just explained why it is desirable to end the war of all against all, or, as he colorfully puts it, "to get some fellows":

> Fellows are gotten either by constraint, or by consent; by constraint, when after fight the conqueror makes the conquered serve him, either through fear of death, or by laying fetters on him; by consent, when men enter into society to help each other, both parties consenting without any constraint. But the conqueror may by right compel the conquered, or the strongest the weaker (as a man in health may one that is sick, or he that is of riper years a child), unless he will choose to die, to give caution of his future obedience. For since the right of protecting ourselves according to our own wills, proceeded from our danger, and our danger from our equality, it is more consonant to reason, and more certain for our conservation, using the present advantage to secure ourselves by taking caution, than when they shall be full grown and strong, and

[66]*Rudiments*, p. 90 (*EW* II:ii).

[67]See, for example, *Leviathan*, p. 189 (*EW* III:116); *Rudiments*, p. 115 (*EW* II:9); and note the odd formulation on children, *Rudiments*, p. 212 (*EW* II:115–116).

[68]See J. Roland Pennock, "Hobbes's Confusing 'Clarity'—The Case of Liberty," *American Political Science Review* 54 (June 1960): 428-436, reprinted in Brown, *Hobbes Studies*, pp. 101–116; and A. G. Wernham, "Liberty and Obligation in Hobbes," in Brown, *Hobbes Studies*, pp. 117–139.

got out of our power, to endeavour to recover that power again by doubtful fight. And on the other side, nothing can be thought more absurd, than by discharging whom you already have weak in your power, to make him at once both an enemy and a strong one. From whence we may understand likewise as a corollary in the natural state of men, that *a sure and irresistible power confers the right of dominion and ruling over those who cannot resist*; insomuch, as the right of all things that can be done, adheres essentially and immediately unto this omnipotence hence arising.[69]

The passage begins harmlessly enough, at least for present purposes. The war of all against all ends by treaty or victory. (Again, Hobbes would do better to stick to sovereignty by institution instead of acquisition, to consent instead of constraint: the latter makes rebellion a tempting option for those counting on a victory in the state of nature.) Next we learn that not only *can* the conqueror compel obedience, he *may* do it, by right. At this point, all this business of the rights of the mighty is so much assertion, with nary a shred of support.

Hobbes's explanation follows. There is an activity named "protecting ourselves according to our own wills"—that is, doing what we think appropriate for safeguarding ourselves. We have a right to engage in this activity. Now, to skip a bit, it is reasonable to ensure our safety by dominating others when they are weak, rather than waiting to deal with them when they are strong and menacing; *reasonable* here, I take it, means "conducive to our ends," here to self-preservation. But the skipped bit is troublesome. Our right of self-preservation proceeds from our danger, which in turn proceeds from our equality. The move from equality to danger is an abbreviation of the argument that the lack of authority produces the war of all against all. But how does the right proceed from the danger? Perhaps Hobbes has in mind the relation between right and reason he sometimes recurs to: "All do grant, that is done by *right*, which is not done against reason."[70] And perhaps we are to slip from "doing something by

---

[69]*Rudiments*, pp. 118–119 (*EW* II:12–13); compare with *Elements*, p. 73 (*EW* IV:85).

[70]*Rudiments*, p. 122 (*EW* II:15); also *Elements*, p. 71 (*EW* IV:83).

right" to "having a right to do something"; that our ends are served by aggressing against the weak would then generate our right to do it. Perhaps; perhaps not. Given the opacity of the passage, any explication must be tentative.

The connection between right and reason needs to be worked out more carefully. Hobbes needs to explain just how the right arises. Instead he goes on to repeat himself: it is reasonable to dominate the weak, so it is unreasonable, or absurd, not to dominate them. Still we want an explanation, but Hobbes instead triumphantly unveils a troublesome general principle. How the principle is a corollary of the narrower claim Hobbes starts with is a puzzle, and why the stark fact of power should be thought to confer a right is a veritable labyrinth. Most perplexing, though, is the essential and immediate adherence of the right to the power. How do rights flow from power relationships? How do moral relations adhere to descriptive ones? Hobbes undoubtedly intends this claim to be the climax of the paragraph and the argument, but it is a profound muddle. Why the necessities of power or nature or anything else should be thought to give rise to moral relations is mysterious. Accordingly, here I dismiss the argument from necessity. It lapses into incoherence just when it needs to be clearest.

I have been probing the argument from necessity not because Hobbes uses it to defend bizarre moral principles, but because the logic of the argument is entirely opaque. Part of the opacity arises not from Hobbes's view of God, or his determinism, or any other aspect of the argument's content. It arises rather from the argument's form, and darkens more appealing principles: Consent obliges. Legitimate governments are those to which we consent. Legitimate governments are those to which we would consent in some special position. The verbal event we call "promising" obliges. Labor creates entitlements. Need creates entitlements. The minority is bound to support the elected outcome or candidate. The majority is bound to support the elected outcome or candidate. In short, rights, duties, obligations, justice, legitimacy, and all the other ghostly inhabitants of the moral menagerie are sired in the real world.

In all these cases, we are presented with a move from descriptive to evaluative or prescriptive, from fact to value, is to ought. The move in each case may be defensible, but surely it needs defense of some kind. (On the fact of it, the only thing separating these principles from Hobbes's more sinister claims about necessity is that we happen to prefer them.) So it will not do simply to propose our favorite moral principles and count on the audience's agreement. Someone may disagree, proposing what strikes us as an eccentric or pernicious principle. If overt disagreement does not create the demand for justification, doubt will. For one may entertain not just the least bit of doubt about our moral and political principles without being extremely stupid, corrupt, or perverse.

Science, Truth, and Morality

Hobbes does more, fortunately, than announce that certain (perfidious) moral relations arise from necessity. He offers a systematic account of truth and science, a foundation on which he self-consciously builds a moral argument. This account enables Hobbes to speak of the truth about morals and politics in the face of his moral skepticism, and to this account I now turn.

Hobbes tells us that "Morall Philosophy is nothing else but the Science of what is *Good*, and *Evill*, in the conversation, and Society of mankind," that "what hath hitherto been written by moral philosophers, hath not made any progress in the knowledge of the truth."[71] I will not attempt a full-dress review of Hobbes's epistemology, but I do want to sketch his views of science and truth. It will prove essential here to exploit the possibility that Hobbes makes false claims about the nature and potential of his argument. We need not, however, say that Hobbes is striving to conceal a philosophic teaching from the vulgar. More workaday (if less reverential) explanations will do the job. We might for example hold that Hobbes was confused. In any case, I suspect that the lion's share of the literature on Hobbes's method goes

---

[71]*Leviathan*, p. 216 (*EW* III:146); *Rudiments*, p. 96 (*EW* II:v). See *EW* VI:362–364 on the science of politics.

awry by concentrating too much on his own glosses on his procedure.[72] Here I would recommend a claim attributed to John
Mitchell during the Watergate controversy: watch what we do,
not what we say. Mitchell's Rule, if I may elevate it to a herme-
neutic principle, provides an incisive guide to the study of political texts as well as political actors.

Hobbes is skeptical about induction: "Though a man hath
always seen the day and night to follow one another hitherto;
yet can he not thence conclude they shall do so, or that they
have done so eternally. Experience concludeth nothing universally."[73] This skepticism does not lead Hobbes to a wholesale
rejection of the belief that we can figure out how the world
works and so control it. Like the good Baconian he is supposed to
be, he holds that "the end of knowledge is power."[74] But "the
natural reason of man, busily flying up and down among the
creatures, and bringing back a true report of their order, causes
and effects" does not, from the sense-data of experience, produce
science: "When one is dealing with the truth of fact, it is not
properly called *science*, but simply *knowledge*."[75]

Science is awfully bleak stuff: "The first grounds of all science
are not only not beautiful, but poor, arid, and, in appearance, de-
formed."[76] Those first grounds are the careful recording of definitions: "All sciences begin with definitions, or otherwise they

---

[72]Critics often focus on the resolutive-compositive method. See, for example, Leo Strauss, *The Political Philosophy of Hobbes*, trans. Elsa M. Sinclair (Oxford: Clarendon, 1936). Strauss also maintains (p. 163) that "the antithesis between classical and modern political philosophy, more accurately between
Platonic political philosophy and that of Hobbes, is that the former orientates
itself by speech and the latter refuses to do so." I believe, for reasons I set out in
this section, that this is wrong. I tend to disagree too with J. W. N. Watkins's
excellent *Hobbes's System of Ideas* (London: Hutchinson University Library,
1965), pp. 37–38. J. Weinberger, "Hobbes's Doctrine of Method," *American
Political Science Review* 69 (December 1975): 1336–1353, an Aristotelian rejoinder to Hobbes, is about "morally intelligible whatnesses" (pp. 1346–1347) and
the like. Finally, Thomas A. Spragens, Jr., *The Politics of Motion: The World of
Thomas Hobbes* (Great Britain: University Press of Kentucky, 1973), is a careful
exploration of continuities and discontinuities between Aristotle and Hobbes.
[73]*Elements*, p. 16 (*EW* IV:18).
[74]*EW* I:7.
[75]*EW* I:xiii; *De Homine*, p. 41. Compare with *Rudiments*, p. 375 (*EW* II:305).
[76]*EW* I:2.

must not be called sciences, but mere verbiage."[77] While typically explication of common usage does the trick, sometimes philosophers may define their own terms: "Whatsoever the common use of words be, yet philosophers, who were to teach their knowledge to others, had always the liberty, and sometimes they both had and will have a necessity, of taking to themselves such names as they please for the signifying of their meaning."[78]

We link all these definitions together in propositions. "A proposition," Hobbes says, "is a speech consisting of two names copulated, by which he that speaketh signifies he conceives the latter name to be the name of the same thing whereof the former is the name; or (which is all one) that the former name is comprehended by the latter."[79] We join (Hobbes would say "add") these propositions into syllogisms, and we pile syllogism upon syllogism. In the end we are manipulating words and definitions, and we arrive at "that conditional Knowledge, or Knowledge of the consequence of words, which is commonly called SCIENCE."[80] For Hobbes, then, a science of politics is a body of knowledge about the meanings and entailments of political concepts. It is not a mass of statistics hammered into lawlike statements. It is not even the study of political regimes. Hobbes is openly contemptuous of observation of the world: "Every man that hath spare money, can get furnaces, and buy coals. Every man that hath spare money, can be at the charge of making great moulds, and hiring workmen to grind their glasses; and so may have the best and greatest telescopes. They can get engines made, and apply them to the stars; recipients made, and try conclusions; but they are never the more philosophers for all this."[81] And since Hobbes equates science and philosophy in his grand schematic of human knowledge, neither are they scientists.[82] Hobbesian scientists, after all, "proceed from most low

[77]*De Homine*, p. 69; also *EW* VII:222, 225.
[78]*EW* I:16.
[79]*EW* I:30.
[80]*Leviathan*, p. 131 (*EW* III:53).
[81]*EW* IV:436.
[82]*Leviathan*, p. 149 (*EW* III:72).

and humble principles, evident even to the meanest capacity, going on slowly, and with most scrupulous ratiocination (viz.) from
the imposition of names they infer the truth of their first proposition; and from two of the first, a third; and from any two of the
three a fourth; and so on."[83] We are a long way indeed from Ba-
con's program.

What does it mean to say a proposition is true? Hobbes sounds
sometimes as though he wants to confine truth to the same analytic framework as science: "When two names are joyned together into a Consequence, or Affirmation; as thus, *A man is a
living creature*; or thus, *if he be a man, he is a living creature*, If the
later name *Living creature*, signifie all that the former name *man*
signifieth, then the affirmation, or consequence is *true*; otherwise
false. For *True* and *False* are attributes of Speech, not of
Things."[84] "Man is a living creature": what better example of a
tautology could we ask for? If truth and falsehood "are attributes
of Speech," how can we possibly understand claims about the
external world as being true or false? Science is but a collection
of tautologies; tautologies are the only examples of true propositions. Or so it might seem; but Hobbes, again, does talk about
"the truth of fact," and he does try to stretch his theory of truth
to handle synthetic propositions: "A *true* proposition is that,
whose predicate contains, or comprehends its subject, or whose
predicate is the name of every thing, of which the subject is the
name; as *man is a living creature* is therefore a true proposition, because whatsoever is called *man*, the same is also called *living creature*; and *some man is sick*, is true, because *sick* is the name of *some
man*."[85] It is a bit artificial to say that "*some man is sick*, is true,
because *sick* is the name of *some man*," but Hobbes needs to say it
in order to hold to his claim that truth "consists in speech, not in
the things spoken of."[86] Still, he does maintain there is a difference between analytic and synthetic propositions: the former he
calls "necessary," and offers as an example "man is a rational liv-

[83] *Elements*, p. 66 (*EW* IV:72–73).
[84] *Leviathan*, pp. 104–105 (*EW* III:23).
[85] *EW* I:35.
[86] *EW* I:35; also *Elements*, pp. 21–22 (*EW* IV:23–24).

ing creature"; the latter he calls "contingent," and offers as an example "every crow is black."[87] Let me note at once that I will not bring in Quine and other critics of the analytic/synthetic dichotomy. While their criticisms would provide a potent line of attack from outside Hobbes's theory, I mean to show that the theory is internally flawed. Accordingly, I will proceed in blithe disregard of recent strictures on the dichotomy.

Hobbes maintains too that "every proposition, universally true, is either a definition, or part of a definition, or the evidence of it depends upon definitions."[88] Now, since Hobbes wants to model moral and political science (or philosophy) after geometry, "the onely Science that it hath pleased God hitherto to bestow on mankind," and since the conclusions of geometry are "indisputable," it might seem that Hobbes would be perfectly content to reserve the name *science* for wholly analytic systems, as I believe he is committed to doing by his account of the matter.[89] But he also wants to incorporate empirically oriented causal models: "till we come to [1] a knowledge of all the Consequences of names appertaining to the subject in hand; and that is it, men call SCIENCE. And whereas Sense and Memory are but knowledge of Fact, which is a thing past, and irrevocable; *Science* is [2] the knowledge of Consequences, and dependence of one fact upon another; by which, out of that we can presently do, we know how to do something else when we will, or the like, another

[87]*EW* I:37–38, italics omitted. Hobbes draws the distinction around whether we can conceive of the proposition being false. Compare Dorothea Krook, "Thomas Hobbes's Doctrine of Meaning and Truth," *Philosophy* 31 (January 1956): 6: "For Hobbes, all truth is 'analytic.'" Hobbes says "that the method of attaining to the universal knowledge of things, is purely *analytical*" (*EW* I:69); but there is nonuniversal knowledge, which is knowledge of fact.

[88]*EW* I:62. Sheldon Wolin, *Hobbes and the Epic Tradition of Political Theory* (Los Angeles: University of California Press, 1970), p. 22, goes too far in saying, "All is changed by the advent of method, for it magnifies human power and certitude. Reason is rendered infallible." *Right* reason is infallible, but we never know if we have right reason; see, for instance, *Elements*, pp. 188–189 (*EW* IV:225); *Rudiments*, p. 303 (*EW* II:220); *Leviathan*, p. 111 (*EW* III:30–31); *EW* V:176, 194. Method, however, surely is important; note *Leviathan*, p. 114 (*EW* III:33); see too *EW* VII:84.

[89]*Leviathan*, pp. 105, 114 (*EW* III 23–24, 33); also *Rudiments*, pp. 91–92, 373–374 (*EW* II:iv–v, 302–303); *EW* I:38; *Elements*, p. 176 (*EW* IV:210).

[56]

time."[90] Consequences of names and consequences of facts, nestled together: Hobbes seems to believe the two are the same, or that somehow attaching causal models to facts makes a body of knowledge of consequences of names.[91]

But how might causation enter this arid world of syllogisms? Hobbes makes three suggestions. First, he exploits his skeptical tendencies. "The doctrine of natural causes hath not infallible and evident principles,"[92] so we must suppose possible causal links between events and, in turn, if a bit mysteriously, between words. Here Hobbes is willing to consider empirical evidence, for even a possible causal connection must not, he thinks, fly in the face of the evidence.[93] Second, in morals and politics, "we ourselves make the principles,"[94] so we can know their causal underpinnings with certainty. Third, Hobbes proposes that we define things by their method of generation, or cause.[95] Yet wherever our causes come from, Hobbes relies on syllogistic inference to preserve the causal connections. Here he confounds logical and empirical necessity, but the two are different. It may be causally necessary that water freeze at zero degrees and normal pressure. We can though conceive of its not doing so, so it is not logically necessary.[96]

Ambitious claims for what Hobbes's science can accomplish must then be discarded. Causal models are not guaranteed correct by the meanings of the terms they are composed of. Nor do any of Hobbes's efforts at patching over the problem succeed. We must, then, turn our attention away from his repeated

[90]*Leviathan*, p. 115 (*EW* III:35).
[91]See McNeilly, *Anatomy of Leviathan*, pp. 59–91; also William Lyons, "Against an Orthodox Interpretation of Hobbes," *Philosophical Quarterly* 27 (October 1977): 302–312.
[92]*EW* VII:3.
[93]See *EW* VII:1–177, particularly 3–4, 88.
[94]*De Homine*, p. 42; also *EW* VII:183–184. Compare the introduction to *Leviathan*.
[95]*EW* I:81–83; compare *EW* I:311–312, *EW* VII:212, and see generally *EW* I:387–388.
[96]Note Richard Peters, *Hobbes* (Harmondsworth: Penguin, 1956), pp. 52–54. Hume, among many others, reproduces the confusion: note J. L. Mackie, *The Cement of the Universe* (Oxford: Clarendon, 1980), pp. 3–28.

glosses of science and philosophy as including causal models, his willingness to call astronomy a science right along with geometry, and his well-known remarks on the resolutive-compositive method.[97] They are flashy, they are provocative, and they are memorable. Unhappily, they are also misleading.

To be sure, Hobbes employs the resolutive-compositive method in constructing the hypothetical state of nature, and he employs causal reasoning to argue, say, that we ought not to limit the sovereign's powers. I do not mean to brush aside these arguments. Rather I want to show that Hobbes grounds a moral argument on the analytic account of science, that he is aware he is doing so, and that this account enables him to claim to have provided the truth about morals and politics, the new political science. I want to show too that Hobbes is sometimes aware that his political science is doomed to triviality.

Consider: "And when a man hath in either manner abandoned, or granted away his Right; then is he said to be OBLIGED, or BOUND, not to hinder those, to whom such Right is granted, or abandoned, from the benefit of it: and that he *Ought*, and it is his DUTY, not to make voyd that voluntary act of his own: and that such hindrance is INJUSTICE, and INJURY."[98] Here Hobbes offers a thumbnail sketch of the terrain of our moral concepts. Notice that he is reporting the ways in which we hook up these concepts: it is said one is obliged on surrendering a right, it is said one ought to let others enjoy rights surrendered to them, it is said it is one's duty, and so on. I take this passage to be an explication of the ordinary usage of the major moral concepts.

Now Hobbes's science comes into play, and these reports of common usage are transformed into true propositions. Hobbes need not limit himself to reporting common usage: he can say that "it is unjust to trespass on others' rights" or that "it is one's duty not to hinder those to whom one has transferred a right in their enjoyment of it." These are true propositions, guaranteed correct by the meanings of the words they are composed of; so

[97] See, for example, *De Homine*, pp. 41–43; *EW* I:82–83; *Leviathan*, p. 682 (*EW* III:664); *EW* I:10, 66; and note the benefits of philosophy at *EW* IV:449–450.
[98] *Leviathan*, p. 191 (*EW* III:119).

they are the building blocks of Hobbes's moral science. It does not matter that Hobbes believes that good and bad are subjective, that he presumably believes that obligation and the rest are epistemologically suspect. We do use the words in an internally coherent framework, and that is all Hobbes the scientist needs in order to go about his work.

Hobbes clearly understands himself as carrying on this sort of scientific inquiry into morals and politics. In the chapter "Of Civil Lawes" in *Leviathan*, he commences by making some observations about the logical features of the concept *law*. He then proceeds to formulate a definition clearly intended as explication of common usage ("in which definition, there is nothing that is not at first sight evident"), and remarks, "Whatsoever can from this definition by necessary consequence be deduced, ought to be acknowledged for truth. Now I deduce from it this that followeth."[99] Crystal clear too is Hobbes's summation of the first two parts of *Leviathan*, a summation he offers at the start of the third part, before he enters into his fantastic disquisition on Scripture: "I HAVE derived the Rights of Soveraigne Power, and the duty of Subjects hitherto, from the Principles of Nature onely; such as Experience has found true, or Consent (concerning the use of words) has made so; that is to say, from the nature of Men, known to us by Experience, and from Definitions (of such words as are Essentiall to all Politicall reasoning) universally agreed on."[100] The argument "from the nature of Men, known to us by Experience" I have been calling the prudential argument; the argument "from Definitions (of such words as are Essentiall to all Politicall reasoning) universally agreed on" I have been calling the argument from ordinary language. I have paid no attention to Hobbes's occasional claim, voiced here, that we consent to the meanings of words. Taking the claim seriously could mean lending moral force to his scientific argument. If consent obliges, and we have consented to the meanings of words, then perhaps we are morally bound to observe conceptual connections. But the sort of consent that we give to the

[99]*Leviathan*, pp. 311–312 (*EW* III:250–252).
[100]*Leviathan*, p. 409 (*EW* III:359). Compare *Rudiments*, p. 367 (*EW* II: 295–296).

meanings of words is surely too tenuous to have any moral import. The introduction of consent only obscures the sense in which Hobbes wants to endorse our conventional views.

Hobbes does not believe that whatever conventional moral views we hold are true simply because we hold them. He believes, on the contrary, that our moral views are abominably confused, that "it would be an incomparable benefit to commonwealth, if every man held the opinions concerning law and policy" that he, Thomas Hobbes, holds. He scorns "vulgar received opinions, which for the most part are erroneous."[101] Nor does he want to enshrine "those hermaphrodite opinions of moral philosophers, partly right and comely, partly brutal and wild; the causes of all contentions and bloodsheds."[102] He wants to concentrate on the logical characteristics of the moral and political concepts; only on these can he construct a scientific system of necessary truths.

Hobbes, then, seems committed to the extravagant view that a purely formal analysis, with a paucity of constraints, will yield substantial conclusions. Only with that commitment will he be able to move past trivialities in his moral and political science. Yet Hobbes labors under no such delusions. He knows that purely formal analysis yields empty conclusions: "It is impossible to be determined by the consent of single men, whom the same things do not please and displease, what actions are, and what not to be blamed. They may agree indeed in some certain general things, as that *theft*, *adultery*, and the like are *sins*; as if they should say that all men account those things *evil*, to which they have given names which are usually taken in an *evil* sense. But we demand not whether theft be a sin, but what is to be termed theft; and so concerning others, in like manner."[103] The quotation is not quite to the point, but the path leading from one to the other is quite short and is well traveled by Hobbes.

---

[101]*Elements*, p. xvi (*EW* IV:xiv); *Rudiments*, p. 231 (*EW* II:137). *Elements*, p. 65 (*EW* IV:71): "Commonly truth is on the side of the few, rather than of the multitude," perhaps because of "the ordinary ignorance, stupidity, and superstition of mankind," *Leviathan*, pp. 474–475 (*EW* III:433). See too *EW* VI:343.

[102]*Rudiments*, p. 98 (*EW* II:xiii). Note *EW* VI:282–283 on "the babbling philosophy of Aristotle and other Greeks"; *EW* VII:75–76; and, of course, the famed chap. 46 of *Leviathan*.

[103]*Rudiments*, p. 283 (*EW* II:196–197).

It is, in fact, one step. Hobbes holds a strikingly modern theory of evaluation and language: "Men, by giving names, do usually not only signify the things themselves, but also their own affections, as love, hatred, anger, and the like."[104] His favorite example is tyranny: "They that are discontented under *Monarchy*, call it *Tyranny*"; but the form of government is still the same, even if "misliked."[105] He says too, for example, that pusillanimity is called "WRETCHEDNESSE, MISERABLENESSE, or PARSIMONY; as it is liked, or disliked."[106] Many concepts, as we might say, have descriptive and evaluative components. Now the moral concepts have evaluative and prescriptive force; if they are to appear in necessarily true propositions, they must be linked to other evaluative and prescriptive concepts. Substantial moral claims—those that assert, say, that we ought to engage in some descriptively understood activity—cannot be necessarily true, since we can conceive of their contrary as being true. We understand, whether we agree or not, the claim that we ought never to aid our neighbors. Here is why, methodologically speaking, Hobbes's moral science does not embrace common moral opinions: not only are they wrong, they have substance.

Theft is wrong, for we mean by theft "wrongful taking of another's property." But we need yet to know just what activities constitute theft. That question is beyond the horizons of Hobbes's moral science. Its findings are true only because they are purged of content; the argument from ordinary language fails, as it must. For "we demand not whether theft be a sin, but what is to be termed theft, and so concerning others, in like manner."

A Substantial Moral Argument?

Hobbes is caught. The prudential argument fails to provide a genuinely moral rationale for obeying the sovereign in all things,

[104] *Rudiments*, p. 192 (*EW* II:93); also *Leviathan*, p. 165 (*EW* III:90).

[105] *Leviathan*, pp. 239–240 (*EW* III:171–172), and pp. 369–370, 722 (*EW* III:315, 706); also *Rudiments*, pp. 192–193 (*EW* II:93–94); *EW* V:215.

[106] *Leviathan*, p. 123 (*EW* III:44). More examples: *Elements*, pp. 37, 38, 43, 109, 114–115 (*EW* IV:40–41, 42, 48, 127–128, 134).

and Hobbes does want a genuinely moral argument. Yet the only argument he can muster to the cause, the argument from ordinary language, is empty: it fails to dictate anything at all. How, then, can he ground a moral argument dictating obedience to an absolute sovereign? Hobbes makes two attempts here. Neither works.

Perhaps uncharitably, I view the first as an attempt to rig the terms of the argument from ordinary language. Hobbes's political science, remember, is concerned with "such words as are Essentiall to all Politicall reasoning." Some of them—"justice," or "right," for example—are specialized moral concepts; but some—"sovereign," or "law", for example—are ostensibly descriptive. Hobbes departs from explication in defining the latter sort: "And in him [Leviathan] consisteth the Essence of the Commonwealth; which (to define it,) is *One Person, of whose Acts a great Multitude, by mutuall Covenants one with another, have made themselves every one the Author, to the end he may use the strength and means of them all, as he shall think expedient, for their Peace and Common Defence. And he that carryeth this Person, is called* SOVERAIGNE, and said to have *Soveraigne Power.*"[107] A sovereign carries the person of the great multitude, each of whom is the author of his acts. Now consider what Hobbes has to say about the "author":

> Of Persons Artificiall, some have their words and actions *Owned* by those whom they represent. And then the Person is the *Actor*; and he that owneth his words and actions, is the AUTHOR: In which case the Actor acteth by Authority. For that which in speaking of goods and possessions, is called an *Owner* . . . speaking of Actions, is called Author. And as the Right of possession, is called Dominion; so the Right of doing any Action, is called AUTHORITY. So that by Authority, is always understood a Right of doing any act; and *done by Authority*, done by Commission, or Licence from him whose right it is.[108]

Actors have a right to do what they are authorized to do; the sovereign, then, *by definition*, has a right to do what he does. Hobbes makes much the same move in discussing law: "It is manifest,

[107]*Leviathan*, p. 228 (*EW* III:158).
[108]*Leviathan*, p. 218 (*EW* III:148).

that Law in generall, is not Counsell, but Command; nor a Command of any man to any man; but only of him, whose Command is addressed to one formerly obliged to obey him."[109] We are, *by definition*, obliged to obey the law. That is what a law is. We are also obliged to obey the sovereign (I leave Hobbes to scientifically transform the transfer of right into obligation: "When a man hath . . . granted away his Right; then is he said to be Obliged"). That is what a sovereign is.

The flaw is obvious enough. If he likes, Hobbes can exercise his privileges as a philosopher and define his terms as he will. He can carefully build the appropriate evaluative and prescriptive components into his definitions of the moral and political concepts. He can then claim that laws and sovereigns ought to be obeyed, and can attach all the splendor of scientific veracity to his claim. But we can demand not whether laws oblige or sovereigns act by right, but what are to be termed laws, what sovereigns, and so concerning others, in like manner. If being a sovereign means, among other things, having the right to do what one does, those we commonly think of as sovereigns (because they wield power in a certain way) may not be sovereigns at all: they may act without right. There may be no sovereigns, no laws, in Hobbes's sense. An argument intended to show that we ought to obey the sovereign cannot commence with that view built into the definitions, else we may fairly decide that its author is trying to smuggle in his own prescriptive views under the guise of describing common usage. Even if common usage made that tie analytic, we could always employ an open-question argument and drive in a skeptical wedge. That is, even if we did commonly understand laws to oblige by definition, we could sensibly inquire whether this putative law really does oblige, whether it "really" is a law at all. Verbal maneuvers don't resolve substantive questions.[110]

The second attempt is more interesting. Hobbes is captivated

[109]*Leviathan*, p. 312 (*EW* III:251).
[110]Compare Anthony Quinton, "On Punishment," *Analysis* 14 (June 1954): 133–142, and John Rawls, "Two Concepts of Rules," *Philosophical Review* 64 (January 1955): 3–32, both reprinted in *The Philosophy of Punishment*, ed. H. B. Acton (New York: St. Martin's Press, 1969). Similar objections may be pressed against the position Ronald Dworkin stakes out in his *Taking Rights Seriously* (Cambridge, Mass.: Harvard University Press, 1980).

by moral disagreement and makes striking claims for its importance: "All controversies are bred from hence, that the opinions of men differ concerning *meum* and *tuum*, *just* and *unjust*, *profitable* and *unprofitable*, *good* and *evil*, *honest* and *dishonest*, and the like; which every man esteems according to his own judgment."[111] The moral concepts are among those of "inconstant signification," since we use them (in part) to express our own affections.[112] Hobbes seems sometimes to believe that the damnable world of human conflict would evaporate if only we could agree on the use of words. "The authors of sedition," he tells us, "be such, as name things not according to their true and generally agreed-upon names; but call right and wrong, good and bad, according to their passions, or according to the authorities of such as they admire, as Aristotle, Cicero, Seneca, and others."[113]

Insofar as language is at stake here, Hobbes is heading precisely backwards. For all the interesting ways in which language shapes our world, it's not that we have conflicting opinions, and so sometimes come to blows, because we use evaluative concepts differently. It's rather that we use evaluative concepts differently because we have conflicting opinions. Regardless, Hobbes is making a beeline for the argument from ordinary language, and we are once again in the world where definition is all-important and the meanings of words reign. This time, though, neither ordinary usage nor the fiat of philosophers or mathematicians is decisive. The verdict of the sovereign is.

To complete the quotation on the importance of moral disagreement: "It belongs to the same chief power to make some common rules for all men, and to declare them publicly, by which every man may know what may be called his, what another's, what just, what unjust, what good, what evil."[114] Here Hobbes's sovereign appears as the ultimate linguistic arbiter, and

---

[111]*Rudiments*, p. 178 (*EW* II:77).

[112]*Leviathan*, p. 109 (*EW* III:28), italics removed.

[113]*Elements*, p. 177 (*EW* IV:211). So should we say that Hobbes's decidedly eccentric explication of the political concepts makes him an author of sedition?

[114]*Rudiments*, p. 178 (*EW* II:77). For one reading of the political implications of the sovereign's linguistic authority, see Sheldon Wolin, *Politics and Vision* (Boston: Little, Brown, 1960), pp. 239–285, especially 257–262.

here Hobbes offers strikingly legalistic accounts of the moral and political concepts: "For not every taking away of the thing which another possesseth, but only another man's goods, is theft; but what is our's, and what another's, is a question belonging to the civil law."[115]

So far Hobbes is still firmly in the realm of the prudential argument. Once we recognize the disastrous effects of moral disagreement and the inconstancy of moral concepts, we should readily flock to the sovereign and slavishly adopt his proffered definitions of the relevant words. Our agreement is more important than what it is we agree on. But this time Hobbes cannot even rely on what little plausibility the prudential argument has. Our moral disagreement is not so important. Nor would the Orwellian maneuver of enforcing a set of definitions remedy conflict. There are real conflicts of interest in the world, far removed from dictionaries. Words can be weapons—we must assent to Hobbes's grim claim that "the tongue of man is a trumpet of war and sedition"[116]—but people wield them for reasons. Without venturing any suggestions on better theoretical frameworks for understanding strife, I do want to suggest, if only editorially, that Hobbes's view of the matter is exotic. Yet he needs that view to head toward the argument from ordinary language.

Hobbes's thoughts on the sovereign and language may seem to lead him to a marriage of the prudential argument and the argument from ordinary language. He insists vehemently on the linguistic powers of the sovereign. He even refers to "him that hath the Power to prescribe the Rules of Right and Wrong; that is, to make Laws" and says that "the civil laws [are] the rules of *good* and *evil, just* and *unjust, honest* and *dishonest*; that therefore what the legislator commands, must be held for *good*, and what he forbids for *evil*."[117] In a section entitled "It pertains to the civil authority, to judge (when need requires) what definitions and what inferences are true," Hobbes says that "the decision of the ques-

---

[115]*Rudiments*, p. 185 (*EW* II:85); also *Leviathan*, p. 328 (*EW* III:269).
[116]*Rudiments*, pp. 168–169 (*EW* II:67).
[117]*Leviathan*, p. 594 (*EW* III:568) and p. 697 (*EW* III:680–681); *Rudiments*, p. 244 (*EW* II:150) and the following pages.

tion, whether a man do reason rightly, belongs to the city."[118] Perhaps Hobbes believes that the sovereign's decreeing something to be the case makes it the case, that truth is a matter of political decree. Certainly Hobbes exalts the state, his *"Mortall God."* Who knows how godlike he thought it? Or, less extravagantly, perhaps Hobbes believes that *true* means "vouched for by the state." Either move would place him in a position to reformulate the argument from ordinary language. He could dress it up as the argument from political decree; with his new account of truth, he could say that civil laws are moral truths. Then he would have a genuinely substantial moral argument (a significantly relativist one, though, since even the least fickle sovereigns change laws, and different sovereigns enact different laws, each of which would be, on this account, true in its time and place).

Such an argument, though, would make mincemeat of our notion of truth. I am inclined to think that Hobbes makes no such argument, and that his apparently contrary statements on the Olympian linguistic powers of the sovereign are just catchy slogans, formulations imposed by his contentiousness.[119] What remains after the sensationalist dust settles is the more straightforward claim: it is in our self-interest to accept the sovereign's verdict on truth and falsehood, just as it is to accept his verdict on what constitutes theft and adultery. We can then place my reading squarely between those of Watkins and Warrender. Watkins claims that Hobbes's sovereign "must be a single determinate body who will fill the natural moral vacuum by issuing laws which will create moral distinctions and regulate relations between men"; Warrender claims that "the sovereign provides conditions which render operative obligations, which previously are but imperfectly effective."[120] Watkins's view, that the sover-

---

[118]*Rudiments*, pp. 329, 344 (*EW* II:268, 269). At *EW* VI:175, Parliament defines *heresy*.

[119]Though we do have Hobbes's demurrer, "I only do reason, I dispute not," *Rudiments*, p. 103 (*EW* II:xx). I wonder what Wallis or Bramhall would say. Note *EW* VII:332–337. For some of Hobbes's marvelous boasting, see *EW* I:ix; *EW* IV:436–437; *EW* VII:242, 471.

[120]J. W. N. Watkins, "Philosophy and Politics in Hobbes," *Philosophical Quarterly* 5 (April 1955): 145 and 141, revised and reprinted in Brown, *Hobbes*

eign creates moral distinctions, is too strong; Warrender's, that the sovereign supplies validating grounds of obligation, is too weak. The moral distinctions are built into the language, but they are empty; it is up to the sovereign to lend them content.

In the end, then, Hobbes can support his contention that we ought to submit to an absolute sovereign only by appealing to prudential considerations. His moral argument remains empty: he can show that we ought to fulfill our obligations, but he cannot show that there is any particular activity we are obliged to engage in. Squeezing obligations into the definitions of *sovereign* and *law* gets Hobbes nowhere; and the marriage of the prudential argument and the argument from ordinary language, even if Hobbes is foolhardy enough to attempt it, is barren.

So I return to a familiar idea: Hobbes offers no satisfactory account of the moral relations between individuals and the state. Nor does his prudential argument succeed. Hobbes's political theory purchases its crystalline precision by forfeiting engagement with concrete issues. As a result, Hobbes fails to justify his conclusions. But perhaps a political theorist willing to go beyond abstract renditions of self-interest and political language will not fail to justify his conclusions. Accordingly, I turn now to John Locke.

Studies, pp. 262 and 258; and Watkins, *Hobbes's System of Ideas*, pp. 138, 144–145, 164; Warrender, *Political Philosophy of Hobbes*, p. 144 and pp. 114–118, though see p. 163.

[CHAPTER TWO]

LOCKE'S
DIVINE POLITICS

I wish here to sketch and probe the social-contract arguments (I think there are three) in Locke's *Second Treatise*. In doing so, I will attempt to reconstruct Locke's moral theory. ("True politics," remarked Locke in 1697, "I look on as a part of moral philosophy."[1]) Such a reconstruction will allow full comprehension of the limits of Locke's contract arguments. I close by showing that while Locke has the makings of a plausible resolution of the Euthyphro dilemma, his moral theory fails to fill out or support his political theory.

Throughout the chapter I cite from the following works by John Locke: *Education* (*Some Thoughts Concerning Education*, in *The Educational Writings of John Locke*, ed. James L. Axtell [Cambridge: Cambridge University Press, 1968]); *Essay* (*An Essay concerning Human Understanding*, ed. Peter H. Nidditch, Clarendon ed. [Oxford: Clarendon, 1979]); *Law* (*Essays on the Law of Nature*, ed. and trans. W. von Leyden [Oxford: Clarendon, 1954]); *Letter* (*Epistola de Tolerantia: A Letter on Toleration*, ed. Raymond Klibansky and trans. J. W. Gough [Oxford: Clarendon, 1968]); *Tracts* (*Two Tracts on Government*, ed. Philip Abrams [Cambridge: Cambridge University Press, 1967]); *Treatises* (*Two Treatises of Government*, ed. Peter Laslett, 2d ed. [Cambridge: Cambridge University Press, 1970]; in the notes, roman numerals I and II following *Tracts* and *Treatises* refer to the number of the tract or treatise); *Reasonableness* (*The Reasonableness of Christianity*, in *Works* VII); *Works* (*The Works of John Locke*, 10 vols. [London, 1823]). Author's italics throughout, unless otherwise noted.

[1]"Locke's Draft Letter to the Countess of Peterborough," in Axtell, *Educational Writings of John Locke*, p. 395. As the Clarendon edition of Locke's works being prepared by Oxford University Press is emerging with glacial speed, I will quote from whatever seems the best edition available for each work.

Three Contract Arguments

"To understand Political Power right, and derive it from its Original," says Locke, "we must consider what State all Men are naturally in," so setting out his plan of attack for the *Second Treatise*.[2] Locke tells us that "Men living together according to reason, without a common Superior on Earth, with Authority to judge between them, is *properly the State of Nature*."[3] It isn't clear whether Locke means to make a substantial observation about what state we are "naturally" in or to offer a stipulative definition of *state of nature*; but for my purposes nothing hangs on the difference. He will investigate what society would be like without politics in order to understand politics.

To offer a quick review of the state of nature: People there are governed by a law of nature, "plain and intelligible to all rational Creatures," however shrouded in mystery it might seem to the reader. Perhaps aware of the mystery, Locke demurs, "Though it would be besides my present purpose, to enter here into the particulars of the Law of Nature, or its *measures of punishment*, yet, it is certain there is such a Law, and that too, as intelligible and plain to a rational Creature, and a Studier of that Law, as the positive laws of Commonwealths, nay possibly plainer."[4] One particular of the law of nature—indeed, the "Fundamental Law"—we do find out: "As much as may be, *all* the Members of the Society are to be *preserved*."[5] And we are treated to a fleeting glimpse of the internal workings of the law of nature: "Men being all the Workmanship of one Omnipotent, and infinitely wise Maker; All the Servants of One Sovereign Master, sent into the World by his order and about his business, they are his Property, whose Workmanship they are, made to last during his, not one anothers Pleasure."[6]

---

[2] *Treatises* II §4 p. 287. Locke believed that there is "a Foundation in Nature" for subjecting women to men (I §47 p. 192; see too II §82 p. 339), and, perhaps accordingly, he generally talks about men. I reluctantly follow him here.

[3] *Treatises* II §19 p. 298; see too *Treatises* II §4 p. 287.

[4] *Treatises* II §124 p. 369, II §12 p. 293.

[5] *Treatises* II §159 p. 393; see too *Treatises* II §16 pp. 296–297, II §134 pp. 373–374, II §183 p. 409; *Education*, p. 226.

[6] *Treatises* II §6 p. 289.

I will try later to extend that glimpse, but now I want to dispose of an apparent blatant inconsistency on Locke's part. Locke appeals to God's ownership of us to explain why we may not commit suicide, why we must not harm each other, and why we may not contract ourselves into slavery.[7] Yet he defends private property rights by suggesting that we gain such rights by mixing our labor with unowned objects or land. That suggestion hangs in turn on our ownership of ourselves: "Every Man," he asserts, "has a *Property* in his own *Person*."[8] So God owns us, and we own ourselves. Is Locke incoherent?

I think not. In each of the passages in the *Treatises* where Locke says we own ourselves, he says we own our *persons*; when he speaks of God's ownership, he says God owns us as *men*. Here, it might seem, is a niggling philosophical distinction; but it is one Locke uses, and it is perfectly serviceable. In the *Essay concerning Human Understanding*, Locke constructs some strikingly modern puzzle cases in his attempt to work out a theory of personal identity. One of those cases is much to the point: "For should the Soul of a Prince, carrying with it the consciousness of the Prince's past life, enter and inform the Body of a Cobler as soon as deserted by his own Soul, every one sees, he would be the same Person with the Prince, accountable only for the Prince's Actions: But who would say it was the same Man?"[9] Locke realizes that his readers may initially frown at the distinction ("I know that in the ordinary way of speaking, the same Person, and the same Man, stand for one and the same thing"[10]), but he thinks it necessary to make it.

Locke contends that *person* is "a Forensick Term," both in the *Essay* and in his veiled "Defence of Mr. Locke's Opinion Concerning Personal Identity."[11] We hold people responsible for

[7]*Treatises* II §6 p. 289, II §23 p. 302, II §135 p. 375, II §168 p. 398, II §172 p. 400.
[8]*Treatises* II §27 p. 305; also *Treatises* II §44 p. 316, II §173 p. 401, II §190 pp. 411–412.
[9]*Essay*, p. 340.
[10]*Essay*, p. 340.
[11]*Essay*, p. 346; John Locke, "Defence," in *Works* III:179–201. Locke distinguishes person from body in *Works* IV:303–334, in arguing that the dead's resurrection need not include their bodies.

their actions; we blame and praise; we do so, in Locke's view, precisely insofar as and because they are the same persons. Persons, therefore, we may take as moral agents, and men as bodies, despite Locke's hesitance on the latter point.[12] God, then, owns us as physical organisms.[13] We may not harm each other, or kill ourselves, because that would be infringing on God's property rights. So Locke typically limits himself to enjoining the preservation of all, to forbidding harm (though he does aver, harshly enough, "I think it every Man's indispensible Duty, to do all the Service he can to his Country: And I see not what Difference he puts between himself and his Cattel, who lives without that Thought"[14]).

A bit more puzzling, but not nonsensical, is the claim that we own ourselves as moral agents.[15] I take Locke to mean that we act freely, not just as God's automatons, and that we are responsible for our actions. Locke insists on such freedom of action, though he discards *free will* as an absurd phrase and admits that he cannot reconcile human freedom with God: "I cannot make freedom in man consistent with omnipotence and omniscience in God, though I am as carefully persuaded of both, as of any truths I most firmly assent to. And, therefore, I have long since given off the consideration of that question, resolving all into this short conclusion, that if it be possible for God to make a free agent, then man is free, though I see not the way of it."[16] The

[12]*Essay*, p. 343. I take Locke's considered view to be like the second advanced on p. 348: "But if to any one the *Idea* of a *Man* be, but the vital union of *Parts* in a certain shape." "Man" must at least include body, else the prince/cobbler puzzle would be no puzzle at all.

[13]Locke, then, cannot be enlisted as a bourgeois ideologist trying to rationalize the quirky claim that laborers own their bodies. Compare Robert Paul Wolff, "A Critique and Reinterpretation of Marx's Labor Theory of Value," *Philosophy & Public Affairs* 10 (Spring 1981): 110.

[14]*Education*, p. 111. Locke's italics removed. Locke regularly demotes the immoral to the status of brutes: see for example *Treatises* II §10 p. 291, II §11 p. 292.

[15]Compare J. P. Day, "Locke on Property," *Philosophical Quarterly* 16 (July 1966): 207–220, reprinted in *Life, Liberty, and Property: Essays on Locke's Political Ideas*, ed. Gordon J. Schochet (Belmont, Calif.: Wadsworth, 1971).

[16]Locke to Molyneux, 20 jan 1692–3, in *Works* IX:305; also *Works* IV:492. Locke grapples with free will and determinism in the *Essay*, pp. 233–271, and discards "free will" at p. 240. Compare C. B. Macpherson, *The Political Theory of*

law of nature commands our preservation because God owns our bodies, and it commands the protection of property rights because we own ourselves. Our owning our labor, and so our gaining property rights in unowned things we mix our labor with, pose additional problems I leave aside. I mean only to acquit Locke of the charge of gross inconsistency.

Let us then return to our story. Locke's anarchy (for that is what his state of nature is) is none too pleasant, and it worsens as Locke considers it. Although people have substantial interests in safeguarding "their Lives, Liberties, and Estates, which," Locke tells us, "I call by the general name, *Property*,"[17] those interests are left insecure. True, the law of nature dictates the preservation of property. But problems arise where everyone is entitled to enforce the law. People are partial in considering their own cases ("'tis easily to be imagined," Locke puckishly observes, "that he who was so unjust as to do his Brother an Injury, will scarce be so just as to condemn himself for it"), and many do not even take the trouble to learn the law. Also, since the unjust may be stronger than the just, even deserved sentences may go unenforced. So men are forced to form a government, or as Locke says are "driven into Society."[18] Locke generally refers to the contract as forming the society, and he has the society go on to entrust a government with the business of politics. He also says, though, that by the law of nature "*Mankind are one Community*, make up one Society distinct from all other Creatures"; and, of course, the state of nature boasts extensive social relations, indeed, all but political ones. It is the formation of a "particular Political Society" Locke takes as decisive in terminating the state of nature.[19] Nothing for my purposes hangs on the re-

---

Possessive Individualism (Oxford: Clarendon, 1962), p. 231. Compare too *Treatises* II §63 p. 327.

[17]*Treatises* II §123 p. 368. I take this extended use of *property* as typical in the *Treatises*, and adopt it myself here. Laslett has a helpful list of references on Locke's use of *property* on p. 341n.

[18]*Treatises* II §13 p. 294, II §124 p. 369; *Treatises* II §126 p. 369; *Treatises* II §127 p. 370.

[19]*Treatises* II §128 p. 370. Note too *Treatises* II §89 p. 343: "the Society, or which is all one, the Legislative thereof." Locke prefers "compact" and "consent" locutions to "contract," generally reserving the lattermost for marriage;

sultant partitioning of humankind into independent political units. Accordingly, here I cast the contract as one to establish a government.

The terms of Locke's contract are familiar enough. People entrust a state with the protection of property. The state's authority is drastically limited. Though it does have a power of prerogative to advance the public good "without the prescription of the Law, and sometimes even against it," it appears more typically as "Umpire," ruling "by settled standing Rules, indifferent, and the same to all Parties."[20] Its exceeding its boundaries represents a violation of the trust, and may in fact be ground for revolution. The state's rights are no wondrous emergent properties created by the concord of individuals: each individual has simply transferred to the executive his power of enforcing the law of nature, to the legislature his power of doing "whatsoever he thinks fit for the preservation of himself and others within the permission of the *Law of Nature*."[21] The law of nature, then, lives on in political society.[22]

All this is fair enough, but we need an account of the status of the contract.[23] Is it a historical event? a metaphor describing how each of us comes to fall under the dominion of the state? a purely hypothetical construct about timeless truths of politics? We need too an account of the uses to which the contract is to be put. Is it a tool in the never-ending polemic against Filmer? a prop for a theory of obligation? for a theory of legitimacy? It is, I want to suggest, all these things, and serves all these functions. I will proceed by sketching out, in idealized form, the three uses

---

though see *Treatises* I §96 p. 230, where "*Contract*" is equated with "*Consent of the People*."

[20]*Treatises* II §160 p. 393; *Treatises* II §87 p. 342. Also *Treatises* II §212 p. 425, II §227 p. 434.

[21]*Treatises* II §128 p. 370.

[22]*Treatises* II §135 p. 376.

[23]My reading of Locke for the rest of this section has been greatly influenced by Hanna Pitkin, "Obligation and Consent," *American Political Science Review* 59 (December 1965): 990–999, and 60 (March 1966): 39–56, reprinted in *Philosophy, Politics and Society*, ed. Peter Laslett, W. G. Runciman, and Quentin Skinner, 4th ser. (London: Basil Blackwell, 1972). My departures from her view should be readily apparent.

for the contract, and then moving closer to Locke's text and exploring some muddy spots.

Locke is clear that we are to understand the contract as a report on our ancestors' behavior. Consider what he has to say about the objection *"That there are no Instances to be found in Story of a Company of Men independent and equal one amongst another, that met together, and in this way began and set up a Government."*[24] He argues that we cannot fairly expect records of this sort of contract, struck after all in very early times, to have survived; and he adduces "evident matter of fact," regaling the reader with instances of the formation of government by contract. Rome and Venice were founded "by the uniting together of several Men free and independent one of another"; "if *Josephus Acosta's* word may be taken," Peru, Florida, the Cheriquanas, and "Bresil" offer still more examples; and finally those who left Sparta with Palantus presumably established a government by contract.[25] The social contract, then, is not just a plausible story about the inception of political society; it actually happened.

At the point in the *Treatises* at which Locke launches into this reading of history, he has already announced that *"every Man's Children* being by Nature as *free* as himself, or any of his Ancestors ever were, may, whilst they are in that Freedom, choose what Society they will join themselves to, what Commonwealth they will put themselves under."[26] If history provides us with no source of obligation, why is he troubling us with crumbled, yellowing tales of antiquity? Locke appeals to history for one of his favorite activities in the *Treatises*: ridiculing Sir Robert Filmer's theories. Filmer's case, as set forth in *Patriarcha*, hinges on the claim that political authority has descended from Adam. Locke, then, can refute Filmer by showing that Filmer's history is wrong. Here is why the historical narrative winds on, leaving the reader dizzied with chronicles of America, Peru, Mexico, the American Indians, Israel, Jephtha, the Ammonites, the Gileadites, Jotham, the Shechemites, Gideon, Midian, Abimelech, Samuel, the Philistines, Saul, Mispah, David, and Hebron:

[24]*Treatises* II §100 p. 351.
[25]*Treatises* II §102 p. 352; *Treatises* II §102 p. 353, II §103 p. 353.
[26]*Treatises* II §73 p. 333.

Locke wants to show where Filmer has gone wrong in his reading of history.[27]

So the historic contract plays a purely negative role in the argument. It is surprising, then, that Hume spent so much time arguing that "force . . . is the origin of almost all the new [governments] which were ever established in the world." Perhaps he had in mind followers of Locke's contract doctrine, not "the most noted of its partisans," the champion of "so refined and philosophical a system."[28] It is surprising too that Josiah Tucker scornfully called "upon the Lockians once more [each to answer separately for him or herself] to name the Year, Month, Week, Day, or Hour, when this Contract was made between the Government of *Great-Britain* on the one part, and A.B. or C.D. or E.F., on the other," and so strenuously insisted that "the true basis of civil government," as against these weirdly historicist "Lockians," was a "quasi-contract," one that bears a striking resemblance to the kind Locke actually uses.[29] To make a methodological suggestion: While there is good sense in holding that accounts of what an author meant should connect up tightly with the way his contemporaries could understand him, we want to be able to say that his contemporaries—even readers as discerning as Hume—misunderstood him. Locke's foray into history may or may not have played an important role in scotching the snake of patriarchalism, but in any case the snake is dead. So we can leave Locke's historical contract behind, where Locke left Filmer and his *"glib Nonsense."*[30] I turn, then, first to Locke's theory of obligation, second to his theory of legitimacy.

Locke poses himself the problem of how we become obliged to the state when he writes, "*Every Man* being, as has been shewed, *naturally free*, and nothing being able to put him into subjection to any Earthly Power, but only his own Consent; it is to be con-

[27]Though not, significantly, in his reading of English legal history. See J. G. A. Pocock, *The Ancient Constitution and the Feudal Law* (New York: Norton, 1967), especially pp. 187–190, 235–238.
[28]David Hume, "Of the Original Contract," in his *Essays: Moral, Political, Literary* (Great Britain: Oxford University Press, 1974), pp. 460, 473, 456.
[29]Josiah Tucker, *A Treatise concerning Civil Government* (New York: Augustus M. Kelley, 1967), pp. 156, 122–146. The brackets and italics are Tucker's.
[30]*Treatises*, preface, p. 155.

sidered, what shall be Understood to be *a sufficient Declaration of a Mans Consent, to make him subject* to the laws of any Government."[31] I say "how we become obliged," not "how it is we are obliged," because Locke holds that children are in no way obliged to obey the law: "*A Child is born a Subject of no Country or Government.* He is under his Fathers Tuition and Authority till he comes to Age of Discretion; and then he is a Free-man, at liberty to decide what Government he will put himself under; what Body Politick he will unite himself to."[32] We need not worry about screaming little banshees, who in Locke's view love authority,[33] being free to wreak havoc; for, of course, they are obliged to obey their parents. Here Locke casts our natural freedom in a refreshingly straightforward way. It's not that people were once, in far-off days of folklore, somehow free; or even that the essence of a human being is to be free, whatever that might mean. It's that each and every one of us is born without political ties and enjoys an opportunity for genuine choice on outgrowing parental authority.

So Locke turns to consent to explain political obligation. A subject is obliged to obey the law, in his account, because he has consented. On reaching his majority, he elected, as Locke would say, to put himself under the laws of England. Consent here appears as an ongoing, inconspicuous process. Each person appends a metaphorical signature to the social contract, signing on a ghostly dotted line upon reaching his majority. That is why, holds Locke, many people imagine that political authority is natural: "*The Consent of Free-men, born under Government, which only makes them Members of it,* being given separately in their turns, as each comes to be of Age, and not in a multitude together; People

[31] *Treatises* II §119 p. 365.
[32] *Treatises* II §118 p. 365; also, for example, *Treatises* II §15 p. 296, II §73 p. 333.
[33] This theme Locke orchestrates most impressively in his *Education*: "Children love *Liberty*. . . . They love something more, and this is *Dominion*" (p. 207); see too *Education*, pp. 179, 229. The theme connects up nicely with Locke's fear of the state's encroachment (*Treatises* I §10 p. 166, I §106 p. 237, II §92 p. 345, II §143 p. 382) and his early perception of the politics of deception (see, for example, *Tracts* I 160, 166).

take no notice of it, and thinking it not done at all, or not necessary, conclude they are naturally Subjects as they are Men."³⁴

If Locke is to say that consent obliges, he needs at the very
least an account of consent on which he can sensibly talk that
way. Locke knows this, of course ("it is to be considered, what
shall be understood to be *a sufficient Declaration of* a Mans *Consent,
to make him subject* to the Laws of any Government"), so he
marches onstage the "common distinction of an express and a
tacit consent, which will concern our present Case."³⁵ What will
Locke take as tacit consent, and how far does it bind?

> And to this I say, that every man, that hath any Possession, or En-
> joyment, of any part of the Dominions of any Government, doth
> thereby give his *tacit Consent*, and is as far forth obliged to Obedi-
> ence to the Laws of that Government, during such Enjoyment, as
> any one under it; whether this his Possession be of Land, to him
> and his Heirs for ever, or a Lodging only for a Week; or whether
> it be barely travelling freely on the Highway; and in Effect, it
> reaches as far as the very being of any one within the Territories of
> that Government.³⁶

If so uninteresting an act as residence suffices to generate the obligation to obey the law, with what iron clamps does express consent shackle us?

> Whereas he, that has once, by actual Agreement, and any *express*
> Declaration, given his *Consent* to be of any Commonweal, is per-
> petually and indispensably obliged to be and remain unalterably a
> Subject to it, and can never be again in the liberty of the State of

---

³⁴*Treatises* II §117 p. 364.
³⁵*Treatises* II §119 p. 365.
³⁶*Treatises* II §119 p. 366. C. B. Macpherson, "The Social Bearing of Locke's
Political Theory," *Western Political Quarterly* 7 (March 1954): 18, reprinted in
Schochet, *Life, Liberty, and Property*, p. 80, reads the "being" in the last clause as
a noun, the person's essence, thereby suggesting a curious existential twist. In
Possessive Individualism, p. 250, Macpherson lends it a rather sinister role in his
class analysis. I take that "being" to be a verb, paralleling "travelling," and so
take Locke to say that merely being inside the boundaries counts as tacit consent.

Nature; unless by any Calamity, the Government, he was under, comes to be dissolved; or else by some publick Act cuts him off from being any longer a Member of it.[37]

Each individual, then, is obliged to obey the law because he has consented; but consent may be as minimal as residence.

Legitimacy, though, is another matter. It is generated by the hypothetical choice of rational agents. Illustrative here is Locke's argument for majority rule. He starts by asserting flatly that it and unanimity are the only feasible choice procedures. "For if *the consent of the majority* shall not in reason, be received as *the act of the whole*, and conclude every individual; nothing but the consent of every individual can make any thing to be the act of the whole," he declares, pointing out that nothing would ever be approved in any public assembly on the unanimity principle.[38] The rather arbitrary exclusion of other alternatives need not detain us here. Note how Locke goes on to reject unanimity: "Such a Constitution as this would make the mighty *Leviathan* of a shorter duration, than the feeblest Creatures; and not let it outlast the day it was born in: which cannot be suppos'd, till we can think that Rational Creatures should desire and constitute Societies only to be dissolved. For where the *majority* cannot conclude the rest, there they cannot act as one Body, and consequently will be immediately dissolved again."[39] We can infer from the contract that people wish to have a government; presumably they wish it to do something; so if people are rational agents, if we can make painfully obvious inferences from their behavior to their ends, we can rule out certain proposals as not meeting those ends.

Locke employs similarly structured arguments again and again. Indeed, he does so extensively enough for us to say that he wields the contract also as a purely hypothetical argument. Regardless of the history of the matter, and regardless of our own consent, tacit or express, we can make observations about the proper behavior of government simply by inferring people's ends

[37]*Treatises* II §121 p. 367.
[38]*Treatises* II §98 p. 350.
[39]*Treatises* II §98 p. 351.

in forming it. Consider: the "power of the Society, or *Legislative
. . . can never be suppos'd to extend farther than the common good*,"
since people leave the state of nature "only with an intention in
every one the better to preserve himself his Liberty and Property; (For no rational Creature can be supposed to change his
condition with an intention to be worse)"; prerogative cannot be
"an Arbitrary Power to do things hurtful to the People," since "a
Rational Creature cannot be supposed when free, to put himself
into Subjection to another, for his own harm"; the legislature
must follow the familiar path of free elections and independent
action, since "the People having reserved to themselves the
Choice of their *Representatives*, as the Fence to their Properties,
could do it for no other end, but that they might always be freely
chosen, and so chosen, freely act and advise, as the necessity of
the Commonwealth, and the publick Good should, upon examination, and mature debate, be judged to require"; and finally,
there must be a rule of law, since "Absolute Arbitrary Power,
or Governing without *settled standing Laws*, can neither of them
consist with the ends of Society and Government, which Men
would not quit the freedom of the state of Nature for, and tie
themselves up under, were it not to preserve their Lives, Liberties and Fortunes; and by *stated Rules* of Right and Property to
secure their Peace and Quiet."[40]

Thinking along these lines, Locke outlines what we would
think of as a theory of legitimacy, laying down the boundaries of
state action beyond which revolution is justifiable: "since it can
never be supposed to be the Will of the Society, that the Legislative should have a Power to destroy that, which every one de-
signs to secure, by entering into Society, and for which the People submitted themselves to the Legislators of their own making;
whenever the *Legislators endeavour to take away, and destroy the
Property of the People*, or to reduce them to Slavery under Arbitrary Power, they put themselves into a state of War with the
People, who are thereupon absolved from any farther Obedience, and are left to the common Refuge, which God hath pro-

[40]*Treatises* II §131 p. 371; *Treatises* II §163 p. 394, II §164 p. 394; *Treatises* II §222 p. 431; *Treatises* II §137 p. 377. See too Locke's *Third Letter for Toleration*, in *Works* VI:212.

vided for all Men, against Force and Violence."[41] Since rational agents would not approve certain behavior, that behavior can be ground for revolution, only thinly disguised in Locke's talk of our divinely allotted common refuge.[42] Not every illicit act either should or will be responded to so violently: "he that *appeals to Heaven*, must be sure he has Right on his side, and a Right too that is worth the Trouble and Cost of the Appeal"; and, of course, "*Great Mistakes* in the ruling part, many wrong and inconvenient Laws, and all the *slips* of humane frailty will be *born by the People*, without mutiny or murmur," for "People are not so easily got out of their old Forms, as some are apt to suggest."[43]

Our consent, then, produces an obligation to obey the law; our ends yield a measuring rod of legitimacy by which we can assess our government. These claims are plausible. But Locke needs a good deal more to fill out this political theory, or so I want to argue.

Let me begin with the theory of obligation. Talk of consent immediately invites cynical sneers, especially from readers aware of the machinations of the modern totalitarian state: suitably stretched and redescribed with loving philosophical care, anything we do can count as consent. Yet for all the slipperiness of consent, an important restriction is built into its very logic. One can take as consent only those acts that allow an alternative, a way of refusing consent. Therefore, if our very being within the territories of the government is to count as consent, we must be allowed to leave. Those governments, then, that deny or im-

---

[41]*Treatises* II §222 p. 430. Locke sometimes says the judge is God, sometimes the people: see *Treatises* II §20 p. 300, II §21 p. 300, II §168 p. 397, II §176 p. 404, II §240 pp. 444–445, II §241 p. 445, II §242 p. 445; *Letter*, p. 129. Note Locke's passing comment in defending this right of revolution: "Are the People to be blamed, if they have the sence of rational Creatures, and can think of things no otherwise than as they find and feel them?" (*Treatises* II §230 p. 436).

[42]Locke indulges here in what I can see only as a touch of mystification: "Rebellion," he says, is "an Opposition, not to Persons, but Authority, which is founded only in the Constitutions and Laws of the Government" (*Treatises* II §226 p. 433). Yet, as Locke himself noted in a manuscript, "Allegiance is neither due nor paid to right or Government which are abstract notions but only to persons having right or government," in John Dunn, *The Political Thought of John Locke* (Cambridge: Cambridge University Press, 1969), p. 148n.

[43]*Treatises* II §176 p. 404; *Treatises* II §225 p. 433, II §223 p. 432.

pede emigration forfeit the claim to authority from tacit consent: "No Government can have a right to obedience from a people who have not freely consented to it."[44] Usurpers and conquerors, Locke tells us, gain no right to rule until the submission of the subjects can plausibly be called free.

Locke must dwell on tacit consent, since express consent is rare; so I will focus my attention on tacit consent here. Schematically speaking, Locke wants to move from some behavior in the world to consent, then (for both express and tacit consent) from consent to obligation. Accordingly, he needs some theory of interpretation on which the behaviors he nominates can plausibly be understood as consent, and he needs some moral theory on which consent generates obligation. The moral theory must also fix terms by showing what sort of consent generates what sort of obligation.

I mean to put off consideration of the moral theory to the next section of the chapter, but it seems worth noting here an elementary confusion in Locke's attempt to fix terms. We need to distinguish between the manner in which consent is given, express or tacit, and the extent of approval that the consent demonstrates, from hearty to grudging. It is sensible to think that hearty approval should generate a more enduring or demanding obligation than should grudging toleration, but Locke appeals instead to express consent. Perhaps he takes it for granted that when we expressly consent, we heartily approve; and when we tacitly consent, we less heartily or only grudgingly approve. That isn't necessarily the case, however. Putative communists signing a vow that they will faithfully uphold the Constitution consent expressly but are only grudgingly tolerant. Staunch conservatives continuing the family structure consent tacitly but are overwhelmingly enthusiastic. Express consent may generally be a good sign of hearty approval, but it is curious that Locke focuses on the manner of consent instead of the extent of the underlying approval.

There are imposing obstacles too in the way of a theory of

---

[44]*Treatises* II §192 p. 412. Compare Theodore Waldman, "A Note on John Locke's Concept of Consent," *Ethics* 68 (October 1957): 47.

interpretation. Hume suggests two pointed criticisms.[45] Some people, he notes, are too poor to emigrate. The alternative required for consent must be more than a logical possibility if consent is to be more than an academic chimera, but the freedom of the poor to leave is purely formal. Hume notes too that since people do not understand that obligation depends on consent, it is "absurd to infer a consent or choice"; should we take consent to contain any element of intentionality or volition, the point is well taken. Locke might wish to say that still we can take certain behavior to signify that the actor would consent. But such a subjunctive consent doctrine would be far removed from Locke's official position, and would itself face serious problems.

A theory of interpretation would also have to show what we consent to. Locke, of course, wishes to say that we consent to the government's rule, but here we can deploy against him his own distinction between state and society. Moving from one state to another is not the casual or even momentous step of some autonomous agent, some desiccated, anomic cell. It means wrenching deep ties with family and friends, perhaps culture and language. If residence indicates consent at all, that consent is to any and all of a set of items bundled together, comprising state and society. One person might consent (though speaking of consent here at all seems contrived) to the country's language, but oppose economic institutions and the state. Another might unpack the bundle we call the state, and consent to the judicial system but oppose a tiresome bureaucracy. It will require investigation in each case to determine to just what (if anything) each individual is consenting. It would be an extraordinary coincidence if all were consenting to the state. Since emigration means leaving state *and* society behind, it functions badly as an alternative showing that residence means consent to the state.[46]

Complications of a different sort arise when we ask whether

---

[45]Hume, "Of the Original Contract," in *Essays*, pp. 461–462.
[46]Those interested in pursuing consent theory to either its logical fulfillment or its *reductio ad absurdum* might consult Herbert Spencer, "The Right to Ignore the State," in his *Social Statics* (New York: Schalkenbach, 1970), pp. 185–194. Spencer removed the chapter from later editions of the book. Similarly, see Lysander Spooner, *No Treason* (Colorado Springs: Ralph Myles, 1973).

this reading is a reconstruction of Locke. For surely three separate contract arguments do not jump out of the pages of the *Treatises*. The text is more evasive. In particular, Locke's deployment of the contract in two different affirmative ways raises a host of questions. We want a theory illuminating the relationships between obligation and legitimacy. True, Locke says that "no Government can have a right to obedience from a people who have not freely consented to it." But that proviso is awfully vague. It will not bear the weight that any concrete line of interpretation will place on it. When is consent free?

Since legitimacy and obligation are generated by independent mechanisms, by (respectively) the hypothetical behavior of rational creatures and the consent of actual ones, there is a possibility they will diverge. A government might be legitimate, but its citizens might not have an obligation to obey the law. We cannot, however, find the converse case, in which citizens are obliged to obey an illegitimate government. For Locke, again, is clear that when the legislature "put themselves in a state of War with the People, [the people] are thereupon absolved from any farther obedience." So legitimacy and obligation are not wholly independent for Locke. One tempting proposal is this: the less completely legitimate the government, the less we are obliged to obey it, for the less free our consent is. But that will depend on just how the government is forfeiting its legitimacy. It may do so in ways that don't even begin to make consent look forced; the crucial alternatives to consent, options such as emigration, may remain completely open. Similarly, it will depend on whether Locke structures consent as a binary concept—one either consents or doesn't—or as a continuum, allowing degrees of consent. There are fascinating complications here that I will not pursue. My point is simply that Locke leaves all questions on these matters unanswered and even unasked.

Faced with such difficulties, scholars have suggested two other ways of interpreting Locke's argument for obligation. Hanna Pitkin has suggested that we forget consent and allow rational choice to do all the work: "For now the Lockean doctrine becomes this: your personal consent is essentially irrelevant to your obligation to obey, or its absence. Your obligation to obey

depends on the character of the government—whether it is acting within the bounds of *the* (only possible) contract."[47] Locke,
though, holds that "only his own Consent" can put a man "into
subjection to any Earthly Power," so Pitkin's reading commits us
to holding that Locke flatly misunderstood his own view. Worse,
it's not clear that consent and rational choice obligate the same
people. On the consent reading, it remains an open question
whether we can be obliged to illiberal but not hopelessly abso-
lutist states, because Locke is not clear about when residence really is consent.[48] Finally, in Locke's account, children are not
obliged to obey the law—quite plausibly on the consent reading,
but only unacceptably ad hoc provisos will make the point pre-
cipitate out of Pitkin's solution.

A. John Simmons acknowledges that "we can believe Locke
when he asserts that he holds personal consent to be the sole
ground of political obligation," but he goes on to find that
"Locke's primary error, then, seems to lie in his confusion of
consent with other grounds which may be sufficient to generate
obligations."[49] Simmons argues that those other grounds are the
enjoyment of benefits, which may oblige by the principle of fairness, or considerations of gratitude. Locke invites such a reading, not as revision but as textual exegesis: "Since the Government has a direct Jurisdiction only over the Land, and reaches
the Possessor of it . . . only as he dwells upon, and enjoys that:

[47]Pitkin, "Obligation and Consent," p. 996 and generally pp. 994–996, in
Philosophy, Politics and Society, ed. Laslett, Runciman, and Skinner, 4th ser., p.
57 and generally pp. 53–57.
[48]The early Locke is especially stubborn in clinging to the view that noxious
laws (not states) oblige to passive obedience; see, for example, *Tracts* I p. 152;
Tracts II pp. 220, 237; *Letter*, pp. 127, 129. Perhaps if there's room for an obligation to bad laws, we can drum up an obligation to not-so-good states by
playing a bit fast and loose with the fallacy of composition; but Locke is rather
nastier about passive obedience in *Treatises* II §228 pp. 434–435.
[49]A. John Simmons, "Tacit Consent and Political Obligation," *Philosophy &
Public Affairs* 5 (Spring 1976): 286, 288. See too Waldman, "Note on John
Locke's Concept of Consent," p. 48; John Dunn, "Consent in the Political Theory of John Locke," *Historical Journal* 10 (1967): 162, reprinted in Schochet,
Life, Liberty, and Property, p. 139. Simmons has pursued these issues further in
"The Principle of Fair Play," *Philosophy & Public Affairs* 8 (Summer 1979):
307–337, and in *Moral Principles and Political Obligations* (Princeton, N.J.:
Princeton University Press, 1979), which incorporates both articles.

The Obligation any one is under, *by Virtue of such Enjoyment*, to submit to the Government, begins and ends with the Enjoyment."[50] Is Locke appealing to the enjoyment itself? Or is consent still the key, enjoyment being merely the sign of consent? Recommending that we take Simmons's view as our explication of Locke is the Procrustean lengths to which we must stretch the concept of consent to make residence fit; militating against it is Locke's repeated claim that his is a consent doctrine. Unfortunately, Simmons's approach seems to yield practical results equivalent to Locke's, or to fall within the same foggy cloud of indeterminacy. For we cannot imagine a case where residence doesn't entail some enjoyments (say, national defense) and feel any assurance as to Locke's views.

Nonetheless, the best bet seems to be that we stick to the consent reading, since political obligation is not the only subject on which Locke employs an attenuated sense of consent. Money "has its *value* only from the consent of Men," and Locke takes its use in turn as a consensual justification of economic inequality: "Men have agreed to disproportionate and unequal Possession of the Earth, they having by a tacit and voluntary consent found out a way, how a man may fairly possess more land than he himself can use the product of, by receiving in exchange for the overplus, Gold and Silver."[51] Flexing heroically liberal muscle, Locke declares, "The *Supream Power cannot take* from any Man any part of his *Property* without his own consent"; but then he concedes, "'Tis true, Governments cannot be supported without great Charge, and 'tis fit every one who enjoys his share of the Protection, should pay out of his Estate his proportion for the maintenance of it. But still it must be with his own Consent, *i.e.* the Consent of the Majority, giving it either by themselves, or their Representatives chosen by them."[52] Most strikingly, in denying that "Property in Land . . . gave any Authority over the

---

[50]*Treatises* II §121 p. 367. I've rearranged Locke's italics.
[51]*Treatises* II §50 pp. 319, 320; see too John Locke, *Some Considerations of the Consequences of lowering the Interest and raising the Value of Money*, in *Works* V:22; John Locke, *Further Considerations concerning raising the value of money*, in *Works* V:139.
[52]*Treatises* II §138 p. 378, II §140 p. 380.

Persons of Men," Locke states that "the Authority of the Rich Proprietor, and the Subjection of the Needy Beggar began not from the Possession of the Lord, but the Consent of the poor Man, who preferr'd being his Subject to starving."[53] A decidedly odd conception of consent animates these claims. If one consents to money and inequality, if one consents when a majority votes, if one consents when the alternative is starving, one may perhaps be pardoned for not cherishing one's right to consent.

Locke has an internally coherent argument for our obligation to obey the law, but the argument is seriously incomplete as it stands so far. He needs an account of why consent is attenuated as residence in the lands of a tolerably liberal state obliges. Indeed, he needs a general account of why consent obliges at all. That account presumably would turn in the *Treatises* on the law of nature, but, again, Locke thinks "it would be besides my present purpose, to enter here into the particulars of the Law of Nature, or its *measures of punishment*," or, for that matter, the status of that law. So we must turn elsewhere. Similarly, Locke has an internally coherent argument for our right to revolt against a patently illiberal state, but that argument too is seriously incomplete as it stands so far. Assuming we are convinced by Locke's arguments that a liberal state serves the protection of property better than an anarchist society would, we still need an account of why it should be thought that we all take as our end the protection of property. That account presumably would turn on some general theory of human motivation and rationality, and might well connect up neatly with a moral theory showing what our ends ought to be. But Locke does not even begin the relevant arguments in the *Treatises*. (He had good tactical reasons for refraining. As we will see, his views on the law of nature were far more unorthodox than anyone could have gleaned from the *Treatises'* vague waves in its direction. His silence thus allows the contemporary reader a placid nod of the head.) So again we must turn elsewhere. Accordingly, I will now attempt a reconstruction of Locke's views on morality, motivation, and rationality.

[53]*Treatises* I §43 pp. 188–189.

Pleasure, Rationality, and Morality[54]

Even the most cursory reading of Locke's *Essay concerning Human Understanding* reveals an author determined to launch a bold attack on received views in epistemology and substitute a thoroughgoing empiricism. We need only glance down the title pages of Book I of the *Essay* to get the point: "No innate Speculative Principles" proclaims one chapter; "No innate Practical Principles" chimes the next, in emphatic chorus. The mind, Locke holds, starts off entirely empty. The imagery, if not the argument, has become the common stock of intellectual company. "The senses at first let in particular *Ideas*, and furnish the yet empty Cabinet"; "white Paper receives any Characters," "white Paper, void of all Characters, without any Ideas." Sense experience and introspection are the sole sources of ideas; since introspection requires something to introspect upon, sense experience is the fundamental source. Discussing "external and internal Sensation," as he calls them, Locke notes: "These alone, as far as I can discover, are the Windows by which light is let into this *dark Room*. For, methinks, the *Understanding* is not much unlike a Closet wholly shut from light, With only some little openings left, to let in external visible resemblances, or *Ideas* of things without."[55] Yet amidst all the thunderous fanfare and clamoring cavalcade, Locke declares: "Nature, I confess, has put into Man a desire for Happiness, and an aversion to Misery: These indeed

[54]The best works I have found in this area are Hans Aarsleff, "The State of Nature and the Nature of Man in Locke," in *John Locke: Problems and Perspectives*, ed. John W. Yolton (Cambridge: Cambridge University Press, 1969); and Patrick Riley, *Will and Political Legitimacy* (Cambridge, Mass.: Harvard University Press, 1982), chap. 3.

[55]*Essay*, pp. 55, 81, 104, 162–163. See too the "Defence of Mr. Locke's Opinion concerning Personal Identity," in *Works* II:194n. ("If the mind was once a mere *rasa tabula*, it will soon appear not only from whence it receives all its furniture"); "Of the Conduct of the Understanding," in *Works* III:272 ("We are born ignorant of every thing"); *Law*, p. 145 ("No principles, either practical or speculative, are written in the minds of men by nature"); *Education*, pp. 115 ("I imagine the Minds of Children as easily turned this or that way, as Water it self"), 275 ("'Tis as impossible to draw fair and regular Characters on a trembling Mind as on a shaking Paper"), 325 ("a Gentleman's Son, who being then very little, I considered only as white Paper, or Wax, to be moulded and fashioned as one pleases").

are innate practical Principles, which (as practical Principles ought) do continue constantly to operate and influence all our Actions, without ceasing: These may be observ'd in all Persons and all Ages, steady and universal."[56] As Locke goes on to argue, the point poses only terminological difficulties for his epistemology. Psychological inclinations are different from knowledge of moral truth. Locke wishes to deny the innateness only of the latter. Still, innate practical principles are the anchor of his moral theory, and I wish to develop his conception.

Suppose we can arrange a monotonically varying spectrum of mental states, from intensely agreeable to intensely disagreeable, and mark off a zero point. Locke proposes to call the positive states pleasure, the negative ones pain: "For whether we call it Satisfaction, Delight, Pleasure, Happiness, *etc.* on the one side; or Uneasiness, Trouble, Pain, Torment, Anguish, Misery, *etc.* on the other, they are still but different degrees of the same thing."[57] We should not take *pleasure*, then, as signifying only hedonistic consciousness, orgiastic ecstasy, and the like. Locke wants to discuss agreeable mental states of whatever sort, and he cares little how we label such states. (Should we, then, take his mention of "the happiness that all Men so steadily pursue, consisting in pleasure"[58] as a linguistic reminder or a slip?) Offhand dismissals of crude libidinal satisfactions will not do when Locke tells us that "things then are Good or Evil, only in reference to Pleasure or Pain. That we call *Good*, which *is apt to cause or increase pleasure or diminish Pain in us*; *or else to procure, or preserve us the possession of any other Good, or absence of any Evil.* And on the contrary we name that *Evil*, which *is apt to produce or increase any Pain*, *or diminish any Pleasure in us*; *or else to procure us any Evil, or deprive us of any Good.*"[59] Locke makes explicit in his *Thoughts concerning*

[56]*Essay*, p. 67. In *Treatises* I §86 pp. 222–223, the desire for self-preservation appears as "a Principle of Actions" God endows us with. In *Education*, p. 159, "God has stampt certain Characters," or "Original Tempers," "upon Men's Minds." But that is perfectly consistent with *Essay*, p. 619, where God "has stamped no original Characters on our Minds," for in the latter discussion the Characters in question are again bits of knowledge.
[57]*Essay*, pp. 128–129; also *Essay*, p. 232.
[58]*Education*, p. 249.
[59]*Essay*, p. 229. Locke readily grants the subjectivism suggested here in *Essay*, p. 268: "The various and contrary choices, that Men make in the World,

Education what he suggests in the *Essay*: "Good and Evil, *Reward and Punishment*, are the only Motives to a rational Creature."[60] It's not that men often happen to be concerned with pleasure and pain. It's rather that this concern and the accompanying calculus comprise the defining core of rationality. (Accumulation of pleasure, not property, is for Locke "the essence of rational conduct."[61])

Despite Locke's tireless refrain that "all we desire is only to be Happy,"[62] his official position in the *Essay* is spelled out differently.[63] Locke knows that we don't always pursue apparent goods, and he appeals to *uneasiness* as the great propellant of human action. We always respond to pains nagging away at us, but more than a recognition of the pleasure-causing properties of something is required for us to strive for it. Required is desire, itself "a state of uneasiness."[64] Locke summarizes the practical implications of his view in his memorable cameo of the drunkard driven by the uneasiness of missing "the tickling of his palate with a glass of Wine, or the idle chat of a soaking club" back "to the Tavern, though he has in view the loss of health and plenty, and perhaps of the joy of another life."[65] Locke's account of human motivation connects up neatly with his elegant if untenable

---

do not argue, that they do not all pursue Good; but that the same thing is not good to every Man alike."

[60]*Education*, p. 152.

[61]Macpherson, "Social Bearing," p. 12, reprinted in Schochet, *Life, Liberty, and Property*, p. 77. Also Macpherson, *Possessive Individualism*, pp. 221, 232–238. It would be easy enough to pile up quotations refuting Macpherson's reading on this point. My favorite: "Covetousness, and the Desire of having in our Possession, and under our Dominion, more than we have need of, being the Root of all Evil, should be early and carefully weeded out, and the contrary Quality of a Readiness to impart to others, implanted" (*Education*, pp. 213–214). Macpherson slips around such passages in *Possessive Individualism*, pp. 236–237. Leo Strauss, *Natural Right and History* (Chicago: University of Chicago Press, 1953), p. 246, also takes Locke as wanting "to prove that the unlimited acquisition of wealth is not unjust or morally wrong."

[62]*Essay*, p. 283; also *Essay*, pp. 274–275, 279, 345, 346; *Education*, p. 222; *Reasonableness*, in *Works* VII:149; John Locke, "Of Ethics in General," in Lord King, *The Life of John Locke* (London, 1829), p. 306; King, *Life of John Locke*, p. 115.

[63]The relevant discussion is in *Essay*, pp. 233–285, especially pp. 250–255.

[64]*Essay*, p. 251.

[65]*Essay*, p. 253.

doctrine of suspension of the will,[66] and much could be made of the import of the whole for understanding those restless souls of liberal society. With due regret, I bring up all these matters only to drop them at once, for they make no difference to Locke's moral theory. Locke bemoans the quirks of human judgment that leave future goods discounted and clearly thinks we ought to respond to pleasure and pain alike.[67] So we cannot object later by saying, "Ah, but that great good doesn't entice us," for Locke can respond simply, "But it should." To avoid needless complications, I simply grant Locke that we ought exclusively to pursue pleasure and avoid pain.

On to morality, *"the proper Science and Business of Mankind in general."*[68] Locke holds that *"Morally Good and Evil* . . . is only the Conformity or Disagreement of our voluntary Actions to some Law, whereby Good or Evil is drawn on us, from the Will and Power of the Law-maker; which Good and Evil, Pleasure or Pain, attending our observance, or breach of the Law, by the Decree of the Law-maker, is that we call *Reward* and *Punishment."*[69] Men judge their actions sometimes by civil statutes, sometimes by the received views of their society; these "laws" are vital in maintaining the social and political world. The "only true touchstone of *moral Rectitude,"* however, is the divine law, or God's commands.[70] The last foundational premise comes in Locke's version of the doctrine that moral considerations are overriding: "The Rewards and Punishments of another Life,

[66]Locke provides no account of why we suspend the will when we do, or why, having done so, we make the decisions we do. In the absence of any such account, both processes are just as plausible subjects for the reign of causal determinism as the initial will buffeted by pleasures and pains.

[67]See the discussion of "wrong judgments" in *Essay*, pp. 272–281, and John Locke, "Thus I Think," in King, *Life of John Locke*, p. 304: "It is a man's *proper* business to seek happiness and avoid misery" (my italics). Locke casts suspension of the will in splendidly Platonic terms in *Education*, pp. 138, 143, 147–148, 151, but the point seems much the same.

[68]*Essay*, p. 646; compare *Essay*, pp. 46, 87, 131, 302, 350–351; *Education*, p. 232; John Locke, "Of Study," in Axtell, *Educational Writings*, pp. 411, 415; Locke, "Of the Conduct of the Understanding," in *Works* III:244–245.

[69]*Essay*, p. 351. See too *Essay*, pp. 69, 74; *Reasonableness*, in *Works* VII:14; *Education*, p. 241; *Tracts* I p. 124; *Tracts* II p. 221; Locke in Dunn, *Political Thought*, p. 1.

[70]*Essay*, p. 352.

which the Almighty has established, as the Enforcements of his Law, are of weight enough to determine the choice, against whatever Pleasure or Pain this Life can shew, when the eternal State is considered but in its bare possibility, which no Body can make any doubt of."[71] We need not let Locke long rehearse his fire-and-brimstone strictures on the "unspeakable rewards and punishments in another world" to begin to sense the project for justifying morality.[72] It is an ambitious project indeed: Locke wants to reconcile self-interest and morality by showing that acting morally is in one's self-interest. By following the rules, his idea is, one goes to heaven and basks in unutterable delight; by breaking them, one goes to hell and flounders in enormities of pain. To carry through the argument, Locke needs to show the existence of God, and how we know what God commands.

First, then, the argument for God. Locke is surpassingly fond of the argument from design. He tells us that "the visible world is constructed with wonderful art and regularity," that "Nature never makes excellent things, for mean or no uses," that "the Wisdom and Goodness of the Maker plainly appears in all the Parts of this Stupendious Fabrick, and all the several degrees and ranks of Creatures in it."[73] God becomes "the Architect," and "after contemplating the beauty of the objects to be observed, their order, array, and motion," we ask "what was the cause, and who the maker, of such an excellent work" and decide that "there must be a powerful and wise creator of all these things."[74] Are you unimpressed by the stunning regularity of the world? Do you look about and see not beauty and order but waste and carnage in nature and politics? Recall that you are a frail being of limited intellectual capacity; in "this our dark and short-sighted state," we cannot hope to fathom the depths of God's wisdom manifest in the world.[75] Humility is called for, since "it will better become the temper of a Christian patiently to obey than to

[71]*Essay*, p. 281.
[72]*Reasonableness*, in *Works* VII:122.
[73]*Law*, p. 151; *Essay*, pp. 113, 148.
[74]*Essay*, p. 447; *Law*, p. 153. See too *Essay*, pp. 89, 560; *Treatises* I §53 p. 197; Locke, "Of The Conduct of the Understanding," in *Works* III:245; *Reasonableness*, in *Works* VII:135.
[75]King, *Life of John Locke*, p. 315.

[91]

presumptuously complain and murmur that God hath not put human affairs into a posture suited to his humour or squared the economy of the world or frame of the Temple according to the model of his brain."[76] Locke's theory itself accounts for our objections to it. That makes it unfalsifiable, but its unfalsifiability is not the result of a series of ad hoc moves designed to save the initial theory. Instead, it is a direct outcome of the initial theory itself. God has created a world ordered in such a complex way that we cannot recognize the order in it. Maybe; maybe not. Theories structured this way can be false. But the concession that we might not recognize the order in God's creation does not strengthen the argument from design; it destroys it. The world's apparent lack of order can hardly serve as a reason for believing in God.

It is not, however, the argument from design that Locke has in mind when he announces, "I have proved there is a God."[77] The proof is the one in the *Essay*, which Locke runs through twice.[78] Here I combine his two presentations:

1. Something cannot emerge out of nothing. ("Non-entity cannot produce any real being.")
2. The cause is superior to the effect. ("That what had its Being and Beginning from another, must also have all that which is in, and belongs to its Being from another too.")

Therefore:

3. The first cause is the most powerful being. ("Whatsoever is first of all things, must necessarily contain in it, and actually have, at least, all the Perfections that can ever after exist.")

[76]*Tracts* I p. 136; see too *Education*, p. 305; *Reasonableness*, in *Works* VII:134. Compare John Smith, "The Excellency and Nobleness of True Religion," in *The Cambridge Platonists*, ed. C. A. Patrides (Cambridge, Mass.: Harvard University Press, 1970), p. 190.
[77]*Works* IV:289; see too *Works* IV:276, 293; *Essay*, pp. 100, 558, 621.
[78]*Essay*, bk. IV, chap. X, pp. 619–630. All quotations in the next two paragraphs are from this chapter. Since Locke can conceive of thinking material substances, I have avoided importing any suggestion of dualism. Note here M. R. Ayers, "Mechanism, Superaddition, and the Proof of God's Existence in Locke's Essay," *Philosophical Review* 90 (April 1981): 208–251.

Now:

4. I know I exist. ("*Man has a clear Perception of his own Being.*")
5. I am a knowing and intelligent being.

Therefore, by (3):

6. That first cause is the supremely knowing, intelligent being.

Concludes Locke: "Our Reason leads us to the Knowledge of this certain and evident Truth, That *there is an eternal, most powerful, and most knowing Being*; which whether any one will please to call *God*, it matters not. The thing is evident, and from this *Idea* duly considered, will easily be deduced all those other Attributes, which we ought to ascribe to this eternal Being."

This proof is a wild tangle of odd premises and faulty inferences. It's not at all clear why (1), which we might call the no-free-lunch principle of metaphysics, or (2), which we might call the all-downhill-from-here principle, should be true. We can conceive of things popping into thin air, and we can conceive, hypostatizing a bit, of evolution dredging human beings out of some primordial gunk. Locke says, unhelpfully, that (2) "is evident." A bit more provocatively, he tells us that we know (1) "by an intuitive certainty," which he likens to a sadly unclear proposition about right angles.[79] But a good deal more argument will be required to ground either premise successfully. Furthermore, I have saved Locke his silliest brummagem inference in restating the argument. Even granted (1) and (2), it does not follow that the first cause still exists. Locke accomplishes this move by a play on words, going from "*Something* must be *from Eternity*," a gloss on (1), to "If then there must be something eternal, let us see what sort of Being it must be."[80] Finally, I wonder what

---

[79]Elsewhere and quite clearly: "'Tis as certain, that there is a God, as that the opposite Angles, made by the intersection of two straight lines, are equal. There was never any rational Creature, that set himself sincerely to examine the truth of these Propositions, that could fail to assent to them" (*Essay*, pp. 94–95).

[80]The point is in J. L. Mackie, *Problems from Locke* (Oxford: Clarendon, 1976), pp. 208–209; see too the treatment in J. L. Mackie, *The Miracle of Theism* (Oxford: Clarendon, 1982), p. 120. The god of this argument rears his head momentarily in "Remarks upon Some of Mr. Norris's Books," in *Works* X:255.

easy deductions will move Locke from his most powerful, knowing being of (6) to an omnipotent, omniscient being.

The existence of God is not all Locke thinks he can demonstrate. He often claims too that "moral Rules are capable of Demonstration: and therefore it is our own faults, if we come not to a certain Knowledge of them."[81] Answering the importunate urgings of Molyneux that "the task must be undertaken," Locke apologizes: "I thought I saw that morality might be demonstratively made out; yet whether I am able so to make it out, is another question."[82] Nonetheless, we can glean the outlines of the proposed demonstration, remarkably more direct than the project on divine command I am sketching in this section, from Locke's comments in the *Essay*.[83] He says, for example, "I am bold to think, that *Morality is capable of Demonstration*, as well as Mathematicks: Since the precise real Essence of the Things moral Words stand for, may be perfectly known; and so the Congruity, or Incongruity of the Things themselves, be certainly discovered, in which consists perfect knowledge."[84] Here Locke is tripped up in his own distinctions. I take it that Locke means *real essence* to denote the actual qualities of things in the external world, *nominal essence* the contents of our concepts. For modes, he says, the two essences coincide.[85] Now the argument goes awry. Locke wields it to prove tautologies, as when he tells us that "*Where there is no Property, there is no Injustice*, is a Proposition as certain as any Demonstration in *Euclid*: For the *Idea* of *Property*, being a right to any thing, and the *Idea* to which the name *Injustice* is given, being the Invasion or Violation of that right; it

---

[81]*Essay*, p. 66. See too *Essay*, pp. 565, 643.

[82]Molyneux to Locke, in *Works* IX:291; Locke to Molyneux, 20 sep 1692, in *Works* IX:294. Tyrrell urged Locke to revise and publish his *Essays on the Law of Nature* (see *Law*, pp. 9, 10). See too Locke to Molyneux, 30 mar 1696, in *Works* IX:377; and *Works* IV:187.

[83]I should note that in *Essay*, p. 549, and King, *Life of John Locke*, p. 120, Locke is unmistakably claiming that the divine command account of morality is demonstrable (though in each passage he also unmistakably refers to the account I'm sketching here). I'll deal with that claim a bit later, in considering Strauss's (mis)construction of the argument.

[84]*Essay*, p. 516.

[85]See *Essay*, pp. 409–471, especially pp. 457–460; also, "Faith and Reason," shorthand journal entry from 27 aug 1676, in *Law*, pp. 278–279.

is evident" that the point is conceptually guaranteed.[86] But then it is evident too that it has no content, no bearing on our conduct, for if property means a right, we can always ask if land or liberty or anything else is properly called property. Perhaps Locke was misled by his erroneous claim that when we name a mode, real and nominal essence coincide, since our meaning starts and stops with our concept. Were that so, were the substances named in moral rules included only in unproblematic ways,[87] and were there such things as tautologies with substance, he could dream of his rigorous demonstration. But modes, the moral terms among them, can sensibly be used to refer to real essences divorced from nominal ones. By *murder*, we may mean to name a certain human activity, and it might require empirical investigation to understand its nature. The tautology problem aside, even moral propositions such as "murder ought to be punished" would be open to question. They could depend on not just a theory of punishment, but beliefs about the efficacy of punishment, the effects of a punishing institution such as the state or of the free employment of vigilantes, and so on. Some moral disagreements, though emphatically not all, rest firmly on factual disagreements. Locke would be the first to insist on the necessity of tackling the factual questions, not trying to evade them by verbal manipulations.[88]

Fortunately, though, the divine-command project is different from this purported demonstration, and the former does not fail

[86]*Essay*, p. 549. In his discussion of trifling propositions (*Essay*, pp. 609–617), Locke tells us we may have certain knowledge of overtly definitional statements, "but 'tis a *verbal Certainty*, but not instructive"; rather surreptitiously he adds that we can have "instructive *real Knowledge*" of "Propositions, which affirm something of another, which is a necessary consequence of its precise complex *Idea*, but not contained in it" (*Essay*, p. 614). But what kind of necessity does Locke have in mind here? Would it be reading too much back into his text to see a glimmer of the synthetic *a priori*? I am inclined to say that the most instructive deductions only point out connections we hadn't noticed, but doubtless all deductive conclusions are contained in the premises. Are moral rules then supposed to be recondite deductive truths? and so illuminating, but empty? Or does Locke have in mind some kind of necessity other than deductive?
[87]*Essay*, pp. 516–517.
[88]See, for example, *Essay*, pp. 591–608, especially pp. 606–608. I am greatly indebted here to Mackie, *Problems from Locke*, pp. 90–93.

as immediately and ignominiously as the latter. I propose to grant Locke the existence of God and continue to follow the project, so I turn to his account of our knowledge of God's will. Here we must first take note of a pronounced shift in Locke's views over the years. He begins by insisting that reason is capable of making out the law of nature. In the early *Essays on the Law of Nature*, we find labyrinthine formulations worthy of, say, Clarke or Cudworth: "What is proper now for the rational nature, in so far as it is rational, must needs be proper for ever, and the same reason will pronounce everywhere the same moral rules. Since therefore all men are by nature rational, and since there is a harmony between this law and the rational nature, and this harmony can be known by the light of nature, it follows that all those who are endowed with a rational nature, i.e. all men in the world, are morally bound by this law."[89] In the *Treatises*, Locke even equates reason and the law of nature.[90] And in the *Essay*, he warns, "I think they equally forsake the Truth, who running into the contrary extreams, either affirm an innate Law, or deny that there is a Law, knowable by the light of Nature, *i.e.* without the help of positive Revelation."[91]

By *The Reasonableness of Christianity* Locke has changed his tune. There he fears "it is too hard a task for unassisted reason to establish morality in all its parts, upon its true foundation, with a

---

[89]*Law*, p. 199; see too *Law*, p. 111.

[90]*Treatises* II §6 p. 289. On a tenuously related problem: Locke writes in *Treatises* II §11 p. 292, "And *Cain* was so fully convinced, that every one had a Right to destroy such a Criminal, that after the Murther of his Brother, he cries out, *Every one that findeth me, shall slay me*; so plain was it writ in the Hearts of all Mankind." That writing looks suspiciously like an innate practical principle of the kind Locke is concerned to deny. The passage ought to be considered in light of *Reasonableness*, in *Works* VII:13, where, in explicating Romans ii.15 on "the law written in their hearts," Locke says easily, "By which . . . it is plain, that under the law of works, is comprehended also the law of nature, knowable by reason." Compare his treatment in "A Paraphrase and Notes on the Epistle of St. Paul to the Romans," in *Works* VIII:265–266. Locke also refers to "the light of nature" as "the transcript of the moral law in the Gospel" ("Error," in King, *Life of John Locke*, p. 283). In these passages, Locke is wrestling with a problem familiar from medieval political theory: how reconcile one's beliefs with apparently opposed passages from Scripture?

[91]*Essay*, p. 75.

clear and convincing light."[92] Finally, in his controversy with Stillingfleet over the *Essay*, Locke seems flatly to deny the very possibility of human reason making out the principles on which the law of nature is based: "Though the light of nature gave some obscure glimmering, some uncertain hopes of a future state; yet human reason could attain to no clearness, no certainty about it."[93] Leo Strauss understood this claim as the surrender of the entire project, and he accordingly offered a reading in which Locke has no genuine account of natural law.[94] That reading rests on holding the late Locke to the early Locke's views, certainly an unsound approach for textual exegesis. We can, of course, search for some univocal teaching that a writer allegedly offers, and we can ruthlessly iron out all the discrepancies and contradictions we find. But political theorists, like the rest of us, can change their minds. Typically, their mature views do not spring from their heads fully formed, like Athena from Zeus's; instead theorists tenaciously struggle over problems, revising their views as they go. It must be an open question in any given case whether we can run together the early and late works. One of the weaknesses of the innocuous idea that a political theorist offers a teaching is that it blinds us to the typical pattern of development, even to the possibility of its holding in a given case. Worse, Strauss overlooked Locke's belief that reason and revelation are complementary, not antagonistic, modes of knowledge. Locke stakes out that position firmly in the *Essay*: "*Reason* is natural *Revelation*," and "*Revelation* is natural *Reason* enlarged by a new set of Discoveries communicated by GOD immediately,

---

[92]*Reasonableness*, in *Works* VII:139; also *Reasonableness*, in *Works* VII:140–147. But see *Reasonableness*, in *Works* VII:13, 157 for explicit affirmations that reason can do the job. It's just that it hasn't, so Locke discards "the declarations of philosophers" as "a wild wood of uncertainty . . . an endless maze" (p. 143).

[93]*Works* IV:489; also *Works* IV:480; John Locke, *A Third Letter for Toleration*, in *Works* VI:493.

[94]Strauss, *Natural Right and History*, pp. 202–230, especially p. 220 ("We thus arrive at the conclusion that Locke cannot have recognized any law of nature in the proper sense of the term"). Strauss thought too that "Honour thy father and thy mother if they have deserved it of you" is a hypothetical imperative, but it is as categorical as "Honour thy father and thy mother" (p. 219): neither hinges on the ends of the addressed agent.

which *Reason* vouches the Truth of, by the Testimony and Proofs it gives, that they come from GOD."[95] The latter point is crucial, for it means to Locke that "*Reason* must be our last Judge and Guide in every Thing."[96]

Reason judges and guides us to the word of God by identifying miracles. Locke defines a miracle as "a sensible operation, which, being above the comprehension of the spectator, and in his opinion contrary to the established course of nature, is taken by him to be divine." (Curiously, Locke chooses to build the indeterminacy problems of identifying miracles into his definition.) Now, enquires Locke, "what shall be a sufficient inducement to take any extraordinary operation to be a miracle?" When apparent miracles conflict, we may take the victorious force as the authentically divine one, "since God's power is paramount to all"—so "the producing of serpents, blood, and frogs, by the Egyptian sorcerers" is not a miracle. By extension, "uncontested revelation will stand too," for "it cannot be supposed God should suffer his prerogative to be so far usurped by any inferior being, as to permit any creature, depending on him, to set his seals, the marks of his divine authority, to a mission coming from him." Yet Locke is decidedly impatient with making out the argument: "The only revelations that come attested by miracles, being those of Moses and Christ, and they confirming each other; the business of miracles, as it stands really in matter of fact, has no manner of difficulty in it; and I think the most scrupulous or sceptical cannot from miracles raise the least doubt against the divine revelation of the Gospel."[97]

The Testaments thus emerge as the word of God, stamped with divine assurance of their veracity. Having been certified by reason, they stand superior to those propositions normally within its jurisdiction. Says Locke, "The holy scripture is to me,

[95]*Essay*, p. 698.

[96]*Essay*, p. 704. See generally *Education*, p. 302; King, *Life of John Locke*, p. 125; John Locke, "A Discourse of Miracles," in *Works* IX:261–262.

[97]Locke, "A Discourse on Miracles," in *Works* IX:256, 259, 260, 261, 258. Locke manages to clear the ground by dismissing "what the Persees say of their Zoroaster, or the Indians of their Brama (not to mention all the Wild Stories of the religions farther East) [as] so obscure, or so manifestly fabulous, that no account can be made of it" (p. 258).

and always will be, the constant guide of my assent; and I shall always hearken to it, as containing infallible truth, relating to things of the higher concernment. . . . I shall presently condemn and quit any opinion of mind, as soon as I am shown that it is contrary to any revelation in the holy scripture."[98] (This position raises difficulties for Locke in his *Letters on Toleration*. Locke declares forthrightly again and again that believing your religion to be true is insufficient for enforcing it: "If that be sufficient to authorize you to use force, it will authorize any other magistrate of any other religion to use force also."[99] Yet in the *Second Letter*, he concedes, "When you can show any commission in Scripture, for the use of force to compel men to hear, any more than embrace, the doctrine of others that differ from them, we shall have reason to submit to it, and the magistrate have some ground to set up this new way of persecution."[100] So a magistrate holding a religious text dictating intolerance ought, on Locke's principles, to coerce away. It could even be a Christian magistrate if, as Locke states, "every one's philosophy regulates every one's interpretation of the word of God."[101] Here we have an instructive spectacle: a foundation threatening the views it is supposed to support.) In *The Reasonableness of Christianity*, Locke again takes miracles to be the foundation of reasoned assent to Christianity; there he also interprets the Testaments. He finds that "immortality and bliss belong to the righteous," though the slightest sin warrants damnation. Yet God supplements that impossibly demanding law of works with the law of faith, by which "faith and repentance, *i.e.* believing Jesus to be the Messiah, and a good life, are the indispensable conditions . . . to be performed by all those who would obtain eternal life."[102]

No theologian, I withhold comment on Locke's reading of the

---

[98]*Works* IV:96; see too *Works* IV:281, 475–482.

[99]Locke, *Third Letter*, in *Works* VI:402. The point is rehearsed endlessly in all four *Letters*. Locke sounds Millian tones on toleration in *A Second Vindication of the Reasonableness of Christianity*, in *Works* VII:376–377.

[100]John Locke, *A Second Letter concerning Toleration*, in *Works* VI:82.

[101]John Locke, "An Essay for the Understanding of St. Paul's Epistles," in *Works* VIII:20. Here again, the medieval problem: what to do with refractory passages in Scripture?

[102]*Reasonableness*, in *Works* VII:10, 105.

Gospel. I do, though, wish to enter the lists on the argument from miracles, for "the most scrupulous or sceptical" may well have objections here. As Locke explicitly notes, we have no first-hand experience of the miracles.[103] Therefore we may have lots of peccadilloes to launch at the argument. We might say that the disciples were lying, or we might have a story to tell about their motives for (mis)understanding the events the way they did.[104] More important, we might wonder whether God takes a positive interest in human affairs and is willing to intervene in them; both points are required for the inference from contested extraordinary event to miracle. It's not clear that God cares, or cares enough to act, or would find acting appropriate. Perhaps Locke thought another easy deduction would show his powerful first cause to be a benevolent meddler, but he offers no argument on the point.[105]

The opacity of God's nature, intentions, and interests in our world disables any argument structured like Pascal's wager. Locke could not respond to the kinds of criticisms I've made of his argument by insisting that things are possibly the way he says they are, for it is also possible that there is a spiteful or Manichaean deity who will reward evildoers, or an absurdist deity who will reward all 5'9" brunettes, and so on. Suppose we take seriously the suggestion that we study the world and adopt a reasonable hypothesis. Locke, after all, need not prove that God exists. He need only show that the likelihood is great enough for one who is maximizing utility to be moral. Estimating the odds will be difficult, to say the least. But the problem of evil militates against the hypothesis of a caring, omnipotent God.[106]

[103]See the imagined dialogue between a pagan and a Christian in Locke, *Third Letter for Toleration*, in *Works* VI:402.
[104]The classic exposition is Hume, "Of Miracles," in his *Enquiry concerning Human Understanding*, in *Enquiries*, ed. L. A. Selby-Bigge, 3d ed. rev. by P. H. Nidditch (Oxford: Clarendon, 1978), pp. 109–131.
[105]Nor is he fond of mystic intuition. The sentiment of the journal formulation of 18 sep 1681—"that there is a God, and what that God is, nothing can discover to us, nor judge in us, but natural reason" (King, *Life of John Locke*, p. 123)—remains with him throughout. Again, reason demonstrates God's existence; revelation reveals his commands.
[106]See Mackie's apt discussion in his *Miracle of Theism*, pp. 150–176.

LOCKE'S DIVINE POLITICS

In developing his moral theory, Locke constructs an impressive intellectual edifice. The argument fails at every turn, however, and I can construct no respectable supports for the flaws in its structure. Still, we must consider how Locke's moral theory meshes with the contract arguments of the *Treatises*. There are puzzles yet in the moral theory, but they are best considered in light of the political doctrine.

An Ungrounded Politics

Suppose, for a wildly ahistorical moment, that Socrates could have turned from his dialogue with Euthyphro and sweetly enquired of Locke, "So, John, is what God commands good just because he commands it, or does he command some independently specified good?" Locke, having no pantheon of disagreeing deities hanging around, would have been in something of a fix. I wish to articulate that fix as clearly as I can, for it lies at the heart of Locke's prescriptive arguments. Socrates's question would strain the limits of Locke's patience and perhaps of his comprehension: "Whoever sincerely acknowledges any law to be the law of God, cannot fail to acknowledge also, that it hath all that reason and ground that a just and wise law ought to have; and will easily persuade himself to forbear raising such questions and scruples about it."[107] What God commands is morality, in this view, and that's that. This dismissal may well seem persuasive as far as our practice goes.[108] For understanding the tenor of Locke's political theory, though, we must persuade ourselves to raise just these questions, to push past the easy identification of God's will and morality.

On the one hand, Locke might believe that whatever God

[107] *Works* IV:188. The remark is in a few pages nestled within the Stillingfleet controversy, apparently addressed to Thomas Burnet's anonymously published *Remarks upon an Essay concerning humane understanding* (London, 1697).
[108] For that reason, it seems silly instantly to throw out Locke's moral theory as a violation of Hume's dictum on is/ought, as does W. von Leyden, "John Locke and Natural Law," *Philosophy* 31 (January 1956): 31 (reprinted in Schochet, *Life, Liberty, and Property*, p. 21). Besides, is/ought, like any other interesting philosophical thesis, is deeply problematic, and needs to be argued for, not produced like a trump card.

commands is morality, just because God commands it. Here morality would be a large-scale system of prudence. Selfish inclinations would be checked by long-term self-interest. Pleasure would be maximized by responding to the allure of heaven and the repulsion of hell, by following whatever rules God happened to lay down for entrance to heaven.[109] We may be inclined to dismiss such a scheme as having nothing to do with morality; but we have read Kant, or come under his influence, and Locke hadn't. Certainly more classical conceptions of morality or virtue are not wrapped in Kantian paper, and indeed it is devilishly difficult to try to understand them in that way.[110]

On the other hand, Locke may intend divine command to supply sanctions for being moral. In this view, morality would exist independent of God's will, but human beings, being fervid pleasure-seekers, would not pay much heed to it for itself. God, observing this sorry state of affairs, would raise the stakes, and his "unspeakable rewards and punishments" would bring human beings into line.

Locke sometimes sounds as though he adopts the first view. Most dramatically, he refers in passing to "the arbitrary Will and good Pleasure of the Wise Architect"—surely a concession that God may command as whimsically as he likes?[111] But a gentle reminder from the *Oxford English Dictionary* is in order. *Arbitrary*,

[109]Recall that repentance for Locke is not simply a momentary mental state, but means rather "an hearty sorrow for our past misdeeds, and a sincere resolution and endeavour, to the utmost of our power, to conform all our actions to the law of God. So that repentance does not consist in one single act of sorrow . . . but in 'doing works for repentance'" (*Reasonableness*, in *Works* VII:105).
Does the last of the *Essays on the Law of Nature* reject this view outright? The argument there is that "each man's personal interest is not the basis of natural law" (*Law*, p. 207). But it's eminently plausible that Locke means here our worldly interests.
[110]Terence Irwin, *Plato's Moral Theory* (Oxford: Clarendon, 1977), is a beautifully executed study of a very different attempt to reconcile self-interest and morality. See generally Philippa Foot's superb *Virtues and Vices and Other Essays in Moral Philosophy* (Berkeley: University of California Press, 1978); and G. E. M. Anscombe's equally superb "Modern Moral Philosophy," *Philosophy* 33 (January 1958): 1–19, reprinted in *The Is-Ought Question*, ed. W. D. Hudson (New York: St. Martin's Press, 1969). And see Alasdair MacIntyre, *After Virtue* (Notre Dame, Ind.: University of Notre Dame Press, 1981).
[111]*Essay*, p. 560.

in a now obsolete usage, means simply "to be decided by one's liking" or, in a legal sense, "relating to, or dependent on, the discretion of an arbiter, arbitrator, or other legally-recognized authority." It need not mean, as we now commonly take it to, capricious or tyrannical. (An etymological guess: repeated experiences of how authorities act are now gloomily reflected in the meaning of the word.) Elsewhere, Locke suggests that "the belief of a God" is "the foundation of all religion and genuine morality," implying that only phony moralities stand without God.[112]

The weight of textual evidence, however, seems to support the second view: God supplies sanctions to a logically prior morality. Take such dictums as "to give a man a full knowledge of true morality I should send him to no other book but the New Testament."[113] Or consider Locke's talk of "the perfections that are in God [as] necessary and unchangeable," "that unchangeably just, wise, good, and all-powerful Being."[114] The only straightforward way of understanding this talk is that God is being measured against an external standard, that of morality.[115] Finally, there are some cryptic comments that make sense only on this reading: "Virtue, as in its obligation it is the will of God, discovered by natural reason, and thus has the force of a law; so in the matter of it, it is nothing else but doing of good, either to oneself or others: and the contrary hereunto, vice, is nothing else but doing of harm."[116] I take it Locke means that virtue and vice

---

[112]*Works* IV:53. See too *Education*, pp. 155–156; "Of Study," in Axtell, *Educational Writings*, p. 420; *Law*, p. 109; *Essay*, p. 720.

[113]"Some Thoughts Concerning Reading and Study for a Gentleman, 1703," in Axtell, *Educational Writings*, p. 400; also "Of Study," in Axtell, p. 409.

[114]"An Examination of P. Malebranche's Opinion of Seeing All Things in God," in *Works* IX:252; "Defence of Mr. Locke's Opinion concerning Personal Identity," in *Works* III:195–196. See too King, *Life of John Locke*, p. 22; *Law*, p. 121; *Essay*, p. 356; *Reasonableness*, in *Works* VII:112; *A Vindication of the Reasonableness of Christianity*, in *Works* VII:356.

[115]Note here the line of criticism in Richard Price, *A Review of the Principal Questions in Morals*, ed. D. D. Raphael (Oxford: Clarendon, 1974), p. 43, excerpted in *British Moralists*, ed. D. D. Raphael, 2 vols. (Oxford: Clarendon, 1969), II:143; also in L. A. Selby-Bigge's edition of the *Moralists*, 2 vols. (Oxford, 1897), II:123.

[116]"Common-place Book," 1661, in King, *Life of John Locke*, p. 292. See too

are (the circularity is only verbal) doing good and doing harm. Divine command provides the incentive to adopt the life of virtue.[117] Entirely comprehensible now is Locke's delightful thumbnail sketch of the history of moral philosophy, worth quoting at length:

> The philosophers, indeed, showed the beauty of virtue; they set her off so, as drew men's eyes and approbation to her; but leaving her unendowed, very few were willing to espouse her. The generality could not refuse her their esteem and commendation; but still turned their backs on her, and forsook her, as a match not for their turn. But now there being put into the scales on her side, "an exceeding and immortal weight of glory," interest is come about to her, and virtue now is visibly the most enriching purchase, and by much the best bargain. That she is the perfection and excellency of our nature; that she is herself a reward, and will recommend our names to future ages, is not all that can be said of her. It is not strange that the learned heathens satisfied not many with such airy commendations. It has another relish and efficacy to persuade men, that if they live well here, they shall be happy hereafter. Open their eyes upon the endless, unspeakable joys of another life, and their hearts will find something solid and powerful to move them. . . . Upon this foundation, and upon this only, morality stands firm, and may defy all competition.[118]

Adopting this view resolves another paradox in Locke. Locke could refer to "innocent pagans, strict observers of what is right, and in no way offending against good morals and the civil law";[119] yet in the same text he insists that "those who deny the

---

Reasonableness, in *Works* VII:144; *Essay*, p. 69; "Of Ethics in General," in King, *Life of John Locke*, p. 312; *Tracts* II pp. 222–223.

[117]Nor is this distinction an idiosyncratic invention of Locke. For example, William Paley, *The Principles of Moral and Political Philosophy*, in Raphael, *Moralists* II:257–260, in Selby-Bigge, *Moralists* II:357–360, employs just the same distinction, and is plausibly understood only as making a claim about why we do and should follow an independently good rule.

[118]*Reasonableness*, in *Works* VII:150–151. Two other provocative passages: *Second Vindication of the Reasonableness of Christianity*, in *Works* VII:229; *Law*, p. 201. Locke's claim about ancient moral theory is surprising: compare the myth of Er, or Scipio's Dream.

[119]*Letter*, p. 113.

existence of the Deity are not to be tolerated at all," going on to explain, "Promises, covenants, and oaths, which are the bonds of human society, can have no hold upon or sanctity for an atheist; for the taking away of God, even only in thought, dissolves all."[120] Heathens and atheists may correctly recognize the morality of keeping compacts, but they cannot be counted on to follow the rule, because they do not believe in the weighty sanctions of an afterlife. The allure of worldly pleasures may attract their attention; unendowed virtue, a poor purchase, may stand spurned.

Now, neither answer to Socrates's query seems quite satisfactory. If whatever God commands is good, we seem to be the victims of a morality tossed down at us, unhinged from our interests in the world. If God commands some independently specified good, the appeal to God in the first place seems superfluous: we might as well argue directly from that independent good. Locke in the end refuses to impale himself on either horn of Euthyphro's dilemma. Instead, he works out an intermediate position that suggests that divine-command theories of ethics have more resources than we tend to think.

It will prove useful here to deploy Locke's distinction between primary and secondary qualities. Whether we take his corpuscularian hypothesis as scientific or epistemological, the distinction is clear. Primary qualities exist on their own; secondary qualities depend for their existence on primary qualities. For example, color, in Locke's view, is not really in the objects we see. Instead, it is a secondary quality, a power the objects have, given their primary qualities, to make us experience what we call color.[121] Suppose we say, then, that primary moral relations ex-

---

[120]*Letter*, p. 135. Locke rails against atheism and demands its exclusion from "all sober and civil society" in *A Vindication of the Reasonableness of Christianity*, in *Works* VII:161. See too *The Fundamental Constitutions of Carolina*, in *Works* X: articles XCV, CI, pp. 193, 195. The exclusion of Roman Catholics from liberal tolerance (*Letter*, pp. 131–135) is in part on different grounds; they have divided political loyalty. But Locke strikes familiar notes in worrying that they believe the Church "can acquit them of all perfidy and perjury" ("Letter to S.H." in *Tracts*, pp. 243–244). See generally on morality and religion Locke's journal for 8 feb 1677, in King, *Life of John Locke*, p. 88; *Law*, pp. 173, 109.

[121]See generally *Essay*, pp. 134–143, 300–303, 535–536, 544–547.

ist independently of God, while secondary moral relations depend on God and on primary relations. Locke suggests one decisively significant primary moral relation: "God has created us out of nothing and, if He pleases, will reduce us again to nothing: we are, therefore, subject to Him in perfect justice and by utmost necessity."[122] The utmost necessity is nothing new: again Locke invites us to cower before the terrifying prospect of eternal punishment. Yet the bond is also one of perfect justice because of a strong obligation of gratitude. Locke says nothing here about God's instructing us that it is just to submit to him. A more plausible reading of this passage is that there is a general moral principle dictating obedience to or consideration for one's maker. The justification of that principle does not turn on God. He is simply one maker to whom it applies. Note the difference between this reason for obeying and the suggestion that it is in one's interest to do so.

This primary moral relation introduces moral reasons for our obeying God's commands. Since God created us, we are fairly beholden to his wishes. That moral relation should splash over into the wishes themselves and lend them a distinctively moral aura. Should God command what Locke would elsewhere call things indifferent, things not already vested with moral significance (the prescribed manner of worship in the Testaments is a likely candidate), those things would emerge as secondary moral relations. Without either God's commands or the moral principle of responding to a creator, the manner of worship would be morally irrelevant. Given the commands and the principle, it takes on moral significance.

The structure of this argument would allow Locke to defuse Socrates's query. Goodness is not some indivisible lump, so we need not accept the terms of the Euthyphro dilemma. Instead, we can say that some moral principles hold regardless of God, while others depend on him. We might still say that, for Locke, what God commands is good because he commands it. But now we need to lend emphasis to "he," in a way that alters the mean-

---

[122]*Law*, p. 187; also pp. 153–154, 183; *Essay*, p. 651. See David Gauthier, "Why Ought One Obey God? Reflections on Hobbes and Locke," *Canadian Journal of Philosophy* 7 (September 1977): 425–446.

ing of the phrase. God commands rightly, not as an ineffable brooding omnipresence, but as our creator.

How, then, can we link this moral theory to the political theory? Recall first where we left Locke's argument for our obligation to obey the law. I sought an account of why consent, even consent as minimal as residence, generates an obligation. Locke could defend that claim by casting it either as a primary moral relation or as a secondary one. Oddly, he seems to cast it both ways.

First, he suggests that we view consent's obliging powers as a primary moral rule: "*Grants, Promises*, and *Oaths* are Bonds that hold the *Almighty*."[123] Then, however, we still need a story about why consent obliges, and here Locke is singularly reticent. "That Men should keep their compacts, is certainly a great and undeniable Rule in Morality," he proclaims. Yet on the very same page, he declares with as much bravado, "*there cannot any one moral Rule be propos'd, whereof a Man may not justly demand a Reason*";[124] so in his view our question is a sensible one. If we have here a primary rule, Locke nowhere provides a justification for it. Such a justification would yield an account of Locke's liberalism not completely wrapped up in religion; it would allow us to bypass his divine-command theory of ethics. Yet no such account is forthcoming from Locke's texts.[125]

Second, Locke suggests that we view consent's obliging power as a secondary moral rule. As to "things not comprehended in" God's will, he writes, "Man is naturally free, but yet so much master of his own liberty, that he may by compact convey it over to another and invest him with a power over his actions, there being no law of God forbidding a man to dispose of his liberty

[123]*Treatises* II §195 p. 414; also *Treatises* I §6 p. 162.
[124]*Essay*, p. 68.
[125]Compare Dunn, *Political Thought*, p. 127. I would modify Dunn's claim that Locke's politics is religious through and through only by adding that it does have conceptual working room for a fairly secular approach. But Locke seems uninterested in filling that room.
Dunn, on the other hand, refuses to pursue the conceptual issues, instead repeatedly dismissing Locke. Note *Political Thought*, pp. xin., 21, 92, 94–95, 163, 221; Dunn, "Justice and the Interpretation of Locke's Political Theory," *Political Studies* 18 (February 1968): 80n.

and obey another. But on the other side, there being a law of God enforcing fidelity and truth in all lawful contracts, it obliges him after such a resignation and agreement to submit."[126] A subject consents to political authority. By itself, the action is uninteresting; but it is vested with moral significance by God's command of fidelity. Accepting this account of consent and obligation would mean placing Locke firmly in the camp of Christian political theorists. It would mean that his liberalism could not be adequately explicated without extensive appeals to God and scripture. We should not be surprised at this possibility. The more typical early view of Locke is that instead of ascending from the consent of the people, political authority descends from God: "Indirectly and by delegated power the will of any other superior is binding, be it that of a king or a parent, to whom we are subject by the will of God. All that dominion which the rest of law-makers exercise over others, both the right of legislation and the right to impose an obligation to obey, they borrow from God alone, and we are bound to obey them because God willed thus, and commanded thus, so that by complying with them we also obey God."[127] Whether or not Locke appeals to consent, an account of the obligation to obey the law hanging on his arguments on pleasure, God, and revelation will not do, for those arguments are deeply flawed.

In the end, then, Locke has no satisfactory account of why consent obliges. Consider next his account of legitimacy. Here I sought an account of why the interests of all rational creatures are served best by the liberal state. We have learned that for Locke rationality consists in maximizing pleasure and minimizing pain. But the issue does not devolve to whether or not a liberal society promises lots of pleasure for one and all in this world. Locke insists that the pleasures and pains of the next world outweigh any that this world has to offer. He needs, then, to show how liberalism falls out of the Testaments, for they are our source of knowledge of God's will. (Liberalism in this ac-

[126]*Tracts* I pp. 124–125.
[127]*Law*, p. 187; also *Tracts* II p. 226. I borrow the heuristic distinction between ascending and descending views from Walter Ullmann, *Medieval Political Thought* (Harmondsworth: Penguin, 1975).

count would lack primary moral significance.) Locke nowhere even begins that effort. (A rumination on the Straussian effort to transform Locke into Hobbes: here Locke needs to imitate Hobbes's fabulous attempt to derive his politics from scripture, but he does not budge in that direction. Locke's expressed attitude toward Hobbes is diffidence.[128])

Alternatively, Locke could proffer some primary moral rule(s) leaving liberalism triumphant. Here again there might be principles independent of God's will that would play into the decisions of rational agents. For example, suppose it were wrong to violate a liberal set of rights, and suppose again that God buttressed that primary rule with the sanctions of the afterlife. Then Locke could offer an account of liberalism not wholly ensnared in religion. Nowhere in his writings, though, does he proceed along these lines.

I conclude that if we pursue the argument of the *Treatises*, we are led farther and farther away from politics. We find ourselves unraveling a tangle of ideas about pleasure, God, and revelation. Locke intends his moral theory to serve as a foundation, but it fails strikingly to support or flesh out his political theory. Like any other foundational structure, Locke's political theory is a house of cards. Should any of the props supporting it be even slightly faulty, the whole structure collapses. But no single prop of this house needs minor adjustment or repair. Instead, major renovation is required.

Perhaps, though, a foundational theory with a far more economical structure will succeed. The modern reader will take Locke's views on pleasure and pain more seriously than his views on religion. And after all, we have a very different theory about the maximization of pleasure on hand, one that proudly disclaims theological commitments and seems perfectly at home in a bureaucratic, scientific world. Accordingly, I now turn to utilitarianism.

[128]*Works* IV:477; *Second Vindication of the Reasonableness of Christianity*, in *Works* VII:420–421. See too Locke, "Of Study," in Axtell, *Educational Writings*, p. 417; *Essay*, p. 68.

[CHAPTER THREE]

AGAINST
UTILITARIANISM

Champions of utilitarianism regularly insist on its thoroughgoing precision and comprehensiveness; even its critics often
grudgingly agree. Here I argue that utilitarianism is intolerably
sketchy and, more important, that we are given no good reasons
to adopt the utilitarian standard.

I proceed by explaining what I take utilitarianism to be and
undertaking some textual exegesis of Bentham, Mill, and Sidgwick. Mill, incidentally, I take to be at most an indecisive, inconsistent utilitarian, whose thought cannot be explicated adequately within the confines of utilitarianism. I include him here
in deference to convention. I go on to reject an all too common
line of attack against utilitarianism, that of showing that it does

Throughout the chapter I cite from the following works by Jeremy Bentham:
Deontology (*Deontology*, ed. John Bowring, 2 vols. [London, 1834]); *Introduction*
(*An Introduction to the Principles of Morlas and Legislation*, ed. J. H. Burns and
H. L. A. Hart [London: Athlone Press, 1970]); *Works* (*Works of Jeremy Bentham*,
ed. John Bowring, 11 vols. [New York: Russell & Russell, 1962]). I also cite
Methods (Henry Sidgwick, *The Methods of Ethics*, 7th ed. [Chicago: University of
Chicago Press, 1962]); *Utilitarianism* (John Stuart Mill, *Utilitarianism*, in *Essays
on Ethics, Religion, and Society*, ed. J. M. Robson, in *Collected Works*, vol. 10
[Toronto: University of Toronto Press, 1969]); *Logic* (John Stuart Mill, *A System of Logic*, ed. J. M. Robson, in *Collected Works*, vols. 7–8 [Toronto: University of Toronto Press, 1973]); *Rational Behavior* (John C. Harsanyi, *Rational Behavior and Bargaining Equilibrium in Games and Social Situations* [Cambridge:
Cambridge University Press, 1977]). Author's italics throughout.

not match our "moral intuitions." The line I adopt instead is that of showing that utilitarianism seems radically incomplete and that the arguments for it are readily refuted. Throughout, I focus on classical utilitarianism, which seems to me the most compelling version. But classical utilitarianism has spawned countless variants, often deemed improvements; so I also examine the theories of Harsanyi, Hare, and Brandt. I conclude with some critical remarks on the foundational structure of utilitarianism.

This chapter wanders away from politics, into terrain occupied largely by economists, and I should explain why. Utilitarianism, with its unswerving devotion to the greatest happiness, presents a marvelously clear picture of the practical syllogism:

> We ought to realize the greatest happiness.
> Doing X will realize the greatest happiness.
> We ought to do X.

Here correct political arrangements would fill in X. I mean to leave aside arguments about what X in fact is. First we need to figure out whether the major premise is right. If it is, then we can worry about the minor premise.

We can note immediately, though, that adopting utilitarianism would mean drastically revising our understanding of politics. It would mean viewing politics as a completely technical activity, simply finding means to a given end, not as anything like a Weberian clash of ultimate ends.[1] This reshaping is only one of the dubious surprises utilitarianism has to offer.

Utilitarianism Characterized

It might be best to begin by explaining what I do not take utilitarianism to be. I take a teleological theory to be one identifying

---

[1] So I must add a note to Nancy Rosenblum, *Bentham's Theory of the Modern State* (Cambridge, Mass.: Harvard University Press, 1978), p. 150: utility may be "unbearable to some" not because it casts "legislation as a continual, indecisive, and unlimited process," but because it misunderstands the source and nature of that endlessness. Compare Max Weber, "Politics as a Vocation," in *From Max Weber*, trans. H. H. Gerth and C. Wright Mills (New York: Oxford University Press, 1980), especially pp. 117–128.

[111]

the right as that which realizes the good, and a consequentialist theory to be one holding that actions, dispositions, rules, and the like are to be evaluated on the basis of their consequences. Both sorts of theories are often called utilitarian, but I wish to reserve the word for a distinctive family of theories that falls within these broader classes.

I take utilitarianism to be any theory holding that the average or total happiness of the group ought to be maximized. Utilitarians differ on their interpretation of happiness: some conceive of it as pleasure or as agreeable mental states of whatever kind; others as preference satisfaction. I insist that happiness be construed descriptively and that it be tightly linked to mental states for a theory to qualify as utilitarian. Utilitarians differ too in their strategies for maximization: act-utilitarians ask agents to calculate the consequences of each and every one of their actions; rule-utilitarians ask agents to follow rules justified in turn by their consequences.[2] Utilitarians also differ on whose happiness is to be maximized: some include the unborn, some those in other societies, some animals. But the crucial element, however elaborated, is maximization of average or total happiness. I do not, for example, consider Moore's "ideal utilitarianism" to be a form of utilitarianism at all, but rather just another teleological theory, for Moore nominated other goods to take the place of happiness.[3]

Suppose we are discussing Bentham's views on dicastic thelematoscopic pathoscopic pneumatoscopic idioscopic eudaemonics, as he named ethics.[4] We all know, without bothering to read Bentham, that his principle of utility dictates striving for the greatest happiness of the greatest number; and indeed there is

[2]On act- and rule-utilitarianism, see Richard B. Brandt, *Ethical Theory* (Englewood Cliffs, N.J.: Prentice-Hall, 1959), pp. 380–385, 396–400. See generally David Lyons, *Forms and Limits of Utilitarianism* (Oxford: Clarendon, 1965).

[3]G. E. Moore, *Principia Ethica* (Cambridge: Cambridge University Press, 1980); and his *Ethics* (New York: Oxford University Press, 1965).

[4]See *Chrestomathia*, in *Works* VIII:82–98, explaining table V, enclosed in the back cover of this edition. Those curious about Bentham's penchant for classification "in the exhaustively-bifurcate mode" should consult *Works* VIII: 102–110, especially 107–108.

textual evidence for that traditional view.[5] Yet, as David Lyons has argued, we actually find in Bentham's writings "a *dual* standard, with community interest the criterion of right and wrong in public or political affairs and personal interest the proper standard for 'private ethics.'"[6] Here I argue that the dual standard is best understood as a strategy for realizing the greatest happiness.

At the beginning of *An Introduction to the Principles of Morals and Legislation*, Bentham offers "an explicit and determinate account of what is meant by" the principle of utility: "that principle which approves or disapproves of every action whatsoever, according to the tendency which it appears to have to augment or diminish the happiness of the party whose interest is in question: or, what is the same thing in other words, to promote or oppose that happiness."[7] Bentham, while hesitant to define *interest*, is clear that "a thing is said to promote the interest, or to be *for* the interest, of an individual, when it tends to add to the sum total of his pleasures: or, what comes to the same thing, to diminish the sum total of his pains."[8] So to understand the explicit and determinate account of the principle of utility, we need know only whose interest is in question. Bentham never, as far as I am aware, argues that when private individuals act, only their own interests are in question, but he apparently holds that view: "By utility is meant that property in any object, whereby it tends to produce benefit, advantage, pleasure, good, or happiness, (all this in the present case comes to the same thing) or (what comes again to the same thing) to prevent the happening of mischief, pain, evil, or unhappiness to the party whose interest is considered: if that party be the community in general, then the happiness of the community: if a particular individual, then the happiness of that individual."[9] These claims are unequivocal. The government is to pursue the happiness of all; I am to pursue my own happiness. That seems a far cry from utilitarianism: it looks

[5]For example, *Works* I:269n.; and *Introduction*, p. 285.
[6]Here I follow, up to a point, David Lyons, *In the Interest of the Governed: A Study in Bentham's Philosophy of Utility and Law* (Oxford: Clarendon, 1973); the quoted passage is from p. vii.
[7]*Introduction*, pp. 11–12.
[8]*Introduction*, p. 12, and 12n.c.
[9]*Introduction*, p. 12; also p. 293. But compare p. 284.

more like utilitarianism for governments, egoism for individuals. The split here is puzzling and demands some explanation.

Let me work backward a moment. Suppose that Bentham's fundamental principle was in fact the greatest-happiness principle as we generally think of it. Why might he have been led to the dual standard? Because, I conjecture, his psychological theories placed obstacles in the way of realizing the greatest happiness in a more direct way. The problem is clear already in the opening flourish of the *Introduction*: "Nature has placed mankind under the governance of two sovereign masters, *pain* and *pleasure*. It is for them alone to point out what we ought to do, as well as to determine what we shall do. On the one hand the standard of right and wrong, on the other the chain of causes and effects, are fastened to their throne."[10] Here Bentham invites cheap criticism. "How convenient!" we might say. "We are determined by Nature to do what we ought to. Immorality is precluded by the laws of causation." But this criticism is too quick. We need to appreciate the gravity of the riddle Bentham poses himself in adopting these views.

Each individual, it seems, seeks his own pleasure, yet (I am supposing) Bentham holds the greatest happiness of all to be the good. If I am causally determined to seek my own pleasure, how can the greatest-happiness principle have any impact? Bentham's hedonism is not purely egoistic. Bentham explicitly allows for simple pleasures and pains of benevolence and malevolence, which he calls "extra-regarding."[11] He does hold, however, that "the only interests which a man at all times and upon all occasions is sure to find *adequate* motives for consulting are his own."[12] With his discovery of the sinister interests blocking the success of utilitarianism, he seems to have become even more firmly convinced of the prevalence of egoism.[13]

For Bentham, there is a second psychological obstacle to ask-

[10]*Introduction*, p. 11.
[11]*Introduction*, pp. 42, 49.
[12]*Introduction*, p. 284. Note too p. 155.
[13]*Deontology* I:13, 18, 28–29, 191; II:15, 35, 72–73, 121, 133, 155; *Works* IX:5–6, X:80. The *Deontology* is of doubtful authenticity, and I will try here not to rest any interpretation on its pages. But I do think it is characteristic Bentham.

ing individuals to pursue the group's good. Bentham is skeptical of the possibility of adequately knowing other minds: "By competent attention and observation every man will be best acquainted with the character of his own sensibilities. By countenance, gesture, deportment, contemporaneous or subsequent conduct, he may give indications to others; but no evidence will be so complete, no testimony so direct, as that of his own feelings: thence it follows that, with the benefit of experience, every man is a more competent judge of what is instrumental to his own well-being than any other man."[14] In Bentham's psychological views, then, we have two good reasons for allowing the pursuit of self-interest. It is what people are most prone to do anyway, and each person knows better than others what makes her happy. Bentham's dual standard thus offers a way of maximizing the utility of a group of largely egoistic agents with basically private mental states.

But the dual standard is unsatisfactory. Bentham claims, "If every man, acting correctly for his own interests, obtained the maximum of possible happiness, mankind would reach the millenium of accessible bliss; and the end of morality—the general happiness—be accomplished."[15] Imagine now, though, that transfers of income, or of other happiness-producing goodies, can on the whole (counting in all the indirect effects Bentham and later utilitarians so strenuously insist on) increase total happiness. Imagine, say, that Bentham is right in arguing from the principle of decreasing marginal utility to economic egalitarianism. Then this claim is wrong. Even a doctrine of the harmony of interests between individual and society, one that Lyons attributes to Bentham in the *Introduction*,[16] may not do the job here, depending on just how we spell out that elusive idea. For

---

[14]*Deontology* I:78–79; see too I:29, 59, 68, 189; II:121, 289–290.

[15]*Deontology* I:12, also I:18; *Works* II:121–122.

[16]Lyons, *In the Interest*, pp. 50–81. This is surely the view in *Deontology* I:18–19, 164; II:36–41, 89, 189–190, 295. Sidgwick, in *Methods*, pp. 87–88n., sees two principles in Bentham and says Bentham reconciles them by holding "that it is always the individual's true interest . . . to act in the manner most conducive to the general happiness"; but as support he cites *Works* X:560, 561, where nothing of the sort is to be found. Nor, as far as I can tell, is the reference a simple typographical error for some similar location. A sound critical edition of the *Methods* is badly needed.

the threat is not exhausted by situations in which I can advance my interests by trampling on yours. Some social settings may present prisoners' dilemmas, situations in which the pursuit of private interests produces results irrational from everyone's point of view.[17]

The dual standard is not the only problematic element of Bentham's utilitarianism. Bentham, as we will see, faces objections for holding that all sorts of mental states are commensurable, and the more he insists on a variety of pleasures and pains—in one manuscript he has fifty-four pleasures and sixty-seven pains[18]—the more plausible the objection seems. He flirts too, especially given his inclination to debunk poetry, with the accusation that utilitarianism is coarse and degrading. Mill, concerned about these issues, introduces a distinction between higher and lower pleasures. He writes that "the creed which accepts as the foundation of morals, Utility, or the Greatest Happiness Principle, holds that actions are right in proportion as they tend to promote happiness, wrong as they tend to produce the reverse of happiness," and adds, "By happiness is intended pleasure, and the absence of pain; by unhappiness, pain, and the privation of pleasure." So far we are on familiar Benthamite ground. Mill, however, holds that "it is quite compatible with the principle of utility to recognise the fact, that some *kinds* of pleasures are more desirable and more valuable than others." There follows his notorious procedure for vindicating the higher pleasures: "Of two pleasures, if there be one to which all or almost all who have experience of both give a decided preference, irrespective of any feeling of moral obligation to prefer it, that is the more desirable pleasure."[19]

The coherence of the utilitarian calculus hangs in the balance here. If we cannot plot all pleasures and pains on the same metric, we cannot make an unequivocal judgment that this action, or

[17]A delightful sketch of this phenomenon, and related ones, is Thomas C. Schelling's *Micromotives and Macrobehavior* (New York: Norton, 1978). Note too Henry Sidgwick, *Elements of Politics*, 4th ed. (London: Macmillan, 1919), pp. 144–151.
[18]*Works* I:205–206.
[19]*Utilitarianism*, pp. 210–211.

rule, or disposition, or whatever else, produces the greatest happiness. One may produce more "higher pleasures," another more "lower pleasures." Perhaps Mill can be successfully defended as a utilitarian here, though the defenses are, I think, a bit too ingenious to rank as compelling interpretations.[20] But Mill presses on, past any recognizably hedonic calculus: "It is better to be a human being dissatisfied than a pig satisfied; better to be Socrates dissatisfied than a fool satisfied."[21] At this point, efforts to show that Mill is a consistent utilitarian seem more foolhardy than courageous.[22] Surely the right hypothesis is that Mill is torn between a Benthamite utilitarianism and an ethic of self-realization.[23] Commitment to self-realization recurs through his works: witness the chapter on "Individuality" in *On Liberty*, his account of his breakdown and sympathy for Coleridge in the *Autobiography*, and the chapter "Of the Probable Futurity of the Labouring Classes" in his *Principles of Political Economy*. The commitment is not readily accommodated, and indeed may be unintelligible, within the Benthamite psychology so conducive to classical utilitarianism.[24] And the commitment is much to his credit. It ought not to be stamped out or glued over to demonstrate Mill's consistency.

Sidgwick hesitates at being described a utilitarian,[25] and he has good reason for doing so, given his views on the duality of practical reason[26] and his critique of hedonism. I will not examine those views here, however. Instead I will take the *Methods of*

[20]See here Rex Martin, "A Defence of Mill's Qualitative Hedonism," *Philosophy* 47 (April 1972): 140–151; Henry R. West, "Mill's Qualitative Hedonism," *Philosophy* 51 (January 1976): 97–101.

[21]*Utilitarianism*, p. 212.

[22]Compare Richard Wollheim, "John Stuart Mill and Isaiah Berlin," in *The Idea of Freedom*, ed. Alan Ryan (Oxford: Oxford University Press, 1979).

[23]The argument for higher pleasures and self-development at the end of *Logic*, p. 952, shows clearly that Mill is willing altogether to surrender a hedonistic conception of happiness.

[24]As aptly noted by Amy Gutmann, *Liberal Equality* (Cambridge: Cambridge University Press, 1980), p. 22: "What would 'self-development' mean in a Benthamite view of personality?"

[25]*Methods*, pp. x–xi.

[26]A lively account is J. L. Mackie, "Sidgwick's Pessimism," *Philosophical Quarterly* 26 (October 1976): 317–327.

Ethics as an argument for utilitarianism, for the exposition and defense of the doctrine there offered is clearer and more elegant than either Bentham's or Mill's.

Sidgwick takes the greatest happiness to mean "the greatest possible surplus of pleasure over pain, the pain being conceived as balanced against an equal amount of pleasure, so that the two contrasted amounts annihilate each other for purposes of ethical calculation," and he takes pleasure and pain "to include respectively all kinds of agreeable and disagreeable feelings."[27] He admits "distinctions of *quality* . . . only in so far as they can be resolved into distinctions of quantity."[28] Finally, he counts the feelings of all sentient beings.[29] It may be appropriate to formalize the notation a bit, for while Sidgwick is aware that calculations will be difficult, he does seek as much scientific precision as he can. A utilitarian wants to maximize

$$U = \sum_{i=1}^{n} (x_i - y_i),$$

where n is the number of beings in the group, x_i is the happiness or pleasure of the ith being, and y_i is the unhappiness or pain of the ith being.

Sidgwick is aware of what must be the case for this view even to be coherent. First, we must be able to place pleasures and pains on a single scale and be able to add and subtract them. More formally, these mental states must be commensurable and cardinal.[30] Second, interpersonal utility comparisons must be possible.[31] It will do no good to tell us to maximize a sum that cannot be summed. If these conditions are prerequisites for the

[27]*Methods*, pp. 413, 120–121.
[28]*Methods*, p. 121.
[29]*Methods*, p. 414; compare *Introduction*, pp. 282–283n.b; *Utilitarianism*, p. 214.
[30]*Methods*, pp. 123–137. Sidgwick plumps for a ratio scale, not merely an interval one.
[31]*Methods*, pp. 144–150, where this point is combined with that of comparing pleasures in the same person at different times.

meaningfulness of utilitarianism, a utilitarian is perforce committed to them. Sidgwick worries about each, but thinks we can make sense of the felicific calculus in at least a rough and ready way.

Maximizing U, the utilitarian holds, is what morality and politics are all about. Utility, writes Bentham, "is itself the sole and all-sufficient reason for every point of practice whatsoever"; Mill takes it "as the ultimate appeal in all ethical questions"; and Sidgwick, despite his hesitations in the *Methods of Ethics*, adopts the principle of utility in his *Elements of Politics*: "For a State, as for an individual, the ultimate end and standard of right conduct is the happiness of all who are affected by its actions."[32]

These claims are extraordinarily bold and sweeping. I have noted already that adopting utilitarianism would mean thinking of politics as a technical activity. Arguably, it would also mean radically reshaping our understanding of moral life.[33] But it would mean, by the same token, a perhaps welcome relief from the endless haggling of moral and political debate. We ought, then, to subject utilitarianism to careful scrutiny to see if we should adopt it.

Utilitarianism Scrutinized

What sort of scrutiny is appropriate? A common procedure is to check utilitarianism against our moral judgments to see if it tells us to do what we know is right. An especially popular argument is that utilitarians are committed to supporting slavery if slavery maximizes utility. Yet, the argument goes on, surely slavery is wrong. The defense has been that the calculations showing slavery to be felicific are incomplete or skewed, that

---

[32]*Works* I:272; Mill, *On Liberty*, in *Essays on Politics and Society*, ed. J. M. Robson, in *Collected Works*, vols. 18–19 (Toronto: University of Toronto Press, 1977), p. 224; Sidgwick, *Elements of Politics*, p. 299; note too *Elements*, pp. 38–40, 609.
[33]See Bernard Williams, "A Critique of Utilitarianism," in J. J. C. Smart and Bernard Williams, *Utilitarianism: For and Against* (Cambridge: Cambridge University Press, 1973).

they don't pay enough attention to indirect consequences, that they ignore deep-seated facts of human nature.[34] (Utilitarians show marvelous ingenuity in developing such defenses, and are lucky to have such a pliable theory.) I want to avoid such discussions, and I will explain why.

Recall the sketch from the introduction on the variety of projects available in moral and political theory: justification, explication, genealogy, and so on. Were utilitarianism to pose as an explication of our moral beliefs, the appeal to slavery and the like would be quite sensible as an objection. Here our moral judgments are appropriately seen as data the theory must fit, and a theory that cannot account for important data is in bad shape. But our beliefs can be explicated whether they are right or wrong, or neither. Utilitarians want to say not that "we all think this is right and wrong, good and bad," but rather that "this *is* right and wrong, good and bad." They are presenting their view as the right one, not necessarily the one we do use, but the one we should use.

So the appropriate considerations are those of justification, not explication. A clear-headed utilitarian can airily dismiss the appeal to the injustice of slavery by saying, "If injustice serves the general happiness, we ought to be unjust." At that point, it will not do to remind the utilitarian that we think slavery is unconditionally wrong. He knows that, and he thinks we are wrong to be so rigid. Why, he might ask, insist on a view so singularly unresponsive to shifting circumstances? Although utilitarians have generally been anxious to minimize the apparent discrepancies between their code and our shared views, they do sometimes take the less timid line I am suggesting. Bentham's *Deontology* may have been extensively revised by Bowring, but it is hard to detect the latter's work here: "If it could be proved that evil, in the shape of a balance of suffering on the whole, grew out of a

[34]For example, Bentham, *Works* I:343–347; R. M. Hare, "What Is Wrong with Slavery," *Philosophy & Public Affairs* 8 (Winter 1979): 103–121. The first clear statement of rule-utilitarianism, R. F. Harrod's "Utilitarianism Revised," *Mind* 45 (April 1936): 137–156, was motivated by a desire to reconcile utilitarianism and our moral views: "I conceive it to be the task of the moral philosopher to determine and explain the subject matter of that body of [common moral] opinion" (p. 137).

given line of conduct, and it were agreed that such line of conduct ought to be called *just*, the consequences would simply be, that *justice* and *virtue* might be opposed to one another, and that to be just would be immoral."[35] Once a utilitarian is willing to take this step, our shared moral views are irrelevant.

What, then, shall we say about the voluminous literature devoted to embarrassing utilitarianism by dreaming up examples in which it has morally counterintuitive implications, and the equally voluminous literature defending it against such attacks? Not only has this line of argument proved inconclusive; it also seems quite beside the point. Once we see the difference between explication and justification, it is tempting to write off this entire literature as simply confused. Still, there are two views that prevent our doing so, views that in different ways threaten the clean logical separation between explication and justification.

The first view is that of Prichard and Ross.[36] I can offer only a bald summary statement here. Suppose there are objective moral truths, and suppose we may discover them by the operation of moral intuition, a sixth sense of sorts. There might be ideal observing conditions: Our intuitions might be most accurate when we are impartial, reflecting in a Butlerian cool moment, and so on. But they would be reports on an autonomous realm of moral truths. We need not litter that realm with scads of judgments. We intuit basic principles, and hammer our way through to individual judgments by applying the principles. So construed, our confident moral judgments are once again data the theory has to fit—but now with a new twist, as they are observational data, automatically true.

This view can perhaps be worked out coherently, but it relies on an extravagant metaphysics and epistemology. Worse, it begs

---

[35]*Deontology* II:58. Note too R. M. Hare, "The Argument from Received Opinion," in his *Essays on Philosophical Method* (Berkeley: University of California Press, 1972); Hare, *Moral Thinking* (Oxford: Clarendon, 1981), pp. 130–140; Peter Singer, "Is Act-Utilitarianism Self-Defeating?" *Philosophical Review* 81 (January 1972): 94.

[36]H. A. Prichard, *Moral Obligation* (Oxford: Clarendon, 1971), especially chap. 1, "Does Moral Philosophy Rest on a Mistake?" reprinted from *Mind* 21 (January 1912): 21–37; W. D. Ross, *The Right and the Good* (Oxford: Clarendon, 1973).

all the really interesting questions about morality. Here I want only to note Bentham's decisive attack on such theories. I refer to the *Introduction*'s scathing footnote on the British moralists, the one Mill quotes as indicative of "the strengths and weaknesses of his mode of philosophizing."[37] Reporting a moral intuition is not the same as giving a reason. Imagine—the case is not counterfactual—two people disagreeing on a basic moral or political question, each sure of being right. In the intuitionist view, we are at a dead end. One or the other is not perceiving the realm of moral truths correctly, but we have no way of checking. *Ipse dixitism*, as Bentham would say, with a vengeance. If we are to have intelligent debate, we will have to find reasons. It would be embarrassing, even for a full-blooded intuitionist, to concede that there is no point to morality.

The second view is that implicitly adopted by Aristotle in the *Nicomachean Ethics*. Justification need not commence with a slate wiped clean of all our views. Instead, we can investigate our view critically, revising them as we go. Nor are our critical standards magically yanked from some hitherto unknown realm. We already have such standards, themselves subject to revision as justification proceeds. Since our views do not form some perfectly coherent whole, we have working room to launch forth on the process of justification. I want to hold this view of justification in abeyance here, since Bentham and Mill offer another view of justification, one promising a much more straightforward account. Not holding a view like Aristotle's, they can afford to sneeze at our shared moral judgments.

I do not mean to cast these two views as rivals. In the *Ethics*, for example, Aristotle actually draws on both; Sidgwick, as a follower of Aristotle, does so too.[38] He appeals, as we will see, to a "fundamental moral intuition" in the argument from egoistic hedonism to utilitarianism. And he writes, "The present argument

[37]*Introduction*, pp. 26–29n.d; "Bentham," in Mill, *Essays on Ethics, Religion, and Society*, pp. 85–86.

[38]See Terence Irwin, "Aristotle's Methods of Ethics," in *Studies in Aristotle*, ed. Dominic J. O'Meara (Washington, D.C.: Catholic University of America Press, 1981). Compare Peter Singer, "Sidgwick and Reflective Equilibrium," *Monist* 58 (July 1974): 490–517.

does not aim at proving an exact coincidence between Utilitarian inferences and the intuitions of Common Sense, but rather seeks to represent the latter as inchoately and imperfectly Utilitarian."[39] So one might well challenge Sidgwick by demanding a viable utilitarian rendition of fairness or justice,[40] but that ground is surely trod well and frequently enough, and I will leave it unexplored.

The appropriate scrutiny, then, is not an appeal to our shared moral judgments. Instead, I want to consider the utilitarians' claims to have provided a clear, all-encompassing theory, and to have given us good reasons for adopting it. Neither of these claims, I argue, can be sustained.

Utilitarianism as Incomplete

Consider:

1. You are floating across the Lake of Lucerne in a canoe on a balmy spring day, admiring the wispy clouds and piping birdsongs.
2. You are about to devour, courtesy of a friend, a triple-fudge cake from Rosie's, your favorite bakery, after a day without food.
3. You are one of a swirling mob exulting over the accession of Charles the Fat to the throne.
4. You finish solving a difficult crossword puzzle.
5. You have an orgasm.
6. You are reinstated with your best friend of thirty years, thought lost in an airplane crash.

These, let us imagine, are all pleasurable.

Now consider:

1. You are caught in a thunderstorm on top of Half Dome and fear death at the hands of wind and lightning.
2. Your promised triple-fudge cake fails to materialize; your friend is playing a practical joke and solemnly brings out an empty plate.

---

[39] *Methods*, p. 427.
[40] See *Methods*, pp. 439–448, for as good a rendition as anyone has offered.

3. You are found hiding during a pogrom.
4. Your first concert performance is poorly reviewed.
5. You break your arm; it is a compound fracture, and your friend swoons at the sight.
6. You receive news of the death of an old friend.

These, let us imagine, are all painful. I trust that I need not disclaim any attempt to show there are six kinds of pleasures and six kinds of pains.

As Sidgwick notes, if we are to sum pleasures and pains, they must be commensurable, cardinal, and interpersonally comparable. Here I will concede cardinality and interpersonal comparability.[41] I want to contest commensurability. We are inclined to think of these twelve pleasures and pains as very different. For commensurability to obtain, there must be some metric, a single scale, along which they can all be placed.

The candidate for the metric, in a utilitarian view, will be agreeability of consciousness. Each experience has a raw feel to it, and the feel has an agreeability or disagreeability. Anticipating the chocolate cake will be less agreeable than the orgasm, say; the broken arm more disagreeable than the fear of death on Half Dome. But does the agreeability refer to any aspect of the experiences, or is it rather a disposition on our part to choose one over another? A full-blown theory of pleasure and pain—not a scientific-minded revision, but merely an account of ordinary usage—will have to move well beyond the supposed feel of the experiences. It will have to draw in, for example, various sorts of behavior. Whatever mentalistic strands the concepts now have do not seem to exhaust their meaning. Yet for the theory to be about happiness construed as a mental state, the metric must not collapse into something like preference satisfaction.

"Well," one might say, "we call them all pleasures and pains, so they must have something in common." The common element might be just our disposition to choose, not an element of the pleasure or pain itself. Yet there need be no common element

---

[41]For a recent suggestive discussion of the latter, see Alfred F. Mackay, "Interpersonal Comparisons," *Journal of Philosophy* 72 (October 2, 1975): 535–549.

at all. We could have a case of family resemblance. As Mill notes, "Names creep on from subject to subject, until all traces of a common meaning sometimes disappear, and the word comes to denote a number of things not only independently of any common attribute, but which have actually no attribute in common."[42] Among all the experiences we call pleasures we find no peculiar tickle, itch, or tingling in common; among the pains, no twinge, burning, or stinging. It is possible that utilitarians are built differently from the rest of us and lead linear mental lives, but that seems doubtful.

That mental states are incommensurable presents more than a technical obstacle for utilitarianism. It is just one part of a general problem: the utilitarian calculus demands a staggering loss of information. Just as utilitarians ask us to forget the differences between orgasms and solving crossword puzzles, they ask us to overlook distributive considerations, risk and uncertainty, and time preference. By focusing now on these three, I hope to show that utilitarians' claims to have provided a complete decision procedure must be rejected.

Suppose an agent has a choice between what Bentham would call a pure pleasure of 6 utils and an impure pleasure of 9 utils with -3 utils (3 units of pain) attached. One would expect a theory of rational choice to describe an agent contemplating two ordered pairs: $(6, 0)$ and $(9, 3)$. Instead we are told, in Sidgwick's words, that we are to strive for "the greatest possible surplus of pleasure over pain, the pain being conceived as balanced against an equal amount of pleasure, so that the two contrasted amounts annihilate each other for purposes of ethical calculation." The agent, then, must be indifferent between $(6, 0)$ and $(9, 3)$—indifferent, for that matter, among all pairs generated by $(6 + x, x)$ for all $x > 0$. Such an agent seems willfully blind or crazy. Sidgwick offers no independent justification for focusing on the surplus. The single number is a technical requirement of the theory. Without it, we would face problems of balance: Mightn't we sensibly prefer a pure pleasure of 10 utils to one of 15 utils mixed with 3 utils of pain?

[42] *Logic*, p. 38; also the superb discussion in *Logic*, pp. 668–697.

Annihilating equal units of pleasure and pain seems worrisome even for an individual pursuing her own happiness. It seems downright perverse for society, and sharpens the nature of the utilitarian's disregard for distributive considerations. Sidgwick notes the possibility that different actions will produce the same greatest happiness score (not merely a formal possibility in his view, since his calculus is rough). In such cases, he tells us, we need "some principle of Just or Right distribution of the happiness," and he suggests "that of pure equality—as given in Bentham's formula, 'everybody to count for one, and nobody for more than one.'"[43] Equality, though, is hardly a complete and clear principle for ranking two or more distributions. Are we to choose that with the lowest standard deviation? with the fewest severely outlying points? or what?

Suppose we choose a social distribution summing to (200,000, 100,000). The surplus is 100,000; if other possible distributions have lower surpluses, we are not supposed to consider them. Yet in this society there are 100,000 units of pain spread around, and we want to know where they are. It is implausible to suggest that for a given individual a given quantity of happiness annihilates an equal quantity of pain. It is extraordinary to suggest that when I am happy and you are unhappy, a given quantity of my happiness annihilates an equal quantity of your unhappiness. Again, we are given no reason to think it should. The simplification is introduced to make sense of the idea of greatest happiness. This technical necessity is why "utilitarianism does not take seriously the distinction between persons."[44]

Were society a colossal organism, we could make sense of focusing on the surplus, on the single number. Each of us would be something like cells in a sponge. But it is hard to see how society literally could be an organism, or to find an author willing to assert explicitly that it is.[45] Perhaps a sponge cell, if conscious,

[43]*Methods*, pp. 416–417.
[44]John Rawls, *A Theory of Justice* (Cambridge, Mass.: Harvard University Press, Belknap Press, 1971), p. 27.
[45]Hard, but alas! not impossible: Herbert Read, "The Philosophy of Anarchism," in his *Anarchy and Order* (Boston: Beacon Press, 1971), writes, "The right kind of society is an organic being—not merely analogous to an organic being, but actually a living structure with appetites and digestions, instincts and passions, intelligence and reason" (p. 50).

would (properly?) care only for the welfare of the entire sponge, but surely that is not the individual's relationship to society. Strikingly, Bentham and Mill both insist, in their very different ways, on criticizing organic conceptions of society. Bentham detects a dread fictitious entity, and pronounces, "The community is a fictitious *body*, composed of the individual persons who are considered as constituting as it were its *members*. The interest of the community then is, what?—the sum of the interests of the several members who compose it."[46] Mill, in the midst of an extremely careful discussion of the logic of the moral sciences, bluntly states, "Human beings in society have no properties but those which are derived from, and may be resolved into, the laws of the nature of individual man."[47] This methodological individualism undercuts a descriptive prop that would help make some sense of the greatest-happiness principle.

Only some sense, though, because there are still more puzzles. I have been writing so far as though we know what the outcomes of our actions are, but of course we don't. Because of our ignorance of the workings of society, we have only an idea of the possible outcomes; and because the causal ripples introduced by one action interact with those introduced by other actions, unintended consequences seem a permanent feature of any remotely complex society. Suppose, in keeping with a rational-choice model, we can formalize for each action we are contemplating the utilities and associated probabilities of a set of possible outcomes. (This is no trivial supposition, even if we take a Bayesian approach to estimating probability.) How ought we to choose among sets?

Economists will be quick to suggest that we maximize expected utility. That is, we collapse each set into a utility score S:

$$S = \sum_{i=1}^{n} p_i U_i,$$

[46]*Introduction*, p. 12.
[47]*Logic*, p. 879. Though it is not clear just what Mill means to deny. He may well believe in emergent properties for this case, but think that those properties must be accounted for by psychology and ethology. If so, I am not sure he would be denying here anything anyone might wish to affirm.

where p_i is the probability of the ith outcome and U_i the utility of that outcome. Recall, however, that we are now considering utility as some agreeable mental state. Maximizing the expected value of this kind of utility is anything but rational; indeed it is absurd. It requires a rational agent to be indifferent between a one-eighth chance of 800 utils and a one-half chance of 200; or, more generally, to be indifferent among all the members of the set defined by $(1/n, kn)$ for all $n > 1$, with $k > 0$ or $k < 0$. This procedure eliminates all reference to risk aversion, and so is at once eminently attractive and decidedly wrongheaded. Attractive, because otherwise utilitarianism again lapses into indeterminacy or arbitrariness. Just how risk averse is it rational to be? (Can levels of risk aversion even be judged as more or less rational?) Wrongheaded, because it again deliberately purges information, leaving us with a travesty of rationality in the interests of meeting the demands of the theory.

Next I wish to consider pure time preference, cases where an agent prefers a sooner good to an equal later good just because it is sooner. Utilitarians often (conveniently) ignore the dimension of time and write as though the happiness produced by an action occurs in an instant. Neglect of time, however, is hardly appropriate to those who insist that we calculate on the basis of consequences, for the consequences of an action stretch through time.

Consider the graphs of Figure 1, where the x-axis is time, the y-axis total utils in society, and the origin the neutral point between pain and pleasure. The two curves represent the utilitarian consequences of two different possible actions. Suppose that the total area under each curve is the same from time 0 to time 10. That is, over the whole time period, each action will give rise to the same amount of pleasure. Which one should we choose? Or is it irrelevant?

Bentham is sometimes fonder of pleasures that occur sooner rather than later. As he writes in the memorable (if obscure) poem in the *Introduction*:

> *Intense, long, certain, speedy, fruitful, pure—*
> Such marks in *pleasures* and in *pains* endure.[48]

[48]*Introduction*, p. 38n. The poem continues with a clear statement of the dual standard.

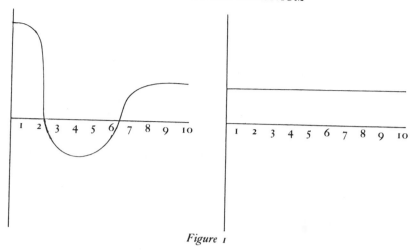

Figure 1

Since *speedy* occurs in the same list as *certain*, we have here a ringing endorsement of pure time preference.[49] In this view, we should choose the first curve—even if the total area under it is less than the total area under the second curve—up to a point depending on the extent of our preference for nearer pleasures. Here we encounter still another source of indeterminacy or arbitrariness. If time preference is to be countenanced, how much time preference? Has rationality anything to say on this score?

In Sidgwick's view, pure time preference is irrational. This view is convenient for utilitarianism, since it avoids the dilemma of choosing a defensible rate of time preference. Unlike the business of pleasures annihilating pains, however, this view is argued for on the merits: "Mere difference of priority and posteriority in time is not a reasonable ground for having more regard to the consciousness of one moment than to that of another."[50] So put, this is but a challenge: why should earlier pleasures be preferred to later ones of equal magnitude? I am not sure that this challenge is unanswerable, but I will grant the point. Time preference, then, is to be discarded.

Regardless, we can exploit the two curves to underline once

[49]See also *Works* I:206; *Deontology* I:62.
[50]*Methods*, p. 381; note too p. 124n. See also Bentham, *Deontology* I:130, 156, 160; II:82–83.

again the curiosity of describing a possible world with a single number. Suppose first that the time units are days. We face a choice between ten days of unbroken serenity and a single tempestuous roller-coaster ride. We may decide it does not matter which we choose. But surely a preference (one way or the other) would be legitimate, for the two alternatives are different. That they leave us at day 10 with the same total amount of happiness is the scantiest description of them. Why should we think that this description captures their only relevant feature for moral or rational choice?

The curves also illustrate the odd conception of society built into the utilitarian calculus. Suppose now that the time units are centuries. We may squander scarce resources and enjoy a cornucopia of consumer delights, falling suddenly into a crevasse of scarcity; yet this limits-to-growth scenario is not all doom, for we will eventually wiggle our way out. We may instead husband scarce resources and keep the welfare of future generations firmly in mind. There are about four centuries of misery in the middle of the first graph, but "society," stretching over a thousand years, is equally happy in the two graphs. It looks as though the utilitarian is committed to the sponge-cell view with a vengeance. That utilitarianism does not take seriously the distinction between persons is a modest way of putting the point. For—imagine now a tiny bit more surface area under the first curve—utilitarians will, in the name of morality, loftily dismiss the life histories of complete generations. (Probably too they will congratulate themselves on transcending the squeamishness of ordinary morality in doing so.)

Handling these points one at a time has cast the difficulties that utilitarianism faces in too charitable a light. A utilitarian choice among alternatives, whether they be rules, acts, character traits, or anything else, will ideally shape up like this: Associated with each alternative will be a set of possible outcomes with probabilities. Choosing between such alternatives will not be easy, so utilitarians will drastically simplify. They will first redescribe each outcome simply as a distribution of pains and pleasures across time and persons. Then they will place all pleasures and pains on a single cardinal axis, however doubtful the availability of such an axis; they will subtract pains from pleasures, and pursue only surpluses of pleasure over pain; and they will pour the mental contents of all persons, each a little receptacle of pain and pleasure, into one great bucket called society. Then, I imagine, they will decide that they are interested in maximizing expected utility, despite the objections to that view, and they will further decide that they have no pure time preference. They will therefore collapse each possible outcome to a single number, multiply each number by the outcome's associated probability, add the numbers in each set, and choose the alternative whose set yields the highest utility score.

I have tried to take Sidgwick's procedure of seeing what is entailed by the notion of maximizing happiness a few steps farther. This procedure, or one much like it, seems to be what is entailed. (Utilitarians who refuse any of the simplifying moves will face problems of indeterminacy or arbitrariness, or will have to supplement their utilitarianism. Worse yet, they will face tradeoffs: how much sooner happiness for how much less pain?) It is, we are told, a model, or the model, of moral decision making. Much of the literature on utilitarianism is reminiscent of the Emperor's New Clothes, and cries out for the same treatment the little boy offers. As far as I know, no one has ever attempted even a sketch of such a decision for any actual problem. (Cost-benefit analysis doesn't even begin to cash out the alternatives into distributions of pleasures and pains.) For good reason, too: we would need to know unfathomably more about consequences and individuals than we do or can know. Attempting even a sketch would discredit the entire project.

Attempting a sketch would also underline a point readily underplayed in abstract discussions of utilitarianism. The sorts of problems I have been discussing are not mere technical obstacles, issues to be handled within the sterile realm of the theory of rational choice. Instead they are fraught with moral and political import. Being forced to consider how to weigh the interests of future generations will put a different face on time preference and uncertainty. The parameters surrounding maximization, telling us just what and how to count, will be morally and politically crucial. Whether we maximize average or total happiness will make all the difference for decisions involving population shifts. Whether we count the happiness of animals will speak volumes on questions about vegetarianism, hunting, vivisection, and the rest. All these issues are morally and politically interesting. None of them could possibly be decided by a utilitarian calculus, since that calculus cannot get started until these issues are resolved. So despite the assurances of Bentham, Mill, and Sidgwick, utilitarianism is not and cannot be the sole principle of morals and politics. Performing its complex calculations might exhaust us, but could not exhaust our moral and political concerns.

Yet even as utilitarianism demands fabulously complicated and detailed calculations, it is singularly narrow-minded in its attention to consequences. Only (un)desirable states of consciousness count. A utilitarian cares not the least for economic or political structure, for culture or society, for themselves. All that is interesting about them is how much happiness they yield. What reason are we given to adopt such a standard?

Justifications of Utilitarianism

Bentham flatly denies the possibility of proving utilitarianism correct: "Is it susceptible of any direct proof? it should seem not: for that which is used to prove everything else, cannot itself be proved: a chain of proofs must have their commencement somewhere."[51] Still, he argues for it, offering a threefold classification of moral principles. There is the principle of utility, those "constantly opposed to it," and those "sometimes opposed to it, and sometimes not, as it may happen." Constantly opposed is the principle of asceticism, which always approves of unhappiness and disapproves of happiness. Sometimes opposed is the principle of sympathy and antipathy, "that principle which approves or disapproves of certain actions . . . merely because a man finds himself disposed to approve or disapprove of them: holding up that approbation or disapprobation as a sufficient rea-

---

[51]*Introduction*, p. 13; also *Deontology* I:276–278.

son for itself, and disclaiming the necessity of looking out for any extrinsic ground."[52]

Bentham is little interested in discussing the principle of asceticism. It "seems originally to have been the reverie of certain hasty speculators" who wished to guard against alluring pleasures fraught with "pains more than equivalent to them" and went on to forget their own devotion to utility.[53] Bentham reserves his concern (as shall I) for principles sometimes opposed to utility and so scrutinizes the principle of sympathy and antipathy. It is, he decides, no principle at all, for, "disclaiming the necessity of looking out for any extrinsic ground," it provides no standard. Since Bentham thinks that "the various systems that have been formed concerning the standard of right and wrong, may all be reduced to the principle of sympathy and antipathy," he makes short work of enshrining the principle of utility.[54]

Bentham is right in holding that an acceptable moral or political principle must direct our attention to reasons, not to our own sentiments, cloaked in "sonorous and unmeaning words" though they be.[55] That we feel something to be wrong is not enough for justification. But it is illegitimate for Bentham to take the principle of sympathy and antipathy as the example of principles sometimes opposed to utility. He makes it seem as though such principles are irreducibly arbitrary, as they would be if pleasure and pain were all that matters.

Bentham observes that "the utilitarian scale vibrates only between good and evil—pain and pleasure—other elements count for nothing in the balance, let them be called by names as pompous as they may."[56] Other scales may not be quite so resolutely unresponsive to other considerations. They may vibrate between freedom and unfreedom, equality and inequality, autonomy and authority, without regard for the felicific consequences. From the point of view of utility, they will oscillate wildly. But provided their standards are suitably well defined and identify con-

[52]*Introduction*, pp. 17, 25.
[53]*Introduction*, p. 21.
[54]*Introduction*, p. 25.
[55]*Deontology* II:11.
[56]*Deontology* II:25.

siderations that vary from utility, they will provide examples of nonarbitrary principles sometimes opposed to utility. Has Bentham anything to say against such principles?

Bentham frequently denies that the moral concepts can be made sense of on nonutilitarian grounds: "Take away *pleasures* and *pains*, not only *happiness*, but *justice*, and *duty*, and *obligation*, and *virtue*—all of which have been so elaborately held up to view as independent of them—are so many empty sounds."[57] This denial surely requires support. Bentham may have such support in mind in referring to the "cloud of misty obscurity [that] has gathered round the term" *obligation*.[58] That view we might speculatively reconstruct. Moral talk is endlessly circular. We ask for an account of rights, and are sent to obligations and permissions, for accounts of those in turn to duties, on to right, wrong, good, bad, legitimate, illegitimate, just, unjust, and so on. We are entrapped, with no escape in sight. Not only is this procedure unenlightening, but it fails to provide a satisfactory standard. Only a purely descriptive concept can provide the bottom line we seek, else moral talk must remain meaningless noise —or so, I suspect, Bentham thinks. One way to meet the argument would be to show that circles big enough to include far-flung elements can be virtuous, not vicious. But a less ambitious approach will do the trick here. Suppose we give a satisfactory descriptive account of freedom and equality and offer a moral principle focusing on them. Bentham would demand of one offering such a principle, "admitting (what is not true) that the word *ought* can have a meaning without reference to utility, let him say whether there is any such thing as a *motive* that a man

[57]*Works* I:206; see too 211, 248; IV:542–543; VIII:290; *Deontology* I:10, 31–32, 136–137. Bentham's famed fusillade against natural rights is at *Works* II:501. None of this talk commits Bentham to defining the moral concepts in terms of pleasure and pain, in which case he would be open to strictures about making his first principle a tautology. His point is rather that the appropriate criteria for using these concepts are pleasure and pain. Though he sometimes writes carelessly—"it is but tautology to say, that the more consistently [utility] is pursued, the better it must ever be for human-kind" (*Introduction*, p. 21) surely does invite such strictures—Bentham himself distinguishes is and ought, so it would be unlikely for him to slip into the fallacy. Note *Works* I:189, 229.

[58]*Deontology* I:10.

can have to pursue the dictates of it"; for if not, the principle looks pointless.[59] Here Bentham explicitly appeals to his hedonistic psychology. I will assume that that psychology is deeply flawed, that we can and do desire things besides pleasure for themselves. Other standards need not be anarchical or horribly vague. It is all a matter of comparison. Attempts to perform a utilitarian judgment would themselves be anarchical and vague.[60] So potentially explosive Benthamite skepticism about nonutilitarian moral talk can be defused.

Like Bentham, Mill cautions the reader that "questions of ultimate ends are not amenable to direct proof." Still, he thinks, "Considerations may be presented capable of determining the intellect either to give or withhold its assent to this doctrine; and this is equivalent to proof." This infamous proof is allegedly encapsuled in one paragraph:

> The only proof capable of being given that an object is visible, is that people actually see it. The only proof that a sound is audible, is that people hear it: and so of the other sources of our experience. In like manner, I apprehend, the sole evidence it is possible to produce that anything is desirable, is that people do actually desire it. If the end which the utilitarian doctrine proposes to itself were not, in theory and in practice, acknowledged to be an end, nothing could ever convince any person that it was so. No reason can be given why the general happiness is desirable, except that each person, so far as he believes it to be attainable, desires his own happiness. This, however, being a fact, we have not only all the proof which the case admits of, but all which it is possible to require, that happiness is a good: that each person's happiness is a good to that person, and the general happiness, therefore, a good to the aggregate of all persons.[61]

Here, it seems, is some blatantly fallacious reasoning, to which we can dutifully rehearse the stock remonstrances. *Desirable* means "*ought* to be desired," whereas *visible* and *audible* mean "*can*

---

[59]*Introduction*, p. 16.

[60]Note Macaulay's politically trenchant attack on utilitarianism as a pliable pretext in Jack Lively and John Rees, eds., *Utilitarian Logic and Politics* (Oxford: Clarendon, 1978), pp. 174–175.

[61]*Utilitarianism*, pp. 207, 208, 234.

be seen and heard," so the analogy breaks down. And only sleight of hand makes the greatest happiness a good to all: "the aggregate of all persons" may not be an entity with a good, and even if it is, Mill gives no reason for any individual to care for others' happiness. No wonder, then, that Bradley professes himself "ashamed to have to examine such reasoning," that Moore finds a "fallacy . . . so obvious that it is quite wonderful how Mill failed to see it."[62]

If Mill were attempting a deductive proof, Bradley's and Moore's derision would be apt enough. But he is not; nor, given his views in the *Logic*, could he be. Though the argument is still faulty, we should try to arrive at a satisfactory understanding of it.[63]

Mill distinguishes in the *Logic* between art and science. The former, he says, concerns what ought to be, the latter what is. Like Bentham, he holds that "a proposition of which the predicate is expressed by the words *ought* or *should be*, is generically different from one which is expressed by *is*, or *will be*."[64] In conceding that if we take a syllogism as an argument, we must grant that it begs the question,[65] Mill commits himself to the view that purely deductive arguments add nothing to what is already contained in the premises. So Mill believes that it is impossible to derive an ought from an is. The conventional view of his proof of utilitarianism, taking him to be attempting just that, is presumably misconceived. We may be driven to hold that Mill simply forgot his own strictures from the *Logic* when he came to write *Utilitarianism*, or that he had changed his mind but some-

---

[62]F. H. Bradley, *Ethical Studies*, 2d ed. (Oxford: Clarendon, 1967), p. 115n.; Moore, *Principia Ethica*, p. 67.
[63]I was encouraged in my thinking along these lines by Everett W. Hall, "The 'Proof' of Utility in Bentham and Mill," *Ethics* 60 (October 1949): 1–18. Richard H. Popkin, "A Note on the 'Proof' of Utility in J. S. Mill," *Ethics* 61 (October 1950): 66–68, uses the *Logic* to buttress Hall's reading. I draw freely from both articles. I cannot, though, follow the interpretation sketched in Norman Kretzmann, "Desire as Proof of Desirability," *Philosophical Quarterly* 8 (July 1958): 246–258.
[64]*Logic*, p. 949.
[65]*Logic*, p. 184.

how never noted the change in his later revisions of the *Logic*. But surely we should first try to find a reading that makes the two works cohere.

We need, then, a view of the proof different from that excoriated by Bradley and Moore. Just what does Mill take to be "considerations . . . capable of determining the intellect?" Look again at part of the proof: "If the end which the utilitarian doctrine proposes to itself were not, in theory and practice, acknowledged to be an end, nothing could ever convince any person that it was so."[66] The point is pragmatic. There is no sense, Mill is suggesting, in nominating moral principles that tell us to pursue ends we take no interest in. We do take an interest in happiness, so "happiness has made out its title as *one* of the ends of conduct, and consequently one of the criteria of morality."[67] Mill goes on to argue that while we do desire other things—money, virtue, music, health—for themselves, we desire them as parts of happiness: "Happiness is not an abstract idea, but a concrete whole, and these are some of its parts"; so "there is in reality nothing desired except happiness."[68]

The argument for our desiring only happiness is the key to the proof, granted Mill's pragmatic strategy. Consider: "We have now, then, an answer to the question, of what sort of proof the principle of utility is susceptible. If the opinion which I have now stated is psychologically true—if human nature is so constituted as to desire nothing which is not either a part of happiness or a means of happiness, we can have no other proof, and we require no other, that these are the only things desirable."[69] Mill's view is that happiness is all we desire, so there is a point to hav-

---

[66] It is surprising that Moore takes Mill to task for "as naive and artless a use of the naturalistic fallacy as anybody could desire" (*Principia Ethica*, p. 66), since Mill does not say, as Moore claims, that "'Good' . . . means 'desirable'" (p. 66). Mill is explicit here that the connection is one of evidence. Elsewhere, though, like Bentham, he flirts with the language of tautology: "What is the principle of utility, if it be not that 'happiness' and 'desirable' are synonymous terms?" (*Utilitarianism*, p. 258n.).

[67] *Utilitarianism*, p. 234.

[68] *Utilitarianism*, pp. 236, 237.

[69] *Utilitarianism*, p. 237.

ing the utilitarian view. Other views may be proposed, but we can return Bentham's challenge: what motive will we have to adopt them?

Mill's psychology is a good deal more complicated than Bentham's and cannot be dismissed as readily. How can we desire things for themselves and as parts of happiness? Moore decides that Mill is talking "contemptible nonsense" and gaily ridicules the idea that jingling coins are a part of happiness.[70] Should we understand happiness as some agreeable mental state, the scorn is deserved. And that is Mill's official view of happiness in his opening account. Moore's reading is hardly fair, however. Mill's conception of happiness shifts emphatically away from a mental state and toward a valuable state of affairs, from a Benthamite to an Aristotelian view. As long as Mill adheres to this latter view, his theory is not utilitarian at all in the sense I have adopted here. Nor is my distinction pointless. It allows us to mark the important differences between a theory telling us to maximize agreeable consciousness and one telling us to maximize valuable states of affairs. (Though talk of maximization will become increasingly mysterious: what could the relevant metric be?) We may concede Mill the psychology he argues for and turn it against utilitarianism. We do take interest in things besides pleasures and pains. So a perfectly reasonable moral theory may direct our attention to those other things.

The argument, then, collapses in broadening happiness. A question remains: How is it supposed to be an argument for utilitarianism and not, say, ethical egoism? How does Mill propose to show that each person ought to attend to the general happiness, and not her own? Mill is moving from (1) my happiness being a good for me, yours for you, and so on, to (2) the general happiness being a good for all, to (3) the general happiness being a good. Since happiness, Mill thinks, is the only good, we may substitute (3') the general happiness being the good. Having reached (3) or (3'), Mill can explain why each person ought to care for the general happiness, even if it makes her miserable: it is simply the good. Here the traditional criticism is more plausi-

[70]Moore, *Principia Ethica*, pp. 71–72.

ble but still miscast. Mill is not offering a faulty deduction; he is getting caught in some linguistic traps. Proposition (2) is doubly equivocal, and only the equivocations make the argument go through. It is equivocal first between "all of us approving all's happiness" and "each of us approving all's happiness"; Mill illicitly slips to the latter meaning. It is equivocal second between "all of us value happiness" and "happiness is objectively good for all of us"; again Mill illicitly slips to the latter meaning. This second slip is all too easily executed, since moral discourse embodies a claim to objectivity.[71]

Mill's argument, then, is an untidy mass of confusions. Sidgwick, characteristically, is clearer on all these matters. He tenaciously clings to a conception of happiness as pleasure or agreeable consciousness, and refutes psychological hedonism; also his keeping the two senses of good clearly distinguished leads him to his worries about the duality of practical reason.[72] His argument for utilitarianism is different from that of Bentham or Mill, but it is not any better. As it is an especially clear specimen of foundationalist thought, I will examine it at some length.

Part of justification for Sidgwick, as I've noted, lies in refining our common moral views. That strand of his approach is subordinate, however. He declares, "We conceive it as the aim of the philosopher, as such, to do somewhat more than define and formulate the common moral opinions of mankind. His function is to tell men what they ought to think."[73] He goes on to seek "fundamental moral intuitions," self-evident axioms to serve as first principles in a moral system.[74] Such an argument courts disaster: it looks as though self-evidence is to be had only at the expense of substance. Tautologies are self-evident but empty, hardly fit to build a substantive moral code on. Sidgwick indeed offers "a word of caution . . . against a certain class of sham-axioms. . . . These are principles which appear certain and self-

---

[71]A lucid account is J. L. Mackie, *Ethics: Inventing Right and Wrong* (Harmondsworth: Penguin, 1977), chap. 1.

[72]*Methods*, pp. 42–54, 497–509.

[73]*Methods*, p. 373.

[74]The exposition in *Methods* is usefully supplemented with Henry Sidgwick, "The Establishment of Ethical First Principles," *Mind* 4 (January 1879): 106–111.

evident because they are substantially tautological." The principles he seeks are to be self-evident yet not tautological. Nor is he satisfied with formal constraints such as universalization, "that whatever action any of us judges to be right for himself, he implicitly judges to be right for all similar persons in similar circumstances." Such constraints, he believes, are "too abstract" to yield any definite account of what we ought to do. They do though offer an insight that may be exploited to other ends. If similar individuals, Sidgwick suggests, make up a "Logical Whole or Genus," there is no good reason to prefer one to another. Therefore, he argues, in a passage worth quoting at length:

> By considering the relations of the integrant parts to the whole and to each other, I obtain the self-evident principle that the good of any one individual is of no more importance, from the point of view (if I may say so) of the Universe, than the good of any other; unless, that is, there are special grounds for believing that more good is likely to be realised in the one case than in the other. And it is evident to me that as a rational agent I am bound to aim at good generally, — so far as it is attainable by my efforts, — not merely at a particular part of it.
>
> From these two rational intuitions we may deduce, as a necessary inference, the maxim of Benevolence in an abstract form: viz. that each one is morally bound to regard the good of any other individual as much as his own, except in so far as he judges it to be less, when impartially viewed, or less certainly knowable or attainable by him.

We already have the formal structure of utilitarianism. There remains only the task of identifying the good with happiness, a task Sidgwick proposes to accomplish "by a more indirect mode of reasoning" than Mill's.[75]

What might the good be? Sidgwick attempts now to eliminate other candidates. It cannot be virtue, since an adequate account of virtue will inevitably mention the good and "involve us in a logical circle" we cannot escape. Nor can it be "the determina-

[75]*Methods*, pp. 374–375, 379, 380–381, 382, 389.

tion of the will to do whatever is judged to be right and to aim at realising whatever is judged to be best," lest we embrace "a palpable and violent paradox": that the good lies in pursuing something that does not itself exist objectively. Like virtue, "talents, gifts, and graces" will not withstand scrutiny: "Reflection shows that they are only valuable on account of the good or desirable conscious life in which they are or will be actualised, or which will be somehow promoted by their exercise." Physical processes of life cannot be ultimately desirable: "So long as we confine our attention to their corporeal aspect, —regarding them merely as complex movements of certain particles of organised matter—it seems impossible to attribute to these movements, considered in themselves, either goodness or badness." Nor is it "all life regarded on its psychical side which we can judge to be ultimately desirable," since there is still pain; instead, it is "Desirable Consciousness." Now we face the initial problem in new disguise. What is to count as desirable consciousness? A crowd of contenders—"cognition of Truth, contemplation of Beauty, Free or Virtuous action, as in some measure preferable alternatives to Pleasure or Happiness"—come bursting in, but Sidgwick bravely fends them off, writing, "I think, however, that this view ought not to commend itself to the sober judgment of reflective persons." Our considered judgment must be that all these things are valuable only because of their "conduciveness, one way or the other, to the happiness of sentient beings." This conclusion coheres well enough, Sidgwick thinks, with the "ordinary judgments of mankind," carefully considered.[76] So goes the argument for utilitarianism.

There is much to criticize here. I will focus on two points: self-evidence and wondering what the good is.

The business of hammering out self-evident axioms to serve as foundations is eminently attractive for quite a few reasons. It exercises just those skills that philosophically inclined writers concerned with morals and politics possess in abundance. It promises to provide a fabulously solid theory, one maybe even immune to attack. It can be done without any attention to con-

[76]*Methods*, pp. 394–402.

tingent facts of society, history, or politics, since it is not at all clear what the seeker of axioms might gain by being steeped in such knowledge of the world. It promises to sail gracefully past more cumbersome approaches which drag in far-flung considerations and wearily force them into less elegant theoretical structures.

The only sticky point is finding the axioms. How do we know when we have stumbled upon a self-evident proposition? Sidgwick offers a four-part test: "The terms of the proposition must be clear and precise"; "the self-evidence of the proposition must be ascertained by careful reflection"; "the propositions accepted as self-evident must be mutually consistent"; and (here he is a bit elusive) we should not find considered disagreement.[77] But the notion of self-evidence, reappearing in the second part of the test, needs a good deal of elucidation. A prosaic attempt would be, "carries its own evidence along with it." That gloss, however, leads straightaway to tautologies, in which Sidgwick is decidedly uninterested. Nor will a purely psychological attempt—say, "seems undeniable"—do, for as Sidgwick notes, "Any strong sentiment, however purely subjective, is apt to transform itself into the semblance of an intuition."[78] We are supposed somehow to scrutinize our beliefs critically from some neutral vantage point, "the point of view of the Universe," Sidgwick would say, and see if they hold up. But just what is that point of view, and how can we take it up? Considering as coolly as I can, I cannot bring myself to believe that Sidgwick's second axiom or intuition (that I am bound to aim at the good generally, sacrificing my own good if need be) is true, let alone self-evident. Lurking here is, once again, the sponge-cell conception of the individual in society, a problematic descriptive view whose contingency smears the epistemic purity of the axiom. On such a conception the plausibility of the so-called self-evident principle rests. Again, the conception is utterly implausible. Sidgwick himself, in his discussion of the dualism of practical reason, concedes as much.[79]

In his pursuit of the good, Sidgwick ascends to increasingly

[77]*Methods*, pp. 338–342.
[78]*Methods*, p. 339. Compare *Logic*, pp. 224–261, especially 238–244.
[79]*Methods*, pp. 497–498.

rarefied considerations and abstract issues. There are two views we might take of such an approach, views I will crudely label Platonic and Wittgensteinian. In the Platonic view, it is only when we reach such questions that the discussion promises to yield genuine knowledge. More strongly put, knowledge of the basic issues must precede anything resembling knowledge in the circumstances of daily life: Lysis cannot really know who his friends are until he knows what a friend is. In the Wittgensteinian view, the relevant concepts can be used meaningfully only within the more or less concrete contexts that contain the criteria governing their use. When we rip the concepts out of context to examine them singly, they have lost meaning, and our inquiry is doomed to failure. A question such as "What is the good?" may then provoke two responses. We may think, "Aha! now we are finally at the heart of the matter; now we can really understand morality." Or we may think, glumly instead of exultantly, "What follows is bound to be nonsensical."

I want to urge the merits of the Wittgensteinian view, or of one much like it. Sidgwick's query, whether it is the physical or mental side of life in which ultimate good is to be found, is baffling. If physical life can be regarded "merely as complex movements of certain particles of organised matter," mental life, I suppose, can be cast as "merely the fluctuations in timbre of experience." So cast, it looks rather uninteresting. Here we can borrow two pages from Hume: "The life of a man is of no greater importance to the universe than that of an oyster"; the point of view of the universe, even if it were available, would dwarf and indeed obliterate all human concerns, interests, and significance. Besides, even contemplating this point of view is disorienting. "We are got into fairy land," as Hume says in a different context;[80] in a realm so foreign to the ones we are familiar with, our responses become erratic, even zany. We can get on perfectly well in discussing good actions, good people, good knives, and all the rest without ever asking what the good is.

We can still learn much of interest by asking what *good* means.

[80]David Hume, "Of Suicide," in *Essays: Moral, Political, and Literary* (Great Britain: Oxford University Press, 1974), p. 590; Hume, *An Enquiry Concerning Human Understanding*, in *Enquiries*, ed. L. A. Selby-Bigge, 3d ed. rev. by P. H. Nidditch (Oxford: Clarendon, 1978), p. 72.

But Sidgwick's question, "What is the good?" is not a request for a definition or explication of the concept. Nor is it a request (more like the actual Platonic ones) for a theory showing what goodness is, how it arises, how we know it, and so on. Instead Sidgwick is asking, as Moore might say, "What things are good?" —but he will accept only an answer showing that one thing is ultimately good, all other goods being instrumental to achieving that good. This requirement seems excessively harsh. Perhaps there is such an ultimate good, but I see no reason whatever to assume that there must be.

Bentham, Mill, and Sidgwick, I conclude, give us no reason to accept utilitarianism. And should the arguments of the last part have any merit, utilitarianism is much too exotic a view to command our allegiance without good reasons.

Contemporary Utilitarianism

Some readers will think that most if not all of my criticisms so far apply only to classical utilitarianism. They will censure me for beating a dead horse, and will urge the merits of contemporary forms of utilitarianism, some of which reject a hedonistic conception of utility. But I think such forms are no better than their classical ancestors. Accordingly, here I examine the theories of three contemporary utilitarians: John Harsanyi, R. M. Hare, and R. B. Brandt.

Harsanyi invites us to consider the common idea that "the moral point of view is essentially the point of view of a *sympathetic* but *impartial* observer."[81] He suggests that we may formulate this point of view in the notation of game theory. Suppose that we denote different (hypothetical) societies, or the same society under different proposed social policies or rules, as A, B, C, and so on. Now, any individual i's objective position in, say, A "can be regarded as a *vector* listing the economic, social, biological, and other variables" describing his position, and can be denoted A_i.[82] Let U_i denote a von Neumann–Morgenstern (from

[81]*Rational Behavior*, pp. 48–49.
[82]*Rational Behavior*, pp. 49, 52.

now on, vNM) utility function for individual i.[83] We may then introduce the social-welfare function. For individual i to be impartial, in the relevant moral sense, in evaluating social situation A, he must pretend uncertainty as to what his position A_i in A would be; accordingly, Harsanyi proposes that the agent assign the same probability, $1/n$, to the chance of coming out in any one of n positions. Thus he says, for some individual i:

> Any given social situation would yield him the expected utility
>
> $$W_i(A) = 1/n \sum_{j=1}^{n} U_j(A)$$
>
> because he would have the same $1/n$ chance of being put in the place of each individual j ($j = 1, \ldots, i, \ldots, n$) and therefore of obtaining the utility amount $U_j(A)$, representing individual j's utility level in situation A. In other words, in making moral value judgments individual i would evaluate each social situation A in terms of the *average utility level* that the n individual members of society would enjoy in this situation.[84]

To choose the morally best situation, one simply chooses the one with the highest expected utility.

The formal similarity between this model and classical utilitarianism should be clear enough. But the introduction of vNM utility functions to replace hedonistically conceived utility marks a striking departure, one that needs emphasis. To review such utility functions: If we make some minimal assumptions about the consistency and sensitivity of a rational agent's preferences, we can find a set of real cardinal numbers, namely her vNM utility function, such that the agent acts as though she were trying

---

[83] I briefly sketch von Neumann–Morgenstern utility below. Expositions may be found in *Rational Behavior*, pp. 32–41; and R. Duncan Luce and Howard Raiffa, *Games and Decisions* (New York: Wiley, 1957), pp. 19–31. An especially clear presentation is Donald Davidson, J. C. C. McKinsey, and Patrick Suppes, "Outlines of a Formal Theory of Value, I," *Philosophy of Science* 22 (April 1955): 152–157.

[84] *Rational Behavior*, p. 50.

to maximize the value of that function. Furthermore, the utility of a lottery ticket of uncertain outcomes will equal the sum of the utility of each outcome multiplied by the probability of that outcome. Such a vivid reinterpretation of the concept of utility changes the whole complexion of utilitarianism.

Some of the objections commonly leveled against classical utilitarianism therefore fizzle as objections to forms of utilitarianism based on vNM utility. There is nothing problematic here about utility being cardinal or commensurable. Nor need we worry about how to handle problem cases of risk and uncertainty; the function effectively incorporates the agent's risk aversion and so gives us her own solution to them. Finally, the perpetual quest for that pure psychic stuff named utility that will serve as the end of all human action happily can be suspended; these utility functions report only preferences, with nary a word on why the agent prefers what she does or how she feels once she gets it. Accordingly, substituting them for the hedonistic conception of utility may seem an unambiguous great leap forward. But vNM utility functions usher in new problems even as they solve old ones.

As Harsanyi recognizes, the relevant sense of preference here is behavioristic: "We shall say that A is preferred (or is *strictly preferred*) to B by the decision maker if he always (i.e., with probability 1) chooses A rather than B whenever he has to choose between them." The utility an agent maximizes, in this view, has nothing whatever to do with mental states.[85] (We could postulate that agents prefer A to B if and only if A yields more of some identifiable mental state. Any such postulate would be unacceptably strong, however; a theory that incorporated it would hardly describe us.) Indeed, an actor could maximize a vNM utility function without even having mental states. Take an automatic vacuum cleaner that propels itself around the room, surveying

---

[85]*Rational Behavior*, p. 27. Yet Harsanyi slips sometimes into thinking of utility as a psychological state, as when he refers to "the basic goal of all morally good actions, viz. to create as much happiness as possible in this world" in his "Nonlinear Social Welfare Functions: Do Welfare Economists Have a Special Exemption from Bayesian Rationality?" *Theory and Decision* 6 (August 1975): 323, reprinted in his *Essays on Ethics, Social Behavior, and Scientific Explanation* (Dordrecht, Holland: D. Reidel, 1976), p. 76.

possible future routes with an electric eye and evaluating them with a minicomputer, gracefully sliding around furniture, rebounding off walls, and adjusting its brushes on different surfaces. We could construct a vNM utility function for such a vacuum cleaner. We might find, of course, that the function was impoverished, that it showed little variation for wide ranges of choices in the machine's environment. (It always goes straight if it sees nothing coming and has not hit anything within the last two seconds.) But that is irrelevant. The vacuum cleaner would act as though it were intent on maximizing its utility. Yet that it darts about the room maximizing utility hardly makes it a purposive agent.

Now, vNM utility functions have the feature that, if U is an individual utility function, so is $V = aU + b$, for all $a > 0$. That is, "we are free to choose a *zero point* and a *utility unit* for U in any way that we wish."[86] For examining the individual decision maker it makes no difference, but now the problem of interpersonal utility comparison is posed in a new, stark form. What are we supposed to be comparing? Again, such utility functions measure quite precisely nothing at all. There have been arguments for interpersonal comparability, and indeed the job may be mathematically tractable.[87] What matters, though, is keeping conceptually clear on what is going on.

As far as vNM utilities go, interpersonal utility comparison is a moral question, not a peculiarly slippery psychological one. There being nothing to measure, problems of ensuring accuracy can hardly arise. We are asking, "How much weight ought we to lend different individuals?"—which invites the ready answer, "Each to count for one, none for more than one." The champion of vNM utility can thus turn what looked like a liability into an additional asset of the theory. We can scale the utility functions so that everyone will assign his best possible outcome a rating of 1, the worst 0. This procedure seems egalitarian; it dispels worries about utility monsters, individuals who experience pleasure

[86]*Rational Behavior*, p. 41.
[87]Richard C. Jeffrey, "On Interpersonal Utility Theory," *Journal of Philosophy* 68 (October 21, 1971): 647–656; Ilmar Waldner, "The Empirical Meaningfulness of Interpersonal Utility Comparisons," *Journal of Philosophy* 69 (February 24, 1972): 87–103.

and pain so intensely that in a felicific calculus they swallow up
the rest of us.[88] And the shift to preferences marks, arguably, a
new concern in utilitarianism for individual autonomy. We need
no longer worry about, say, forcibly implanting electrodes in
people's brains and inducing constant ecstasy.[89]

Again, there may well seem to be unequivocal gains in shifting
to the economist's conception of utility. I mean to concentrate
once more on the attempts given to justify utilitarianism, but I
would like to note one serious difficulty that the shift to vNM
utility creates. As long as an individual's preferences are appropriately sensitive and consistent, we can construct the utility
function. It does not matter whether those preferences are egoistic, altruistic, malicious, or psychopathological. By using the
functions, we lose all ability to criticize the individual's preferences. We lose too all ability to discuss the good life, for the
question "What ought our preferences be?" must be rendered, in
a view like Harsanyi's, "What do we prefer our preferences to
be?" The new preferences introduced to rank our existing preferences are themselves unimpeachable. Nor does a regress—
"What do we prefer our preferences for our preferences to be?"
and so on—seem at all illuminating. Note the wide range of concepts, from very different theories, that we cannot accommodate
in a vNM view of utility: false consciousness, delusions, vicious
dispositions, misunderstandings of one's interests, worthless or
meaningless life plans, and so on. If in a classical utilitarian view
Brave New World offers a tempting vision of the good society because its people are happy, in a vNM utilitarian view that same
society is tempting just because its individuals would not prefer
other states. The loss of information here, the draining of all
kinds of pregnant categories into the sink of preference, is appall-
ing.

But perhaps I move too quickly. Harsanyi, after all, is willing
to censor individual utility functions: "In our opinion individual
i will be perfectly justified in disregarding *j*'s actual preferences

[88]Robert Nozick, *Anarchy, State, and Utopia* (New York: Basic Books, 1974),
p. 41.
[89]J. J. C. Smart, "An Outline of a System of Utilitarian Ethics," in Smart
and Williams, *Utilitarianism*, pp. 18–21.

in cases where the latter are based on clearly *antisocial* attitudes, e.g., on sheer hostility, malice, envy, and sadism. After all, the entire basis for *i*'s interest in satisfying *j*'s preferences is human sympathy. But human sympathy can hardly impose on *i* the obligation to respect *j*'s preferences in cases where the latter are in clear conflict with human sympathy."[90] Here Harsanyi conflates two very different senses of sympathy. The first is that of empathy, identifying completely with another. The second is that of approval, going along with another. Harsanyi uses the first sense in constructing the social-welfare function. Each of us is to sum $U_j(A)$, to compute *j*'s utility level in state A (not, as we might expect, to compute how he feels about being *j* in A). Only in the second sense, though, does sympathy censor antisocial preferences; and the second sense will not begin to yield a utilitarian calculus.

Harsanyi, then, offers no satisfactory reasons for censoring utility functions. Nor does he offer any satisfactory reasons for employing them in the first place. He claims that his social-welfare function "can be obtained by a conceptual analysis of the nature of moral preferences (moral value judgments)."[91] Being moral, the idea is, just means computing and observing these utility functions; if we want to be moral, we must do so. Presumably Harsanyi has this sort of necessity in mind when he claims, somewhat obliquely, "quasi-hypothetical objective validity" for the moral rules yielded by his theory.[92] Surely, though, the purported conceptual analysis is flawed. Utilitarianism, however conceived, is hardly the only putatively moral doctrine available; it is only one such doctrine.

---

[90]*Rational Behavior*, p. 52; see too John C. Harsanyi, "Morality and the Theory of Rational Behavior," *Social Research* 44 (Winter 1977): 647. Identifying "antisocial attitudes" will be no mean trick: compare the likely candidates of a Marxist, a libertarian, and a fundamentalist.

[91]Harsanyi, "Nonlinear Social Welfare Functions," p. 313, in Harsanyi, *Essays*, p. 65; see too Harsanyi, "Cardinal Welfare, Individualistic Ethics, and Interpersonal Comparisons of Utility," *Journal of Political Economy* 63 (August 1955): 310, in Harsanyi, *Essays*, p. 7; Harsanyi, "Ethics in Terms of Hypothetical Imperatives," *Mind* 67 (July 1958): 309, in Harsanyi, *Essays*, p. 28; *Rational Behavior*, p. 49.

[92]Harsanyi, "Ethics in Terms of Hypothetical Imperatives," p. 315, in Harsanyi, *Essays*, p. 34.

I conclude that Harsanyi's variant of utilitarianism is unsatisfactory. While the shift from pleasure to preference may seem promising, again we are given no good reason to adopt the utilitarian standard.[93] Yet the appeal of Harsanyi's strategy of justification—that of anchoring controversial claims on some formal analysis—is clear. Harsanyi's analysis of morality will not do the job, but Hare has pursued a more promising line of attack. Hare wants to ground a moral theory in the logic of the moral concepts. He thinks that "once the form of morality is accepted in our thinking, it quite narrowly circumscribes the substance of the moral principles that we shall adopt."[94]

Indeed, Hare now argues that we will find ourselves constrained to be utilitarians. He has arrived at this position only gradually. In his first book, where the program of studying the logic of the moral concepts is already laid out, Hare notes in passing the possibility of a conflict between justice and utility.[95] That book, however, is occupied chiefly with the moral concepts. In his second book, Hare tries to draw a moral code out of his theory of the moral concepts, and he arrives at a position near utilitarianism. I will take the liberty of paraphrasing the argument.

[93]Harsanyi also offers two mathematical proofs of his theory, and he has complained that "some critics of my concept of an additive social welfare function have apparently failed to notice the fact that in order to refute my conclusions they would have to refute *all three* arguments" (*Rational Behavior*, p. 293n.5). The proofs are flawed not by the mathematics, but by the axioms labeling certain preferences moral preferences.

Harsanyi also appeals to conceptual analysis to resolve moral issues. First, on who is to be included in the social welfare function, he opines, "We would like to have an operationally meaningful *analytical* criterion that would help us to decide whether to include, e.g., higher animals, human idiots, unborn babies in their mothers' wombs, more distant future generations" (*Rational Behavior*, p. 60). But it is a moral dilemma, again not soluble by conceptual analysis of "society." And on the choice between maximizing mean or total utility, Harsanyi declares flatly that "in my view, the mean utility criterion gives incomparably superior results" ("Morality and the Theory of Rational Behavior," p. 633n.) —pretty heady stuff from one who in the same article discards intuitionist doctrines as "crude forms of obscurantism in ethics" (p. 625).

[94]R. M. Hare, "Adolescents into Adults," in his *Applications of Moral Philosophy* (Berkeley: University of California Press, 1973), p. 60.

[95]R. M. Hare, *The Language of Morals* (Oxford: Clarendon, 1952), pp. 56–57.

Moral judgments properly understood, in Hare's account, must be universalizable. Should I hold that some state of affairs is good, or some action wrong, I am logically committed to holding that all relevantly similar states of affairs are good, all relevantly similar actions wrong. So much is guaranteed by the moral concepts. (Other concepts work similarly. Should I hold that X is striking, or large, or infuriating, or sticky, I must grant the same of all relevantly similar Ys.) Hare presses on further, demanding of us "a certain power of imagination and readiness to use it" in making our judgments. B "must be prepared to give weight to A's inclinations and interests as if they were his own."[96] That B's desires are his own counts for nothing, Hare holds, from a moral point of view. They are simply another set of desires, to be taken no more (or less) seriously than anyone else's. A large part of morality has to do with safeguarding people's interests, and Hare flirts with the idea that prescribing universally for the satisfaction of everyone's interests will mean maximizing satisfactions.[97]

But a most important obstacle stands in the way of an argument from universalization to utilitarianism. That obstacle is the existence of ideals, conceptions of human excellence, aesthetic preferences, preferred states of the world of whatever kind. Someone might be willing, in the pursuit of an ideal, to flout others' interests systematically. Hare has unkind things to say about such a person. He calls him a fanatic and says that his ideal may be a perverted one. But a universalization argument, he recognizes, cannot show why one genuinely devoted to an ideal ought not to attempt to realize it. Hare conjures up a Nazi willing to affirm that, were he a Jew, he should be exterminated. The world, holds the Nazi, would be better off that way. Such a Nazi is universalizing his ideal, and Hare concedes that he can catch him in no violation of the logic of the moral concepts. He may be, as Hare urges, a rare specimen; but he prevents the argument for utilitarianism from going through successfully.[98]

[96] R. M. Hare, *Freedom and Reason* (Oxford: Clarendon, 1963), p. 94.
[97] Hare, *Freedom and Reason*, p. 123.
[98] See generally Hare, *Freedom and Reason*, pp. 137–185.

In his recent third book, Hare polemically champions utilitarianism. The book is concerned chiefly with rebutting those criticisms of utilitarianism that appeal to our moral intuitions. Hare argues that those intuitions serve utilitarian ends in most cases, but they are after all only a guide. The "critical level" of moral thinking enables us to move beyond appeals to intuition, to extract the nugget of utilitarianism hidden in the logic of the moral concepts. Perhaps because of the polemical animus of the book, Hare never quite explains how that logic yields utilitarianism.[99] In an earlier paper, however, he does offer a clear explanation, so I will focus on that paper.[100] Hare first explicitly endorses the view that universalistic concern for interests leads to a maximizing view: "If I am trying to give equal weight to the equal interests of all the parties in a situation, I must, it seems, regard a benefit or harm done to one party as of equal value or disvalue to an equal benefit or harm done to any other party. This seems to mean that I shall promote the interests of the parties most, while giving equal weight to them all, if I maximise the total benefits over the population; and this is the classical principle of utility."[101] Hare makes a deceptively simple attempt to meet "the problem of the fanatic, who has given me so much trouble in the past": "In so far as, in order to prescribe universally, I have to strip away (*qua* author of the moral decision) all my present desires, etc., I shall have to strip away, among them, all the ideals that I have. . . . This means that for the purposes of the moral decision it makes no difference *who has* the ideal. It means that we have to give impartial consideration to the ideals of ourselves and others."[102] Morality thus requires that child abusers sus-

---

[99]Consider, for example, Hare, *Moral Thinking*, pp. 94–95, where Hare flatly asserts that we must forget our own preferences in considering others' positions.

[100]See here R. M. Hare, "Ethical Theory and Utilitarianism," in *Contemporary British Philosophy*, ed. H. D. Lewis, 4th ser. (London: Allen & Unwin, 1976). Two other key papers: R. M. Hare, "Wrongness and Harm," in his *Essays on the Moral Concepts* (Berkeley: University of California Press, 1973), and Hare, "What Makes Choices Rational?" *Review of Metaphysics* 32 (June 1979): 623–637.

[101]Hare, "Ethical Theory and Utilitarianism," in Lewis, pp. 116–117.

[102]Hare, "Ethical Theory and Utilitarianism," in Lewis, p. 121. Hare dismisses the possibility of a Nazi so devoted to his cause that his desire outweighs

pend their own ideals and pay heed to those of friends of the disabled—and vice versa. Once Hare's Nazi gives impartial consideration to other ideals, he will be unable to recommend realizing his own; and again, that they are his own is uninteresting.

Hare's theories have been criticized widely, and I do not wish to rehearse those criticisms here.[103] I mean instead to press one point. Even on a generous construction of universalization, utilitarianism could only with great difficulty be universalized.

Universalization may be construed in quite a few senses, and Hare shifts a bit erratically among them.[104] The crucial phrase is "give equal weight to the equal interests of all the parties in a situation," a phrase which allows two competing interpretations. In the first, we may keep the interests glued firmly to the persons, and construe equal interests as something like "interests equally important in realizing life plans." In the second, we may allow the persons as bearers of the interests to fade away, leaving the interests free-floating, and construe equal interests as something like "wants experienced with equal psychological urgency."

The second interpretation yields Hare a recognizably utilitarian view. Once the persons disappear, all that is left is to maximize the realization of the interests. Questions of distribution cannot arise, for there is no one to distribute to. Why, though, should we take up this gloss of universalization? Surely it does not flow from a formal study of the logic of the moral concepts. The first interpretation is a more plausible candidate for the uni-

---

all competing ones as extremely unlikely and so irrelevant for our common reactions. This statement suggests that were such a Nazi to exist, he ought to be catered to; and Hare implicitly affirms that he should in *Moral Thinking*, pp. 171–172.

[103]Outside the territory of the battle Hare as prescriptivist has waged especially with Philippa Foot and G. E. M. Anscombe as descriptivists, a lucid critique is Robert K. Fullinwider, "Fanaticism and Hare's Moral Theory," *Ethics* 87 (January 1977): 165–173. Jan Narveson, "Liberalism, Utilitarianism, and Fanaticism: R. M. Hare Defended," *Ethics* 88 (April 1978): 250–259, is a response to Fullinwider and Alan Gettner, "Hare and Fanaticism," *Ethics* 87 (January 1977): 160–164.

[104]See here Don Locke, "The Trivializability of Universalizability," *Philosophical Review* 77 (January 1968): 25–44, and, more generally, Mackie, *Ethics*, chap. 4.

versalization embedded in morality, and it simply will not yield anything like utilitarianism. I am unable to universalize a view that might condemn a minority (or a majority with flaccid mental lives) to be used as fodder for others, for I take seriously the possibility of being one so used. Nor could I affirm a system in which I profited by others' being so used. What is called for by the first view of universalization is a view structured like a rights view, or a welfare view with minimal levels guaranteed to each individual—some view on which, generally at least, each individual's interests are safeguarded.

The assumption that causes the trouble here is that morality must be a matter of maximizing something, and all we need do is figure out what.[105] This view prods Hare toward utilitarianism and forces him to such an odd construal of universalization. It is not that the formal study of the moral concepts yields utilitarianism; it is rather that, with some arm-twisting, it can be made to. The source of the twisting, however, lies outside the formal theory. Regardless, the maximization assumption requires defense. With his meager conception of ethics as "the logical study of the language of morals,"[106] Hare will be unable to defend the assumption. And once we wrest free of the hold that conflating rationality, maximization, and morality has on us, we may well wonder whether the assumption is defensible at all.

I pause to notice a strikingly counterintuitive implication of the program of deriving moral content from moral form, undertaken in different ways by Harsanyi and Hare. Were the program successfully executed, it would show that all other moral theories are, in fact, not moral theories at all. Note that it could

[105] Hare's commitment to using the language of morality as it stands is at once the center and the chief flaw of his approach, for surely we are entitled to revise that language if we see fit. His resisting that conclusion perhaps explains his suggestion that in the end all different moral theories come to pretty much the same thing; were that so, escaping our vocabulary might be more difficult. Note Hare, "Rules of War and Moral Reasoning," *Philosophy & Public Affairs* 1 (Winter 1972): 167–173, reprinted in *War and Moral Responsibility*, ed. Marshall Cohen, Thomas Nagel, and Thomas Scanlon (Princeton, N.J.: Princeton University Press, 1974), pp. 47–53; Hare, "Rawls' Theory of Justice," *Philosophical Quarterly* 23 (April 1973): 144–155, and 23 (July 1973): 241–252, pp. 150–155, reprinted in *Reading Rawls*, ed. Norman Daniels (New York: Basic Books, n.d.), pp. 88–95.
[106] Hare, *Language of Morals*, p. iii.

not show that they were wrong, or unacceptable, just that they were not properly described as moral in the first place.[107] Harsanyi and Hare are committed, strictly speaking, to saying that the theories of Plato, Aristotle, Kant, Rawls, and Nozick cannot properly be described as moral theories at all. That commitment invites an open-question argument of the kind both Harsanyi and Hare insist on.[108] Once we focus on the descriptive component of the concept *morality* or on the workings of what we call the moral concepts, it is perfectly sensible to ask, "Why should I be moral?" This question would mean, addressed to Harsanyi, "Why should I take up the position of your impersonal spectator?" To Hare it would mean, "Why should I universalize in this way?" Harsanyi would respond, "Because that is what it means to be moral." But someone debating opting out of a social practice such as morality—or, more to the point here, pursuing a competing conception of morality—would not be swayed by linguistic reminders.[109] Hare, officially leery of giving conceptual answers to substantive questions, has sketched an argument reminiscent of Plato and Aristotle that prudence is best served by the cultivation of dispositions to be moral.[110] The limits of these sorts of arguments aside, the alternatives Hare should be considering are not morality and egoism, but his brand of morality and others. That he implicitly assumes his is the only brand available shows that he still assumes that *morality* just means his theory. In that sense, his position is no better than Harsanyi's. Given these dilemmas, would it be premature to recommend abandoning the attempt to derive moral content from moral form?

Brandt takes a different tack in arguing for utilitarianism. His

[107]Note the ambiguity between two senses of *moral* (contrasting with nonmoral and immoral) carefully laid out by Onora Nell, *Acting on Principle* (New York: Columbia University Press, 1975), pp. 2–4.

[108]Harsanyi, "Ethics in Terms of Hypothetical Imperatives," p. 308, in Harsanyi, *Essays*, p. 27; Hare, "Universalizability," in his *Essays on the Moral Concepts*, p. 20; Hare, *Freedom and Reason*, pp. 108, 116; Hare, "Descriptivism," in *Essays on the Moral Concepts*.

[109]Compare John R. Searle, "How to Derive Ought from Is," *Philosophical Review* 73 (January 1964): 43–58, and Hare, "The Promising Game," *Revue internationale de philosophie* 18 (1964): 398–412; both reprinted in *The Is-Ought Question*, ed. W. D. Hudson (New York: St. Martin's Press, 1969).

[110]Hare, *Moral Thinking*, pp. 188–205.

Theory of the Good and the Right is in part an attempt to develop "an account of concepts suited for a scientific psychological explanatory conceptual framework."[111] Accordingly the book bulges with elaborate views of rationality, desire, and so on. I mean to bypass discussion of those views. Brandt proposes that we understand questions about the good and the right as questions about choices that a fully rational person would make with ideally vivid representations of the alternatives. A fully rational person, in his view, is one whose desires and aversions have been flooded with all available information, and so restructured. The effects of this cognitive psychotherapy, Brandt realizes, will depend on the starting point of the individual undergoing it. So the theory will not converge on a unique solution: "It would be nice if we could demonstrate that all fully rational persons would support one and the same moral system. We shall in fact have to settle for something short of that."[112]

Nonetheless, Brandt thinks, "rational persons would probably opt for one within a narrow range of what we might loosely call 'utilitarian' moral systems; that is, ones the currency of which would maximize the expectable happiness or welfare of some large group, the size of the group depending on the benevolence of the chooser."[113] His argument is brief and a bit elusive. He tries to show that both perfectly benevolent and perfectly selfish rational individuals would choose a utilitarian view, and he infers that those with middling benevolence would do so as well.

Take first the benevolent chooser: "I define a 'perfectly' benevolent person as one who, between two options, always prefers the one associated with the greater long-term sum of expectable net happiness, irrespective of who is to receive it." Unsurprisingly, Brandt decides that "the main inference is quite obvious"; such a fellow will choose utilitarianism. The definition, though, begs the question. Why should benevolence dictate disregard to all distributive considerations?

The argument from the rational selfish chooser warrants quotation at length:

[111]R. B. Brandt, *A Theory of the Good and the Right* (Oxford: Clarendon, 1979), p. 25.
[112]Brandt, *Good and Right*, p. 200.
[113]Brandt, *Good and Right*, p. 208.

The serious options open to a perfectly selfish man, however, are restricted by the requirement of viability. Let us suppose, for the moment, that the persons in the group with whom he will interact and with whom he must form a moral community are equally as selfish as himself. Obviously a moral system which serves his interests at their expense would not enlist their loyalty, and there is no point in his supporting it. . . . If the selfish chooser wants, as he will, protection against crimes against the person, such as assault, negligent injury, and libel, he must choose a moral system which provides the same protection for others, thereby restricting his activities and giving them what they surely want. A selfish person who supports a rule which provides a desired circumstance for all because it, among feasible options, maximizes expectable welfare for him is inadvertently also supporting a rule which will maximize expectable welfare for the group (put each one on a higher 'indifference curve').[114]

But there is no reason to think that maximizing the utility of each individual means maximizing the utility of the group. The group's utility may be increased by lowering the utility of some to get a greater increase in the utility of others. That possibility creates the conflict between rights theorists and utilitarians, so prominent in recent literature, yet Brandt seems unaware of it. The confusion here is the confusion animating Bentham's dual standard, and was noted by Sidgwick. It is disheartening, to say the least, to see it reappearing at this late date.

Since we have no reason to think that the extremes of benevolence (as generally understood) and selfishness lead to utilitarianism, we need not explore the possibility that the spectrum is discontinuous, that those in the middle would deliberate differently.

Foundational Structure of Utilitarianism

Utilitarianism, for all its vaunted precision, cannot tell us what to do. It frames a choice procedure only by purging information, reducing descriptions of outcomes to distributions of

[114]Brandt, *Good and Right*, pp. 215, 217, 218–219.

pleasures and pains, and reducing those distributions to one summed surplus of pleasure over pain. Even then, it sets out an incomplete choice procedure which does not guide us in cases of risk and uncertainty. Indeed, that choice procedure can never get off the ground, since pleasures and pains are a wildly assorted host of incommensurable experiences. Neither classical nor modern utilitarians offer any satisfactory justification of utilitarianism, any account that would give us some reason to redouble our efforts to solve these problems. I therefore propose that we write off utilitarianism as incomprehensible.

However incomprehensible it actually is, though, utilitarianism seems at least to permit, indeed to enjoin, the redistribution of felicific goodies. This redistribution is mandated not to render the lives of the poor dignified, not in the name of fairness, justice, or equality, but to maximize the utility score of some mystic whole named society. Suppose that throwing eggs at Jack will make us very happy, happy enough to offset Jack's unhappiness and any indirect disutilities. (Rule-utilitarians may suppose that a practice of throwing eggs at people like Jack would be felicific. Hare may suppose that critical moral thinking would approve the cultivation of a moral intuition that it is right to throw eggs at people like Jack.) Then utilitarianism is a theory about the moral rightness, indeed obligatoriness, of splattering people with raw egg, on the ground that "society" is happier if we do so. That, surely, is a view we need not take seriously as a leading moral and political theory.

A utilitarian may protest the mention of such an example. "Didn't you forswear the appeal to our moral intuitions? And aren't you doing just that here, inviting us to realize that utilitarianism enjoins behavior we think of as pernicious or just plain silly?" Actually, my point is different; it's that society becomes a mystical whole in utilitarianism. But it is worth noting one last puzzle arising here. Again, utilitarians do often insist that, properly understood, utilitarianism coheres beautifully with our moral judgments. A sophisticated utilitarianism, it has been argued, can accommodate our commitments to liberty, equality, even autonomy. It would not dictate egg-splattering, even for the uniformly unpopular. This move, however, gives up the fight. If utilitarianism yields the same judgments we do, why insist so strenuously on it? What would be at stake in adopting or rejecting it? Utilitarians too eager to show the fit between utilitarianism and our settled views invite a pragmatic response: if two theories make the same prescriptions, they are for all intents and purposes the same theory. Nor can utilitarians suggest that they at least have a theory, while we have nothing but muddled intuitions. If our intuitions are so perfectly utilitarian, we might as well stick with them; and given its difficulties, it's not clear that utilitarianism delivers the benefits a real theory is supposed to.

Still, there are attractive features of utilitarianism, features attractive enough to explain the support it has commanded during its long and illustrious history. It demands no exotic metaphysical or theological commitments. It makes human welfare the point of morality. It offers (or seems to offer) reasons for its conclusions, reasons that have a nicely hard-boiled air about them. (If for example we challenge Bentham's economic egalitarianism, we are not directed to the misty realm of rights, human dignity, and the rest. Instead we receive a brisk argument about diminishing marginal utility; if we challenge the force of that argument, we are told triumphantly that it follows deductively from the greatest-happiness principle.) It allows facts to affect and even determine our moral principles. Finally, it is in some ways a perfectly egalitarian theory: "each to count for one, none for more than one," as the injunction goes. Yet these features are caught up in a foundational structure that causes lots of problems and solves none. I will conclude by mentioning two problems posed by the structure of the theory.

Utilitarianism poses the is/ought problem, that of justifying a move from the realm of description to that of evaluation and prescription, in a peculiarly sharp way. The move occurs all at once, in the claim that pleasure (or preference satisfaction) is the good. Once that premise is employed as a foundation, the weight it bears—no less, in the utilitarian view, than that of supporting a complete moral and political theory, of serving as "the sole and all-sufficient reason for every point of practice whatsoever"— makes the demand for a justification all the more pressing. The utilitarian widens the is/ought gap and makes it look unbridgeable. Nor are hopes of constructing a sound bridge encouraged by the flimsy attempts utilitarians make to justify their theory.

Utilitarianism is further embarrassed by the reappearance of moral notions in the foundation allegedly supporting them. Much of our pleasure and pain is parasitic on moral notions.[115] Agents take pleasure in acting morally and feel remorse at acting immorally. Even if a friend would live his happiest possible life staring at soap operas all day, we are glad when he discards the television and takes up some more challenging life plans. Will utilitarians count these pleasures and pains? Will they count those we feel because we hold nonutilitarian moral views? (It will be much easier to show that slavery is unfelicific if we count the rage and resentment arising from the nonutilitarian understanding that slavery is wrong.) Similarly, Hare's demand that we universalize our moral judgments is in fact a demand for fairness, for refusing to exploit the contingencies of superior position. We cannot cleanly separate pleasure or universalization from morality. So neither will properly serve as a foundation for morality.

We want, if we can, to retain utilitarianism's attractive features and discard both its foundationalist structure and its tendency to purge information. I turn now to David Hume and Adam Smith, who, I think, show that we can.

[115]That the *Deontology* contains a lengthy discussion of the morality of "emission of gas from the alimentary canal" (II:237–240) is perhaps neither a sign of Bentham's senility nor a sign of editorial betrayal, but rather an attempt to evade this issue. Compare David Baumgardt, *Bentham and the Ethics of Today* (Princeton, N.J.: Princeton University Press, 1952), pp. 491–492.

[CHAPTER FOUR]

THEORY IN CONTEXT: HUME AND SMITH

In the works of Hume and Smith, we find a strategy of justification strikingly different from the foundationalism of Hobbes, Locke, and the utilitarians. But we find nothing so dramatic as a radical break with foundationalism. The quest for foundations exercises the charm of the Sirens, to which neither Hume nor Smith is wholly immune. Still, each one develops powerful justificatory arguments rooted in social contexts, arguments with no foundations. These are the arguments I mean to commend as an alternative to foundationalism.

Throughout the chapter I cite from the following works by David Hume: *Enquiry concerning Morals* (*An Enquiry concerning the Principles of Morals*, in *Enquiries*, ed. L. A. Selby-Bigge, 3d ed. rev. by P. H. Nidditch [Oxford: Clarendon, 1978]); *Enquiry concerning Understanding* (*An Enquiry concerning Human Understanding*, in *Enquiries*, Selby-Bigge, ed.); *Essays* (*Essays: Moral, Political, and Literary* [Great Britain: Oxford University Press, 1974]); *History* (*History of England*, new ed., 6 vols. [Boston: Little, Brown, 1872]); *Letters* (*The Letters of David Hume*, ed. J. Y. T. Grieg, 2 vols. [Oxford: Clarendon, 1969]); *Natural History* and *Dialogues* (*The Natural History of Religion and Dialogues concerning Natural Religion*, ed. A. Wayne Colver and John Valdimir Price [Oxford: Clarendon, 1976]). I also cite the following works by Adam Smith: *Jurisprudence* (*Lectures on Jurisprudence*, ed. R. L. Meek, D. D. Raphael, and P. G. Stein, Glasgow ed. [Oxford: Clarendon, 1978]); *Moral Sentiments* (*The Theory of Moral Sentiments*, ed. D. D. Raphael and A. L. Macfie, Glasgow ed. [Oxford: Clarendon, 1976]); *Wealth of Nations* (*An Inquiry into the Nature and Causes of the Wealth of Nations*, ed. R. H. Campbell, A. S. Skinner, and W. B. Todd, Glasgow ed., 2 vols. [Oxford: Clarendon, 1979]). Author's italics throughout.

I commence by reviewing Hume's case against various foundations. Next I explore his defenses of virtue, especially justice, officially grounded in his own preferred foundation. I then examine his account of political obligation, whose foundationalist moorings are cut, and sketch his argument on the English constitution, an argument which finds him happily at sea. Turning to Smith, I first establish some points of contact between Hume and Smith. Next I explain in what sense the *Wealth of Nations* offers a defense of capitalism. Finally, I argue that Smith's account of the downfall of feudalism, an elaboration on Hume's, embodies a perfectly sensible combination of descriptive and evaluative analysis.

Dismissing Reason, God, and Nature

Hume brusquely dismisses three traditional foundations of moral and political theory. He argues that reason, God, and nature are incapable of doing the work they are often assigned. Here I sketch his arguments.

In Hume's theory of mental activity, reason occupies no vaunted place. It leaves us fairly helpless in a dizzying world of sense-data. As "the discovery of truth and falsehood," reason can investigate "relations of ideas" and "matter of fact."[1] It can, for example, pronounce on "quantity and number"; and it can, once experience provides constant conjunctions, tell us what cause produces what effect, from history and politics to astronomy and chemistry.[2] This conception of reason brings Hume to one of his more notorious "skeptical" conclusions: "When we run over libraries, persuaded of these principles, what havoc must we make? If we take in our hand any volume; of divinity or school metaphysics, for instance; let us ask, *Does it contain any abstract reasoning concerning quantity or number?* No. *Does it contain any experimental reasoning concerning matter of fact and existence?* No. Commit it then to the flames: for it can contain nothing but

[1] *Treatise*, p. 458 (and generally pp. 458–460, 73); *Enquiry concerning Understanding*, p. 35, also pp. 163–164.
[2] *Enquiry concerning Understanding*, pp. 163–165.

sophistry and illusion."³ Nor does Hume vindicate a more exalted conception of reason when he turns to human action. Here
he offers a model of reason and the passions which connects up
neatly with the structure of means and ends. Neither demon-
strated relations nor factual truths can move us to action, he
holds. Our passions set our ends; reason, by investigating matters of fact, figures out how to reach those ends. "Reason is, and
ought only to be the slave of the passions, and can never pretend
to any other office than to serve and obey them."⁴ Reason has
nothing to say about the ends themselves. "'Tis not contrary to
reason to prefer the destruction of the whole world to the
scratching of my finger," Hume declares. Lest we think reason is
essentially egoistic, he immediately adds, "'Tis not contrary to
reason for me to chuse my total ruin, to prevent the least uneasiness of an *Indian* or person wholly unknown to me."⁵

Reason's modest concern with truth and its inability to move
the will neatly equip Hume for his final blow: reason is not the
source of morality. (The neatness is no accident if, as Kemp
Smith thought, Hume commenced with ethical issues.⁶) Here
Hume is battling against the ethical theories of such predecessors
as Samuel Clarke and William Wollaston. Clarke held that "certain necessary and eternal differences of things, and certain consequent fitnesses or unfitnesses," provide moral distinctions.
Unless one's understanding was "either very imperfect, or very
much depraved," one would correctly perceive these fitnesses.
Indeed, they would be every bit as evident as the findings of ge-
ometry.⁷ Wollaston offered another cognitively based theory of
ethics. In his account, actions (and omissions) can be understood
as expressing propositions, and so may be true or false. (Here we

³*Enquiry concerning Understanding*, p. 165. As the old joke goes, here Hume
instructs us to burn the *Enquiry*.
⁴*Treatise*, p. 415, generally pp. 413–418.
⁵*Treatise*, p. 416.
⁶Norman Kemp Smith, *The Philosophy of David Hume* (London: Macmillan,
1941), pp. 12–20, 538–540.
⁷Samuel Clarke, *A Discourse of Natural Religion*, excerpted in *British Moralists*,
ed. D. D. Raphael, 2 vols. (Oxford: Clarendon, 1969), I:198, 201–202; also in
L. A. Selby-Bigge's edition of *Moralists*, 2 vols. (Oxford, 1897), II:11, 12, 15–
16.

have an inversion of Austin's theory of performative utterances.⁸) "If a body of soldiers, seeing another body approach, should fire upon them, would not this action declare that they were enemies; and if they were *not* enemies, would not this military language declare what was *false?*" Now comes the punchline: morally right acts are those that express truths; wrong acts are those that express falsehoods. "If a man steals a horse, and rides away upon him," he implicitly declares that the horse is his. Yet that declaration is false, so the action is wrong.⁹

These theories provide the relevant context for Hume's attack on reason. Clarke is surely the imagined interlocutor in the first appendix to the second *Enquiry*. There Hume professes himself "altogether at a loss to understand" how morality could be like mathematical relations. He insists that "it is impossible that, in any particular instance, this hypothesis can so much as be rendered intelligible, whatever specious figure it may make in general declamations and discourses."¹⁰ Wollaston is the object of Hume's attention in the *Treatise*, where he examines the theory that "falsehood is the foundation of all guilt and deformity." Hume misconstrues Wollaston by taking the falsehood to be that of the judgment others are likely to make, instead of that expressed by the action itself. Some of his more mischievous counterexamples, then—"a person, who thro' a window sees any lewd behavior of mine with my neighbour's wife, may be so simple as to imagine she is certainly my own"—do not touch Wollaston's position. Yet Hume does refute the position: "Besides, we may easily observe, that in all those arguments there is an evident reasoning in a circle. A person who takes possession of *another*'s goods, and uses them as his *own*, in a manner declares them to be his own; and this falsehood is the source of the immorality of injustice. But is property, or right, or obligation, intelligible, without an antecedent morality?"¹¹ Once we see the ob-

---

⁸J. L. Austin, *How to Do Things with Words*, ed. J. O. Urmson and Marina Sbisà, 2d ed. (Cambridge, Mass.: Harvard University Press, 1977). The resemblance is noted by J. L. Mackie, *Hume's Moral Theory* (London: Routledge & Kegan Paul, 1980), p. 20.

⁹William Wollaston, *The Religion of Nature Delineated*, excerpted in Raphael, *British Moralists* I:240, 248–249; in Selby-Bigge, *Moralists* II:362, 368.

¹⁰*Enquiry concerning Morals*, pp. 288, 287; also *Treatise*, pp. 463–464.

¹¹*Treatise*, pp. 461n., 461, 462n.

jection, the naivete of Wollaston's position is surprising. Truth and falsehood were supposed to serve as the foundation of right and wrong. Yet now we find that right and wrong are being smuggled in under the foundation.

Hume generalizes his case against Clarke and Wollaston into an argument that sentiment, not reason, is the source of morality. (In his theory of mental activity, there is after all no other choice.) Morality can be no relation, since any relation between people can be found between inanimate objects: "A young tree, which over-tops and destroys its parent, stands in all the same relations with Nero, when he murdered Agrippina; and if morality consisted merely in relations, would no doubt be equally criminal."[12] Nor is morality found in the world as a fact: "Take any action allow'd to be vicious: Wilful murder, for instance. Examine it in all lights, and see if you can find that matter of fact, or real existence, which you call *vice*. In which-ever way you take it, you find only certain passions, motives, volitions and thoughts. There is no other matter of fact in the case. The vice entirely escapes you, as long as you consider the object." You find the viciousness of murder only when "you turn your reflexion into your own breast, and find a sentiment of disapprobation, which arises in you, toward this action."[13]

Hume thus satisfies himself that morality is not sired by reason. I cannot forbear adding two points. First, we cannot sensibly enlist Hume as an emotivist. Granted, Hume declares, "So that when you pronounce any action or character to be vicious, you mean nothing, but that from the constitution of your nature you have a feeling or sentiment of blame from the contemplation of it."[14] But he is not out to debunk a common understanding that moral argument is meaningful and partly cognitive. Instead, he is striving to puncture the exalted imagery of theorists like Clarke and Wollaston, so he permits himself a rhetorical flourish. The putatively emotivist claim is supposed to jolt the reader out of any rationalist reveries. The point is simply that human

[12]*Enquiry concerning Morals*, p. 293; also *Treatise*, p. 467.
[13]*Treatise*, pp. 468–469; compare *Enquiry concerning Morals*, pp. 291–293; "The Sceptic," p. 165, and "Of the Immortality of the Soul," p. 601, both in *Essays*. See here Mackie, *Hume's Moral Theory*, pp. 51–63.
[14]*Treatise*, p. 469.

approval, not eternal and immutable fitness, is the key to morality. (Note Hume's strikingly parallel claim about causation: "When we say, therefore, that one object is connected with another, we mean only that they have acquired a connexion in our thought"; but that is still "a conclusion which is somewhat extraordinary,"[15] one designed to unsettle us, not simply an attempt to account for our ordinary notions.) Second, the famous ironic denial that *ought* can be deduced from *is*[16] is not some bloodless principle of logic; it rests on Hume's epistemology and psychology. Only with those background commitments can he indulge himself ironically.[17]

The way to challenge Hume's skeptical account of the place of reason in ethics, then, is to attack his epistemology and psychology. Here I want to make two points about Hume's psychology. The means/end scheme is a useful heuristic device in some settings, but it hardly captures the full range of human action. Witness Sidgwick's paradox of hedonism: happiness is apparently an end; yet if we deliberately strive for it, we will not attain it.[18] Also, reason and the passions, in the eighteenth century's extended sense of passion, are tools too clumsy to do finely discriminating work in the psychology of action. We need to distinguish spontaneity, guilt, conscience, playfulness, morbid dependency, and so on. (Note Hume's discussing "calm desires . . . such as benevolence and resentment, the love of life, and kindness to children," and his lumping low time preference together with the passions.[19]) Still, I do not mean to suggest that we can reject Hume's conclusions.

It would be especially difficult to reject Hume's conclusions on religion. From the *Treatise* to the *Dialogues concerning Natural*

---

[15]*Enquiry concerning Understanding*, p. 76.

[16]*Treatise*, pp. 469–470, quoted at length in the introduction to this volume.

[17]Compare on both points the readings of Hume in the opening section of W. D. Hudson, ed., *The Is-Ought Question* (New York: St. Martin's Press, 1969); Jonathan Harrison, *Hume's Moral Epistemology* (Oxford: Clarendon, 1976), pp. 63, 112–113.

[18]Henry Sidgwick, *The Methods of Ethics*, 7th ed. (Chicago: University of Chicago Press, 1962), pp. 136–140. The point is poignantly explored by John Stuart Mill, *Autobiography*, in his *Autobiography and Literary Essays*, ed. John M. Robson and Jack Stillinger, in *Collected Works*, vol. 1 (Toronto: University of Toronto Press, 1981), pp. 137–147, especially 145, 147.

[19]*Treatise*, p. 417; *Treatise*, p. 536; *Enquiry concerning Morals*, p. 239.

Religion, Hume does occasionally recite some platitudinous paean to God and orthodox relief. Yet typically such passages have an ironic twist.[20] Hume's considered judgment, argued with devastating brilliance in the *Dialogues*, is that there is no reason whatever to believe in a deity with any of the predicates we typically ascribe to him. If the universe has a first cause, it may well be a spider or a vegetable.[21] A Lockean position, "that *Faith* was nothing but a Species of *Reason*, that Religion was only a Branch of Philosophy, and that a Chain of Arguments, similar to that which establish'd any Truth in Morals, Politics, or Physics, was always employ'd in discovering all the Principles of Theology, natural and reveal'd," looks thoroughly incredible by the end of the *Dialogues*.[22] And if the universe may be presided over by a vegetable, Locke's dangling the afterlife before the eyes of his audience will seem fatuous.

Nor is it only natural religion that falls to Hume's onslaught. "Our most holy religion is founded on *Faith*, not reason": here Hume seems to embrace a position modern theologians would gladly accept, but he presses on. If we survey, say, the Pentateuch, "we find it full of prodigies and miracles. . . . I desire any one to lay his hand upon his heart, and after a serious consideration declare, whether he thinks that the falsehood of such a book, supported by such a testimony, would be more extraordinary and miraculous than all the miracles it relates." The inference is obvious: "The *Christian Religion* not only was at first attended with miracles, but even at this day cannot be believed by any reasonable person without one."[23] The conclusion is of course paradoxical, since Hume has just argued that we can never infer that any event, however extraordinary, is a miracle. The paradox ironically underlines what Hume considers the stupendous idiocy of religion. Not only "the *Roman Catholic* religion" will fall as "strange superstition" in Hume's views.[24]

Hume, then, will not appeal to reason or God to justify his po-

---

[20]See generally John Valdimir Price, *The Ironic Hume* (Austin: University of Texas Press, 1965).

[21]*Dialogues*, pp. 201–208.

[22]*Dialogues*, p. 156.

[23]*Enquiry concerning Understanding*, pp. 130–131. See generally *Enquiry*, pp. 109–131; *Treatise*, pp. 232–251.

[24]*Treatise*, p. 99.

[167]

litical theory. Nor will he appeal to "the word, Nature, than which there is none more ambiguous and equivocal."[25] In Hume's view, nature, far from being a critical standard, is a multiple homonym that courts confusion. Sometimes opposed to miracles, sometimes to what is "rare and unusual," sometimes to "artifice," the concept shifts its meaning insensibly.[26] The concept of nature does serve as a critical standard in a teleological system, but here Hume is a mechanist with a vengeance. He unceremoniously rejects final causes: "For as our idea of efficiency is deriv'd from the constant conjunction of the objects, wherever this is observ'd, the cause is efficient; and where it is not, there can never be a cause of any kind."[27] The final cause, that fruition to which things naturally tend to develop, is a linchpin of teleology. Discarding it strips the concept of nature of its traditional normative overtones.

Hume does seem to embrace a purposive nature that scornfully rejects his skeptical conclusions. At the end of Book I of the *Treatise*, Hume depicts the helpless confusion his skeptical arguments leave him in. Yet he takes comfort: "Nature herself . . . cures me of this philosophical melancholy and delirium. . . . I dine, I play a game of back-gammon, I converse, and am merry with my friends; and when after three or four hour's amusement, I wou'd return to these speculations, they appear so cold, and strain'd, and ridiculous, that I cannot find in my heart to enter into them any farther."[28] Is a teleological nature stealing in the back door and guiding Hume away from his despair? Kemp Smith, urging Hutcheson's influence, suggests that for Hume, "Man . . . lives under the tutelage of Nature, and must find in *its* dictates . . . the ultimate criteria alike of belief and of action."[29] Yet Hume wrote to Hutcheson, "I cannot agree to your Sense of *Natural*. Tis founded on final causes; which is a Consideration, that appears to me pretty uncertain & unphilosophical."[30]

[25]*Treatise*, p. 474. See too *Dialogues*, p. 205; *Enquiry concerning Morals*, p. 307.
[26]*Treatise*, p. 474; *Enquiry concerning Morals*, p. 307n.
[27]*Treatise*, p. 171.
[28]*Treatise*, p. 269. Also, *Treatise*, pp. 183, 187, 215, 269–272, 455; *Enquiry concerning Understanding*, pp. 9, 41, 55; *Enquiry concerning Morals*, pp. 213n., 229n.; "The Epicurean," in *Essays*, pp. 140–141.
[29]Kemp Smith, *Philosophy of Hume*, p. 45; see too pp. 130–131, 564–565.
[30]Hume to Francis Hutcheson, 17 sep 1739, in *Letters* I:33.

Hume is picturesquely putting a descriptive point far more mundane than Kemp Smith suggests. It is a psychological truth, one part of the enormous causal mechanism Hume calls nature, that in the world he cannot maintain his skeptical stance. Philosophers, "immediately upon leaving their closets," fall back on ordinary views.[31] We need not appeal to a critical standard of nature to explain the point.

Human Nature, Virtue, and Justice

Banishing reason, God and nature from moral and political theory deprives Hume of three traditional foundations. But rhetorically, at least, Hume is no critic of foundationalism. Announcing a Copernican revolution in philosophy, he proposes "to leave the tedious lingring method, which we have hitherto followed, and instead of taking now and then a castle or village on the frontier, to march up directly to the capital or center of these sciences, to human nature itself. . . . In pretending therefore to explain the principles of human nature, we in effect propose a compleat system of the sciences, built on a foundation almost entirely new, and the only one upon which they can stand with any security."[32] Again, Hume's study of human nature will be purely descriptive. He wants to find out what mechanisms move us, not what final causes tug us toward the good.

How will this "only Science of man" work?[33] Over and over, Hume is pulled in two opposite directions. Referring to "the constant and universal principles of human nature," he offers apparently universal truths: "The generality of mankind" are "great dupes," and "To declaim against present times, and magnify the virtue of remote ancestors, is a property almost inherent in human nature," to name but two.[34] Yet he also holds that "man is a

---

[31]*Treatise*, p. 216, generally pp. 216–218.
[32]*Treatise*, p. xvi.
[33]*Treatise*, p. 273.
[34]*Enquiry concerning Understanding*, p. 83; "Of Public Credit," in *Essays*, p. 369; "Of Refinement in the Arts," in *Essays*, p. 285. See too on invariant human nature *Natural History*, p. 92; "Of Eloquence," in *Essays*, p. 108, a reference to which Abigail Gutmann Doyle inadvertently drew my attention; "Of the Rise and Progress of the Arts and Sciences," in *Essays*, p. 114. On popular stupidity:

very variable being, and susceptible of many different opinions, principles, and rules of conduct."[35] How do these two views cohere? The answer is apparently simple: people vary, but they vary according to regular principles.

What, then, are the sources of human variation? Hume declines to follow Montesquieu's lead: "Nor do I think men owe any thing of their temper or genius to the air, food, or climate."[36] Instead, Hume tries to demonstrate the primacy of "moral causes," a rubric for "all circumstances fitted to work on the mind as motives or reasons, and which render a peculiar set of manners habitual to us. Of this kind are, the nature of the government, the revolutions of public affairs, the plenty or penury in which the people live, the situation of the nation with regard to its neighbours, and such like circumstances."[37] Hume's moral causes are what we would call social context; I will use the latter term here.

Formally, at least, Hume has a perfectly coherent position. Unvarying principles of human nature give rise to colorful and varied outcomes in different social contexts. In practice, though, Hume is still tugged two ways. Sometimes social context does the explanatory work. Consider for example Hume's sociological analysis of the soldier and the priest, who obtain their characters from the conditions of their lives.[38] Yet sometimes the account is emphatically psychological, and the invariant principles do the explanatory work. Consider again Hume's comments on the stupidity of the masses. Yet another tension emerges in Hume's comments on political science. Here, paradoxically, the very importance of social context makes a science of politics viable: "So great is the force of laws, and of particular forms of government, and so little dependence have they on the humours and tempers

National History, pp. 49–50; "Of the Protestant Succession," in *Essays*, p. 492. On preferring the past: "Of the Populousness of Ancient Nations," in *Essays*, pp. 420, 451; *History* IV:528n.W.

[35]"Of Commerce," in *Essays*, p. 261. Also "The Sceptic," in *Essays*, p. 173; "Of Some Remarkable Customs," in *Essays*, p. 372.

[36]"Of National Characters," in *Essays*, pp. 205–206.

[37]"Of National Characters," in *Essays*, pp. 202–203.

[38]"Of National Characters," in *Essays*, pp. 204–205 and 204–206n.2; also *Treatise*, p. 402; *Enquiry concerning Morals*, p. 255.

of men, that consequences almost as general and certain may sometimes be deduced from them, as any which the mathematical sciences afford us."[39] Yet Hume's sense of the sweeping variations in social context dampens his enthusiasm: "I am apt, however, to entertain a suspicion, that the world is still too young to fix many general truths in politics, which will remain true to the latest experience."[40] We cannot extrapolate to unobserved social contexts.

Or can we? Hume pictures "a traveller, returning" with stories of "men, who were entirely divested of avarice, ambition, or revenge; who knew no pleasure but friendship, generosity, and public spirit." We know he is "a liar, with the same certainty, as if he had stuffed his narration with stories of centaurs and dragons, miracles and prodigies."[41] Hume will not even allow the traveler to explain what differences in social context give rise to such fabulous differences in character. If human nature is putty, it is refractory, not infinitely pliable. Such talk invites us to dismiss Hume as a pigheaded doctrinaire, certain that he has latched onto true and invariant human nature. But we have seen already that Hume is aware of the importance of social context. Though we can quibble with his inference, the passage has a political point worth noting. Hume's emphasis on social context opens an inviting loophole to the radical. If men are avaricious, ambitious, and vengeful, the radical will reflect, it is because their social context makes them that way. So if we restructure society, we can make men into saints. Hume has a far more sober view of the possibilities for reforging human nature, and as we will see he cringes at the very thought of revolutionary politics. To douse radical ardor, Hume lumps his traveler's tales with talk of centaurs.[42]

The tensions in Hume's science of human nature—in particular, his vacillations between psychologically and sociologically oriented arguments—provide the context within which I want

[39]"That Politics May Be Reduced to a Science," in *Essays*, p. 14.
[40]"Of Civil Liberty," in *Essays*, p. 89.
[41]*Enquiry concerning Understanding*, p. 84; also *Treatise*, pp. 402–403.
[42]See here in *Essays* "Of Commerce," p. 266; "Of Refinement in the Arts," p. 287.

to consider Hume's account of morality and justice. I will limit my discussion to the streamlined version of the argument Hume offers in his *Enquiry concerning the Principles of Morals*, "which, in my own opinion (who ought not to judge on that subject), is of all my writings, historical, philosophical, or literary, incomparably the best."[43]

Hume commences as a scientist, a detached observer trying to arrive at a satisfactory explanatory account of our moral beliefs: "It is not my present business to recommend generosity and benevolence, or to paint, in their true colours, all the genuine charms of the social virtues."[44] Since morality is founded on a sentiment of approbation, the question is simply: of what qualities do we approve? "Personal Merit," concludes Hume, "consists altogether in the possession of mental qualities, *useful* or *agreeable* to the *person himself* or to *others*."[45] Human nature is equipped with psychological mechanisms, most notably sympathy (more prominent in the *Treatise*), that lead us to approve such qualities, not others. Sociological mechanisms have a role, too: language, for example, forces us to take up an impartial point of view to communicate meaningfully.[46]

Hume's conclusion is largely formal. He need not commit himself to any account of what we find useful or agreeable. There is then no good reason to consider Hume a utilitarian, if again we take utilitarianism to be the view that the happiness of the group ought to be maximized. Hume's use of *utility* in the *Enquiry* is undeniably sloppy. Sometimes he ties utility explicitly to happiness, and we can find inklings in his work of a hedonistic psychology.[47] Yet I take his considered view to be that "usefulness is only a tendency to a certain end," leaving open what the end is.[48] The term *utility* ought not to blind us to the salient dif-

[43]"My Own Life," in *Essays*, p. 611; in *History* I:vii; in *Letters* I:4.

[44]*Enquiry concerning Morals*, p. 173. See too *Enquiry concerning Understanding*, pp. 5–16; *Treatise*, pp. 619–621.

[45]*Enquiry concerning Morals*, p. 268.

[46]*Enquiry concerning Morals*, pp. 228–229; see too *Treatise*, pp. 580–587.

[47]*Enquiry concerning Morals*, pp. 178, 198, 286; *Treatise*, pp. 301, 311, 438–439.

[48]*Enquiry concerning Morals*, p. 219; also *Enquiry*, pp. 179, 218, 237, 241, 245, 286. That Hume is not a utilitarian, despite his reputation, is pretty well estab-

ferences between Hume's view and, say, Sidgwick's. Sidgwick thought we should maximize the happiness of the group, and he diligently pursued the ramifications of that claim into the niceties of mental arithmetic. Yet even if we grant that by utility Hume always has (tendency to) pleasure in mind, we will be nowhere near a view like Sidgwick's.

The very formality of Hume's scientific conclusion, his choosing not to identify the useful and agreeable, prompts worries about relativism. What will we say about those with different views about which qualities are useful and agreeable? If "the particular manners and opinions of our age and country"[49] lead to variations in morality, what can we say about those variations? If morality lies in a faculty of approbation, what can we say about those who approve of what we disapprove of? Despite Hume's easy assurances that "the sentiments, which arise from humanity, are . . . the same in all human creatures and produce the same approbation or censure,"[50] we can detect the workings of social context a scant few pages away. Cleanliness, Hume holds, is a virtue.[51] Part of the surprise of this suggestion lies in the obvious rejoinder that only in a certain social context, one rather like Hume's, is cleanliness particularly agreeable.[52]

Hume attempts to quell worries about relativism in "A Dialogue," where he treats the reader to a deliberately lurid account of the exotic customs of Fourli. There, Palamedes informs us, he found homosexual favors swapped for philosophy tutoring, to

---

lished in the Hume literature. See Mackie, *Hume's Moral Theory*, pp. 151–153; David Gauthier, "David Hume, Contractarian," *Philosophical Review* 88 (January 1979): 3–38; Knud Haakonssen, *The Science of a Legislator: The Natural Jurisprudence of David Hume and Adam Smith* (Cambridge: Cambridge University Press, 1981), pp. 40–41; David Miller, *Philosophy and Ideology in Hume's Political Thought* (Oxford: Clarendon, 1981), pp. 190–191; and especially Aryeh Botwinick, "A Case for Hume's Nonutilitarianism," *Journal of the History of Philosophy* 15 (October 1977): 423–435. Note too *Treatise*, p. 472, on the varieties of pleasure.
[49]"Of the Standard of Taste," in *Essays*, p. 249.
[50]*Enquiry concerning Morals*, p. 273.
[51]*Enquiry concerning Morals*, p. 266; *Treatise*, p. 611.
[52]Note too the discrepancy between *Enquiry concerning Morals*, p. 261n., where unanimity of approval is required for virtue, and p. 272, where a majority will suffice.

the applause of all; murder, parricide, the assassination of close friends, infanticide, and suicide, all esteemed; and the marriage of siblings taken as a matter of course. Palamedes reveals triumphantly that Fourli is a composite of ancient societies, especially Athens. He then delivers the relativist challenge: "I only meant to represent the uncertainty of all these judgments concerning characters; and to convince you, that fashion, vogue, custom, and law, were the chief foundation of all moral determinations. . . . How shall we pretend to fix a standard for judgments of this nature?"[53] Palamedes's interlocutor, appearing in a very Humean first person, argues that the differences arise mainly from factual disagreements. The ancients thought assassination conducive to liberty, but the moderns dissent. The moral disagreement hinges on estimation of the consequences. There are some issues for which social context is decisive and generates authentically moral disagreements.[54] There are others where all that matters is that a line be drawn, not precisely where it is drawn. But, the argument goes, all those disagreements are confined to a narrow range, and throughout, we still find people approving of the useful and agreeable: "All the differences, therefore, in morals, may be reduced to this one general foundation."[55]

Setting aside worries about relativism, I want here only to emphasize the place that descriptive considerations have in Hume's account of morality. Some moral differences can be both explained and resolved if we sharpen our understanding of how the world works. Note too the role that descriptive considerations play in disposing of the challenge Palamedes poses when he introduces two champions of "*artificial* lives and manners," Pascal and Diogenes.[56] Pascal led an odd life, says Palamedes. He cultivated a sense of his own dependency and worthlessness; he suffered for the sake of suffering, and denied himself innocent pleasures; he strove to maintain an air of indifference toward his loved ones. Diogenes's life was odd in precisely contrary ways.

[53]"A Dialogue," in *Enquiries*, Selby-Bigge, ed., p. 333.
[54]Compare "Of the Standard of Taste," in *Essays*, pp. 231–255.
[55]"A Dialogue," in *Enquiries*, Selby-Bigge, ed., p. 336.
[56]"A Dialogue," in *Enquiries*, Selby-Bigge, ed., p. 341.

He thought himself superior; he submitted to suffering only for discipline and sought out pleasure; he loved his friends and so scolded them. Both were odd, yet both are celebrated as paragons of virtue. The interlocutor impeaches their virtue, arguing that "the natural principles of the mind play not with the same regularity, as if left to themselves, free from the illusions of religious superstition or philosophical enthusiasm."[57]

Is Hume none too surreptitiously reintroducing the banished critical standard of nature? Here again the reference to natural principles is mundane. It is simply a matter of fact, Hume thinks, that without their meretricious beliefs, Pascal and Diogenes would have entertained no such extravagant views of virtue. Even if we say that only their passions are different, there is one relevant derivative sense in which Hume will allow reason to judge the passions. If the passion is "founded on false suppositions," we may, a bit elliptically, call it unreasonable.[58] Pascal's religious beliefs, Hume thinks, are thoroughly indefensible. His conception of virtue can therefore be discarded without any appeal to a critical standard of nature. Here again descriptive considerations are relevant in assessing evaluative positions. Similarly, Hume could rebut Diogenes's position by explaining why the descriptive props of philosophical enthusiasm are illusory.

Far more powerful than his general analysis of virtue is Hume's account of "the cautious, jealous virtue of justice."[59] Here Hume's assumptions about invariant human nature are relatively innocuous, and he takes up more of a social perspective. I simply outline his intricate argument.[60]

Suppose we inhabit a world where cooperation is fruitful, and we have not enough goods to supply all our desires. Suppose too that while we are concerned chiefly for our own interests, we can respond to claims of equity (and, perhaps more importantly, to our own long-term self-interest). Suppose further that we are

[57]"A Dialogue," in *Enquiries*, Selby-Bigge, ed., p. 343; see too *Enquiry concerning Morals*, p. 270.
[58]*Treatise*, p. 416.
[59]*Enquiry concerning Morals*, p. 184.
[60]I follow the exposition in *Enquiry concerning Morals*, pp. 183–204; see too *Treatise*, pp. 477–534. See here the superb account in Mackie, *Hume's Moral Theory*, pp. 76–96.

more or less equal, in the sense that no single group can obviously overpower the rest. Suppose finally that we are social beings, capable of cooperating and adopting a division of labor. These suppositions constitute Hume's circumstances of justice. Having the traits and living in the world we do, we face a problem. If we could trust each other, we could gain the payoffs of cooperation. Yet since we are largely egoistic, trust would be imprudent. The situation is a large-scale prisoners' dilemma.

Hume's comments on how we could work our way out of this dilemma are somewhat elusive. He appeals to a convention that is not a promise, one that involves the tacit coordination of many individuals. It is unclear how this coordination could arise and flourish, though it will cheer some to note that Hume's suggestions have been strikingly confirmed by recent work on prisoners' dilemmas.[61] In any case, Hume need not produce a plausible story. All that matters is that we are better off with justice than without it. Justice, which Hume understands largely as the rules defining property rights, solves the problem posed by the facts of our world. If for example we believe that contracts oblige, and in turn we enforce the obligation, we can trust each other. Obligations in this view are not ghostly entities with a puzzling ontological status. They are part of our understanding of social institutions and rules.

Hume wants to say that justice, so understood, is the only viable solution to the problem. He explicitly rejects the Aristotelian understanding of justice. Just as Hume discards final causes, the linchpin of a teleological view of nature, he severs the tie between justice and merit or desert, the linchpin of a teleological view of morality and politics. No longer can we entertain the thought of distribution in accordance with desert, a distribution contributing to the pursuit of the good life: "Were mankind to

<hr/>

[61]For an imaginative exegesis of Hume, see Mackie, *Hume's Moral Theory*, pp. 88–90. Hume aside, for a game-theoretic treatment, see Robert Axelrod, "The Emergence of Cooperation among Egoists," *American Political Science Review* 75 (June 1981): 306–318; compare Robert Jervis, "Cooperation under the Security Dilemma," *World Politics* 30 (January 1978): 167–214. And note Hume's hesitation on whether men perceive the role of justice: *Enquiry concerning Morals*, pp. 187, 192, 195, 200–201, 203.

execute such a law; so great is the uncertainty of merit, both from its natural obscurity, and from the self-conceit of each individual, that no determinate rule of conduct would ever result from it; and the total dissolution of society must be the immediate consequence."[62] Only a practice of observing property rights will keep the peace and allow us to cooperate. Just how those rights are transferred is largely irrelevant: there is nothing essential about signing on the dotted line. Still they must be transferable.

Not only does Hume break with Aristotle; his view is also far removed from the rationalist flights of fancy of Wollaston and Clarke. From within the social institution of justice, we do tend to take its demands as sacrosanct, so talk of truth and fitness is plausible. But to emphasize, however impishly, his point that justice is a social institution, not an eternal fitness, Hume describes the workings of justice from an external point of view: "I may lawfully nourish myself from this tree; but the fruit of another of the same species, ten paces off, it is criminal for me to touch. Had I worn this apparel an hour ago, I had merited the severest punishment; but a man, by pronouncing a few magical syllables, has now rendered it fit for my use and service."[63] Again Hume deliberately jolts the rationalist reader. Hume's irony accomplishes a task essential for making his philosophical point.[64] The detached description of property makes it look mysterious, even magical. And so, Hume presses, it would be— every bit as much as religious superstition—were it not for its utility. Hume is so intent on emphasizing utility that he commits a logical blunder. Outside the scope of any of the four suppositions constituting the circumstances of justice, he argues, justice would be useless, so we would ignore it. We can grant this point, yet deny Hume's inference that "the beneficial consequences of

---

[62]*Enquiry concerning Morals*, p. 193; see too *Treatise*, p. 502.
[63]*Enquiry concerning Morals*, p. 199. Note the use of the external stance on property in the long footnote in the *Treatise* starting on p. 599, and Hume's use of ironic detachment to ridicule religion in *Natural History*, pp. 66–69. See too the dark humor in *History* I:251–252.
[64]Compare Price, *Ironic Hume*, pp. 65–67.

this virtue are the *sole* foundation of its merit."[65] The confusion is like that between necessary and sufficient conditions. The circumstances can be a necessary condition of the social practice of justice without wholly accounting for its virtue.

Still, Hume's positive accomplishment here is no mean feat. For his accounts of both virtue and justice, he has tried to develop simultaneously a genealogy, an explication, and a justification. Hume explains the origins of our views on virtue by appealing to psychological mechanisms such as sympathy and sociological mechanisms such as the use of language and the influence of social context. He offers a structure for those views in holding that personal merit consists in qualities useful and agreeable to oneself and others. Similarly, he explains the origins of justice by appealing to human convention and structures our views by sketching a scheme of rights, largely in property. He then tries to justify the life of virtue.[66] Hume casts his project as satisfying the egoist that he has good reason to embrace the life of virtue, and so runs into the problems we might expect. Hume appeals to vanity to persuade the egoist that he should cultivate qualities agreeable to others. Coming to justice, Hume concedes that "a Man, taking things in a certain light, may often seem to be a loser by his integrity."[67] Since the egoist's acts of injustice will not destroy the social practice of justice, he may propose to profit twice, first by others' acting justly and second by his getting away with injustice. In short order, Hume urges that the life of such a man will not allow him peaceful and approving self-contemplation, that he may well be caught, and that the "worthless toys and gewgaws" we call wealth do not warrant the injustice aimed at gaining them.[68]

This is not the strategy of justification for which I mean to commend Hume. As a justification for living a moral life, it is

---

[65] *Enquiry concerning Morals*, p. 183; note especially p. 188. For a case that Hume's circumstances are too narrow, see D. Clayton Hubin, "The Scope of Justice," *Philosophy & Public Affairs* 9 (Fall 1979): 3–24.

[66] *Enquiry concerning Morals*, pp. 278–284.

[67] *Enquiry concerning Morals*, p. 280; also *Treatise*, p. 535.

[68] *Enquiry concerning Morals*, p. 283. Compare the opening in "Of Impudence and Modesty," in *Essays*, p. 547.

open to obvious objection. The introduction of vanity tells us more about Hume's moral psychology, or perhaps Mandeville's influence on Hume, than it does about the life of virtue. And should our egoist be a thoroughgoing blackguard, his contemplation of himself will be perfectly peaceful. He may be caught, but then again he may not be, and he may be willing to take the risk. He may also not embrace Stoic sentiments on material prosperity. Hume's views on sympathy allow him to dissolve the putative tension between self-interest and morality. Oddly, though, he does not take advantage of those views in trying to justify morality.

In the *Treatise* Hume nowhere addresses the problem of the egoistic free-rider.[69] We ought not to think of the omission as an oversight or a failure to tackle the really interesting problems. Instead, the omission is a merit of the account. As far as political theory goes, the egoist seems irrelevant. Collectively, we are better off with justice than without it—we can enjoy the fruits of trust and cooperation—and that suffices as a justification. (I also think that moral theorists need not devote themselves to meeting the egoist's challenge, but that is a longer and separate story.)

This argument departs from foundationalist views in some ways. Though officially based on invariant human nature, it hinges primarily on social considerations. And Hume makes no attempt to provide a formal standard for ranking alternative outcomes. He never suggests, for example, that we can show that worlds with justice have twice as much happiness as worlds without it, and that the differential is what makes them better. But the argument is reminiscent of foundationalist views in its attempt to legislate timelessly. Hume, like Hobbes, writes about a particular set of facts—his circumstances of justice—as though they were endemic to the human condition. The argument will succeed, however, only in those times and places in which the circumstances hold. In this sense a Humean account of justice is less solid than we might initially like. But the very fluidity of the account, I want to suggest, is perhaps its greatest

[69]See *Treatise*, pp. 619–621, where Hume briefly plays the moralist without addressing the free-rider, and pp. 492 and 497, where he writes his way around him.

merit. I can make that point more clearly in considering Hume's account of political obligation.

Political Obligation

Hume rejects social-contract arguments. He thinks they are historically extravagant and parochial, and he argues tellingly that the contract theorist cannot sustain the understanding of consent that is needed.[70] Hume attacks the view not just to destroy it, but to clear the ground for his own account of political obligation. Here I sketch his argument. Then I defend his account against a recent line of criticism.

The structure of Hume's account of political obligation is disarmingly simple. It proceeds in much the same way as his argument for justice. Given certain facts about human nature and society, we face a problem to which political obligation is the solution. The best place to begin is with Hume's introduction of the state. Why do we need more than the social practice of justice? Why isn't Hume an anarchist, another eighteenth-century prophet of natural society? Politics is partly the organization and administration of justice: "We are . . . to look upon all the vast apparatus of our government, as having ultimately no other object or purpose but the distribution of justice, or, in other words, the support of the twelve judges."[71] More importantly, however, politics enables us to overcome three problems accompanying the prisoners' dilemma of trust and cooperation. "Some extraordinary circumstances may happen," Hume concedes with impressive optimism, "in which a man finds his interests to be more promoted by fraud or rapine, than hurt by the breach which his injustice makes in the social union."[72] Men may also miscalculate and think that injustice is in their interests when it is not.[73] Most important in Hume's view, however, is the moti-

---

[70]"Of the Original Contract," in *Essays*, pp. 452–473.

[71]"Of the Origin of Government," in *Essays*, p. 35.

[72]"Of the Origin of Government," in *Essays*, pp. 35–36. See the bleaker sentiments on justice in international politics in *History* II:63–64.

[73]*Enquiry concerning Morals*, p. 205.

vational problem generated by time preference. Justice may be in our long-term interest, and we may recognize that it is. Yet even then, given our "narrowness of soul," we may leap to gain some tantalizing present good at the expense of the very justice in our weightier long-term interests.[74] The refrain by now should be familiar: "This great weakness is incurable in human nature."[75]

Hume's emphasis on human nature once again invites skeptical rejoinders. Is human nature so inflexible? Are there no interesting sociological dimensions to this problem and its solution? Hume, sensitive to the instability of solutions to prisoners' dilemmas, meets the objection by adding an observation: "You have the same propension, that I have, in favour of what is contiguous above what is remote. You are, therefore, naturally carried to commit acts of injustice as well as me. Your example both pushes me forward in this way by imitation, and also affords me a new reason for any breach of equity, by shewing me, that I should be the cully of my integrity, if I alone shou'd impose on myself a severe restraint amidst the licentiousness of others."[76] The logic is much the same as in Hobbes's observations on the law of nature's binding *in foro interno*. Here, though, the sword of the sovereign does not prevent the war of all against all, but guards against the breakdown of justice, a fragile solution which individuals can work out.

So we need a state to maintain justice. But why should people obey the law? Ensuring justice aside, Hume offers political arguments by exploring counterfactual worlds. How, he asks, would the world be if people believed that they were free to disobey the law? The spectacle is not pretty: civil war, insurrection, and violence of all kinds would materialize. Magistrates, fearing an unruly populace, would rule harshly; even if the political system did not topple, it would be tyrannical.[77] Hume dwells on the gap between the principles people hold and the way, sometimes

---

[74]*Treatise*, p. 537. Also "Of the Origin of Government," in *Essays*, p. 36; *Enquiry concerning Morals*, p. 205.
[75]"Of the Origin of Government," in *Essays*, p. 36.
[76]*Treatise*, p. 535.
[77]"Of Passive Obedience," in *Essays*, p. 475.

misinterpreting the principles, they behave. He is investigating what we might call the acceptance-utility of competing principles of political obligation. Hume does think that "on some occasions, it may be justifiable both in sound politics and morality, to resist supreme power"; yet, he continues, "'tis certain, that in the ordinary course of human affairs nothing can be more pernicious and criminal."[78] If we teach the masses that they ought not to disobey, they will properly obey most of the time. "Nor is there any danger that mankind, by this prudent reserve, should universally degenerate into a state of abject servitude."[79] When the time comes that people should in fact disobey, they will, regardless of what principle they hold. Perhaps because of his contempt for human intelligence and his conviction that men are invariably impetuous, Hume's position is essentially that we should trick people. He does not shrink from this implication: "If ever on any occasion, it were laudable to conceal truth from the populace, it must be confessed, that the doctrine of resistance affords such an example; and that all speculative reasoners ought to observe, with regard to this principle, the same cautious silence, which the laws in every species of government have ever prescribed to themselves."[80] "Force," Hume urges finally, "is always on the side of the governed [and so] the governors have nothing to support them but opinion."[81] If the opinion has to incline a little toward the side of excess obedience, so be it. The element of deception here is unattractive, but it stems from Hume's rather bleak estimation of popular responsibility, not from the structure of his account. Human interests are the key to the problem. They are served by obedience, not by disobedience.[82] The work of justification is accomplished by the estimation of real and counterfactual consequences. Thus in Hume's view to say that we are obliged to obey is, perhaps surprisingly,

[78]*Treatise*, p. 553.
[79]*History* V:274.
[80]*History* V:274; also *Treatise*, p. 558.
[81]"Of the First Principles of Government," in *Essays*, p. 29.
[82]See especially "Of the Original Contract," in *Essays*, p. 468, where Hume taunts the contract theorist with the question, "Why ought we keep our word?"

to say something about nearby possible worlds as well as the real one.[83]

More surprisingly, what should be the heart of the account is well nigh missing. Hume makes no serious effort to explain why disobedience yields such horrible consequences. He capitalizes on British history, on memories of Jacobites and bonnie Prince Charles, and so illicitly wins the argument. As it stands, though, his exposition is just too pat to be persuasive. Maybe disobedience is better than obedience. In any case, we can only gain by working out a theory showing under what circumstances what sort of disobedience yields what consequences. That Hume only gestures in the direction of such an account must be deemed a major shortcoming of his political theory. For all the merits of the structure of his account, Hume gives us insufficient reason to hold that we are in fact obliged to obey.

I can clarify Hume's account by reconsidering it in light of a recent critique. A. John Simmons, in a volume devoted to arguing that no moral principle yields an obligation to obey the law, swiftly disposes of Hume's account. Here I argue that Hume's account is immune to the criticisms that Simmons levels against it. I will not decide whether Hume's account meets Simmons's criteria for a satisfactory account of political obligation. I do though hope to clarify Hume's use of consequences and rules, as well as to say something (not everything) about the role that consequences can play in moral and political theory.

Simmons frames his search for political obligation by laying out four considerations.[84] First, political obligation does not exhaust the question of obedience. Instead, having a political obligation is, roughly speaking, having a special kind of good reason to obey. That reason, however, may be outweighed by competing considerations. Second, our political obligations must bind us specially to our own government. If for example someone ar-

---

[83]The appearance of subjunctives here should deepen our understanding of Hume's dictum, "Every thing in this world is judg'd by comparison" (*Treatise*, p. 323; compare pp. 372, 557).

[84]See generally A. John Simmons, *Moral Principles and Political Obligations* (Princeton, N.J.: Princeton University Press, 1979), pp. 29–38.

gues that we have a general duty to promote just governments, she will not have an account of political obligation. Even if our government is just, it is merely one just government among others. Third, political obligation need not arise from just one source. Fourth, it need not be the case that everyone turns out to have political obligations. A satisfactory theory might reveal that only a scattered few are obliged.

Simmons sandwiches Hume into his discussion of utilitarianism, which he takes "very loosely [as] any theory which holds that the only acts (or kinds of acts) which are morally right are those which promote (or tend to promote) 'social utility' or 'the general happiness.'"[85] Now, says Simmons, Hume is an act-utilitarian; that is, he believes that one should apply the test of utility directly to each proposed instance of disobedience. If disobedience serves utility, disobey; if not, obey. The principle of utility does all the work, leaving no room for obligations. If utilitarians suggest that we cast political obligation as a convenient rule of thumb—most of the time, we know, obedience serves utility—we can rebut them by insisting that still the principle of utility does all the work: "Where the general happiness can obviously be served by disregarding the rule of thumb, we must do so, for the rule has no prescriptive force independent of the principle of utility."[86] Suppose now that utilitarians embrace rule-utilitarianism; that is, they say that one should follow rules justified in turn by the principle of utility. Then, Simmons says, we need only note that rule-utilitarianism is indefensible. Citing the work of David Lyons and J. J. C. Smart, Simmons claims, "One committed to maximizing social utility could not consistently act on the kinds of rules sanctioned by rule-utilitarianism." This judgment is perhaps unfortunate, since "the rule-utilitarian's principles of obligation will have the kind of force we want in providing an account of political obligation."[87]

Why is rule-utilitarianism supposed to be untenable? The gist of the argument in Lyons and Smart, on whom Simmons de-

[85]Simmons, *Principles and Obligations*, p. 45. The following discussion is taken from pp. 45–54.
[86]Simmons, *Principles and Obligations*, pp. 48–49.
[87]Simmons, *Principles and Obligations*, p. 52.

pends, is simple. Following a rule-utilitarian's rules would typically maximize utility. Most of the time, then, the rule-utilitarian and the act-utilitarian agree. Sometimes, though, the rules will diverge from the dictates of utility. In such cases, what are we to do? If we break the rules and follow the act-utilitarian's instructions, rule-utilitarianism collapses into act-utilitarianism. If we follow the rules, we expose ourselves "to the accusation of rule worship."[88] Why adhere to a rule justified by utility when we know adherence will not be felicific?

Simmons thus tries to impale Hume on the horns of a dilemma. As an act-utilitarian, Hume has no conceptual working room for obligations. Even if he were a strict rule-utilitarian, he would have an indefensible theory. I want to deny that Hume is either an act-utilitarian or a rule-utilitarian. His position is best viewed as a variant of rule-consequentialism that escapes the objections of Lyons and Smart.

Simmons's use of *utilitarian* is broad; I would prefer to reserve the term for those urging that we maximize the happiness of the group. Note the striking differences between Hume's theory and utilitarianism. Hume allows for goods besides happiness. He is not committed to maximizing anything at all. His appeal to consequences does not involve fabulously detailed and complex calculations. Accordingly, I propose that we call Hume a consequentialist. Simmons's case remains, however.

Why does Simmons think that Hume's account of justice and obedience is act-consequentialist? Hume, after all, explicitly affirms the central place of rules in his theory: "The rules, which we follow . . . are such as can best be contrived to serve farther the interests of society."[89] He also affirms, contrary to what Simmons claims, that not every defensible act of justice need be useful, as long as the practice is: "A single act of justice is fre-

---

[88]J. J. C. Smart, "An Outline of a System of Utilitarian Ethics," in J. J. C. Smart and Bernard Williams, *Utilitarianism: For and Against* (Cambridge: Cambridge University Press, 1973), p. 10; also p. 44. See too David Lyons, *Forms and Limits of Utilitarianism* (Oxford: Clarendon, 1965), p. 144. I will not discuss Lyons's case against variants of rule-utilitarianism not drawing on our actual rules; neither his primitive nor his ideal rule-utilitarianism (pp. 119–160) is to the point here.

[89]*Enquiry concerning Morals*, p. 192.

quently contrary to *public interest.* . . . But however single acts of justice may be contrary, either to public or private interest, 'tis certain, that the whole plan or scheme is highly conducive, or indeed absolutely requisite, both to the support of society, and the well-being of every individual. 'Tis impossible to separate the good from the ill."[90] Defending his view, Simmons appeals to Bentham's authority, refers the reader to several passages in Hume, and asserts, "Many other passages . . . support this reading."[91] The passages he cites do have an unmistakably act-consequentialist ring, but the inconsistency is understandable in the context of eighteenth-century ethics. The position Hume stakes out, tying justice and obedience to human interests, is radically different from those of his contemporary rationalist and theological opponents. In a narrower context, where the broad outlines of his view were more generally accepted, Hume might well have fine-tuned his position. As it stands, it would be perverse to blame Hume for not anticipating the more technical distinctions of twentieth-century ethics.

Still, there are two reasons for holding Hume's considered views to be rule-consequentialist. First, Hume does focus his attention on the workings of social institutions embodying rules. Second, he holds that "all political questions are infinitely complicated, and . . . there scarcely ever occurs in any deliberation, a choice which is either purely good, or purely ill. Consequences, mixed and unmixed, may be foreseen to flow from every measure: and many consequences, unforeseen, do always, in fact, result from every one."[92] Hume is not claiming that we cannot estimate consequences at all. We can, he thinks, show that on the whole obedience is better than disobedience; but in any particular instance, we cannot be sure.

These two points defuse Lyons's and Smart's argument. Hume's cannot be "the law worship of the rule-utilitarian, who would say that we ought to keep to a rule that is the most generally optimific, even though we *knew* that obeying it in this partic-

---

[90]*Treatise*, p. 497; note too *Enquiry concerning Morals*, pp. 304–305. Compare Simmons, *Principles and Obligations*, p. 53.
[91]Simmons, *Principles and Obligations*, p. 208n.29.
[92]"Of the Protestant Succession," in *Essays*, p. 492.

ular instance would have bad consequences."[93] In Hume's account, the supposition does not arise. We do not know whether obedience would serve the public interest in each case, but we do know that on the whole it does. So it makes sense to have a presumption that obedience is right. This position does not denigrate the presumption of obedience to a mere rule of thumb, a practical aid we use to save the time that calculation in each case would involve or to protect ourselves from the temptation to skew the calculations in our own favor.[94] For the case-by-case calculation is simply unworkable. And Hume need not try to reform our existing practice of obedience to exclude the kinds of cases where disobedience is "optimific." It is impossible to distinguish kinds of actions by identifying all their causal consequences, and it is absurd to think of framing social practices around the extremely complicated rules needed to exclude the appropriate cases.[95] Besides, if we have an existing practice, and I exempt myself, I encourage others to follow my example. It may then be impossible to create a social practice that does not include the suspect applications of the existing rule. These considerations explain why "'tis impossible to separate the good from the ill."[96]

Hume's position, then, is best viewed as a variant of rule-consequentialism. We believe we are obliged to obey the law. The obligation, again, is not some ghostly entity with a puzzling ontological status. Rather it frames a social practice of obedience. That practice has relatively good consequences: disobedience would mean insurrection, tyranny, and so on. The justification for obedience lies in its beneficial consequences.[97]

---

[93]Smart, "System of Utilitarian Ethics," in Smart and Williams, *Utilitarianism*, p. 44.

[94]Lyons, *Forms and Limits*, p. 149.

[95]Compare the treatment in Lyons, *Forms and Limits*, pp. 30–61, which assumes omniscience.

[96]Note especially *Treatise*, p. 535, and compare Mackie, *Hume's Moral Theory*, pp. 91–92, and Jonathan Harrison, *Hume's Theory of Justice* (Oxford: Clarendon, 1981), pp. 66–74.

[97]Robert Paul Wolff, "A Reply to Reiman," in his *In Defense of Anarchism* (New York: Harper & Row, 1976), pp. 105–109, protests against double-counting political obligation as something added to such useful consequences.

Change the (real or counterfactual) consequences, and the justification of the obligation ceases. Only in some social contexts would the consequences Hume appeals to materialize. Suppose that obedience has the unfortunate consequence that the magistrates feel free to exert arbitrary power on a passive citizenry and that disobedience could mean preventing such abuses. Suppose that, to prevent disobedience from having the grave consequences Hume ascribes to it, we carefully delimit the appropriate sort of disobedience. Perhaps we will insist that it must be public and peaceful and that the disobedient must be willing to accept the penalty. Disobedience of that sort would not promote widespread violence or injustice; nor need it force the government into a ruthlessly repressive stance. If the consequences of such disobedience are acceptable, we may say it is permissible. If the consequences of obedience are grave and can be remedied by disobedience, we may say there is an obligation to disobey.

My concern here is not to structure a justification for civil disobedience but to show how Hume's account invites disagreement and permits meaningful debate. Just what are the consequences of our regular behavior? What would be the consequences of adopting some new practice? These questions are basically factual or descriptive, but they are where the work of justification takes place in Hume's political theory. If the consequences of disobedience are what Hume claims they are, the case is properly closed; it would be quite odd to ask for an account of what's wrong with violence, injustice, or tyranny. The point holds as well for Hume's account of justice. Competing descriptions alter the justification. For example, if we show that private property is not the only way to achieve social peace, or if we can refute Hume's claim "that a man either has a full and perfect property, or none at all,"[98] the way is clear to consider other schemes. Then we will want to ask: How would these schemes work? What problems would they solve? What new problems

---

But political obligation, we can say, exists because of those consequences and adds no force to them. Such a stance seems proof too against Wolff's worries about mystification, worries a Humean consequentialist can share.

[98]*Treatise*, p. 529. Hume is willing to concede that property rights may be "bounded in time or degree" (p. 530), but we may want to say more than that.

would they create? Hume's focus on real and counterfactual consequences assuages worries that his putative emotivism will not permit meaningful moral or political debate. Before sentimental approval, "it is often necessary, we find, that much reasoning should precede, that nice distinctions be made, just conclusions drawn, distant comparisons formed, complicated relations examined, and general facts fixed and ascertained."[99] To justify a political position, we need to know how the (social and political) world works.

England's Constitution and the Rule of Law

So one may sensibly turn to history to develop a normative political theory. That, I will argue, is precisely Hume's interest and accomplishment in the *History of England*. It need not be a regrettable "love of literary fame, my ruling passion"[100] which wrenches Hume from the skeptical philosophy of his beloved chamber and consigns him to the winding corridors of English history. "The question"—Hume makes the point in a discussion of the tendencies of the British constitution, but it applies far more broadly—"is not concerning any fine imaginary republic, of which a man forms a plan in his closet."[101] While it can be fun to flee "the common botched and inaccurate governments" and try to outdo Harrington in a brief disquisition, the public "will be apt to regard such disquisitions both as useless and chimerical."[102] Instead, Hume, as a political theorist, writes a *History of England*. I mean to avoid asking whether that *History* is liberal or conservative, Whig or Tory, court or country in inclination. Duncan Forbes, recognizing Hume's critique of "vulgar Whiggism," has sought to enlist him as a "sceptical Whig"; David Miller, suggesting that only after the French Rev-

---

[99]*Enquiry concerning Morals*, p. 173. See too "Of the Standard of Taste," in *Essays*, p. 237.
[100]"My Own Life," in *Essays*, p. 615; in *History* I:xii; in *Letters* I:7.
[101]"Whether the British Government Inclines More to Absolute Monarchy or to a Republic," in *Essays*, p. 52; see too in *Essays* "Of Commerce," p. 266, and "Of Refinement in the Arts," p. 287.
[102]"Idea of a Perfect Commonwealth," in *Essays*, p. 500.

olution does the distinction between liberal and conservative take shape, has argued that Hume would then have sided with Burke and so can serve admirably as a model conservative.[103]

Redoubling a point Forbes makes, I would urge that trying to pigeonhole Hume's political thought will not contribute much to our understanding of it. Hume thought the political positions of his day were jumbled, and he strove to hammer out a nonpartisan view. "It is no wonder," he muses in the closing pages of the *History*, "that these events have long, by the representations of faction, been extremely clouded and obscured. No man has yet arisen, who has paid an entire regard to truth, and has dared to expose her, without covering or disguise, to the eyes of the prejudiced public."[104] No man so far, that is; but Hume could boast, "I have the impudence to pretend that I am of no party, and have no bias."[105] Here I take Hume's claim to have escaped the bias of party at face value.

Most striking about Hume's *History* is the unequivocal emergence of social context as the pivot of justification. Surveying very early English history, Hume ventures some remarks that undercut his philosophical treatment of politics. Britain, a "remote province" of the Roman empire, was beset by marauding barbarians through the fifth century. Appealing to Rome for defense, the Britons were twice granted a legion; "but the Romans, reduced to extremities at home, and fatigued with those distant expeditions, informed the Britons that they must no longer look

---

[103]Duncan Forbes, *Hume's Philosophical Politics* (Cambridge: Cambridge University Press, 1975), chap. 5; Miller, *Philosophy and Ideology*, pp. 187–205. Both these studies are useful in setting out the context of Hume's political theory. I found especially useful Isaac Kramnick, *Bolingbroke and His Circle* (Cambridge, Mass.: Harvard University Press, 1968), for the decades leading up to Hume.
   The question of Hume's political affiliation is an old one. See here Sheldon Wolin, "Hume and Conservatism," *American Political Science Review* 48 (December 1954): 999–1016; James Conniff, "Hume on Political Parties: The Case for Hume as a Whig," *Eighteenth-Century Studies* 12 (Winter 1978–79): 150–173; Ernest Campbell Mossner, "Was Hume a Tory Historian? Facts and Reconsiderations," *Journal of the History of Ideas* 2 (April 1941): 225–236; and, for a somehow simultaneously republican and court Hume, Garry Wills, *Explaining America* (Garden City, N.Y.: Doubleday, 1981).
[104]*History* VI:319.
[105]Hume to Matthew Sharp of Hoddam, 25 feb 1754, in *Letters* I:185.

to them for succor," and deserted them. Thus England attained her independence, after subjection of "near four centuries." Yet, Hume continues, "the abject Britons regarded this present of liberty as fatal to them."[106] Hume can rhapsodize over "that noble liberty, that sweet equality, and that happy security, by which [the English] are at present distinguished above all nations in the universe."[107] He recognizes, however, that liberty will be no prize if it means being left to suffer barbarian invasions.

Consider too Hume's comment on his adored Alfred, who ruled England several hundred years later. Alfred came to power and succeeded in expelling the Danes, who had long been trampling English life and liberty underfoot. Still, "the kingdom was in the most wretched condition; desolated by the ravages of those barbarians" and full of wandering Danish marauders reducing the English "to the most extreme indigence" and anarchy. Here England's problems stemmed not from invariant human nature or unalterable circumstances of justice, but from historical contingency: "These were the evils for which it was necessary that the vigilance and activity of Alfred should provide a remedy." Alfred hammered out a rude system of justice. Laying out a meticulous system of districts and requiring everyone to register a permanent residence, he established a system of criminal justice where "every man was obliged from his own interest to keep a watchful eye over the conduct of his neighbours; and was in a manner surety for the behaviour of those who were placed under the division to which he belonged."[108] To keep the system working, Alfred made it difficult for men to move. These measures look decidedly harsh compared to Elizabeth's star chamber proceedings. Yet while Hume indicts the star chamber in no uncertain terms,[109] he condones Alfred's innovations. Granted, Hume is interested for other reasons in discrediting Elizabeth, and he wants to lavish praise on Alfred for originating (as it turns out) the jury system and the common law. We need

---

[106]*History* I:10, 11.
[107]*History* IV:200; also II:482.
[108]*History* I:75–77.
[109]*History* IV:186: "I much question whether any of the absolute monarchies in Europe contain at present so illegal and despotic a tribunal."

[191]

not, however, explain away Hume's benign rendition of Alfred. The problems of ninth-century England were different from those of sixteenth-century England. Hume makes it clear that social context is the key that explains why Alfred's institutions were good: "Such a regular distribution of the people, with such a strict confinement in their habituations, may not be necessary in times when men are more inured to obedience and justice; and it might perhaps be regarded as destructive of liberty and commerce in a polished state; but it was well calculated to reduce that fierce and licentious people under the salutary restraint of law and government."[110]

Social context unlocks another puzzling passage, where Hume briskly tosses off a reference to "the customs of the feudal law, which was then universally established in the southern countries of Europe, and which suited the peculiar circumstances of that age."[111] Hume's account of justice leaves no room for feudalism. In the *Treatise*, he insists that justice is universal: "The interest, on which justice is founded, is the greatest imaginable, and extends to all times and places. It cannot possibly be serv'd by any other invention." He insists too that property must be transferable by consent.[112] Yet these positions crumble under the weight of his own *History*. Primogeniture and entails subvert Hume's picture of free exchange; the feudal scheme of property is different from the scheme he insists is uniquely possible. In Hume's commendation of feudalism, we find real history overtaking the natural history of justice. One of the allegedly permanent circumstances of justice—rough equality—did not obtain in feudalism, for there it was clear that very powerful lords, with their retainers, could overcome lesser lords. Private property solves a problem posed by invariant human nature; feudal institutions solved a historically contingent problem posed by marauding barbarians. By keeping property in large lots allowing for organized military defense, feudalism permitted some semblance of social flourishing in the face of constant invasion. That is why feudalism suited the times.

---

[110]*History* I:77–82. Hume is even willing to condone star chamber proceedings in some contexts (II:609n.Y).
[111]*History* I:116. Note too *History* II:476.
[112]*Treatise*, pp. 620, 514–516.

The introduction of history also sheds light on Hume's political science. At the close of his narration of the reign of Henry VII, Hume canvasses a number of developments in the period which left England much as it was in his time. "Here, therefore," he concludes, "commences the useful as well as the more agreeable part of modern annals. . . . As each incident has a reference to our present manners and situation, instructive lessons occur every moment during the course of the narration."[113] Despite Hume's didactic tone, the passage is illuminating. "Like causes still produce like effects," in all different contexts.[114] But the *History*'s caution is crucial. Hume has at least a glimmering of awareness that in a very different social context talk about like causes will be elusive. Here the historian's sobriety tones down the enthusiasm of the political scientist.

I turn now to the central instructive lesson of the *History*, the truth, as Hume will have it, about the English constitution. Hume wants to deny the mainstays of what Forbes calls the vulgar Whig interpretation of the events of 1688: that the English people reclaimed the liberties of the ancient constitution from tyrannical James II. To demolish the melodramatic contrast between Stuart despotism and Tudor liberty, Hume turns a searching eye to the reign of Elizabeth, celebrated with "unbounded panegyrics" by the Whigs. Elizabeth enjoyed "unlimited authority," he argues, and indeed the portrait in appendix III of the *History* is not flattering: the court of star chamber had "unlimited discretionary authority" to punish "all sorts of offences, contempts, and disorders that lay not within the reach of the common law." The court of high commission investigated the relatively "undefinable" crime of heresy in ways "contrary to all the most simple ideas of justice and equity." Any subject could be thrown in jail without legal remedy. Extrajudicial torture was common, and in the courtroom "timid juries, and judges who held their offices during pleasure, never failed to second all the views of the crown." Seamen were pressed into service. Hume even likens Elizabeth's government to that of Tur-

---

[113]*History* II:566–567. Compare *History* II:474–475, 482; "Of the Study of History," in *Essays*, pp. 560–562.

[114]*Treatise*, p. 401; also "That Politics May Be Reduced to a Science," in *Essays*, p. 22.

key, constantly held up as a spectacle of despotism: the sultan permits "bashaws" to take bribes and enjoys his share; Elizabeth erected monopolies of all kinds, threatening always to impoverish England as she enriched herself. Extorting interest-free loans and outright "gifts" from helpless subjects, issuing frivolous proclamations, granting and denying permission for noble marriages and travel, trampling on freedom of speech, and, worst of all, by common consent above the law, Elizabeth was decidedly popular.[115]

In that paradox resides a distinction crucial for Hume's political theory. Hume thinks of liberty in two ways. Liberty is the rule of law; here it is opposed to prerogative, arbitrary power, star chamber proceedings, and the like, and here Elizabeth looks despotic. Yet liberty is also being left alone; here it is opposed to endless interference in the largely extrapolitical life of the subjects, and here Elizabeth does fairly well, for all her authority and prerogative was exercised infrequently and in a small scope.[116] These two senses of liberty are different and deserve different names. I will call the first the rule of law, the second liberty. They are also connected, however. Only under a rule of law can the people enjoy liberty in security. Unrestrained by the rule of law, Elizabeth could at any moment have trampled on her subjects' liberty. Perhaps the connection inspires Hume to call both concepts liberty, but in any case the rule of law is "that noble liberty" which so distinguishes Hume's England.[117] Hume's views prepare what is for him perhaps the most decisive contrast in English history: "In the ancient feudal constitution . . . there was a mixture not of authority and liberty, which we have since enjoyed in this island, and which now subsist uniformly together; but of authority and anarchy, which perpetually shocked with each other, and which took place alternately, according as circumstances were more or less favourable to either of them."[118] Elizabethan England did not enjoy the happy subsistence of au-

[115]*History* IV:184–201.
[116]*History* IV:200.
[117]See *History* V:317; "Of the Rise and Progress of the Arts and Sciences," in *Essays*, p. 125.
[118]*History* IV:534n.LL.

thority and liberty. Even the members of Parliament were "entirely negligent" of liberty and the rule of law, and their "persecuting statutes . . . accustomed the people to the most disgraceful subjection."[119]

Elizabeth, then, is no model to be held up to castigate the Stuarts. Hume further subverts the contrast between Stuart despotism and Tudor liberty by arguing that Elizabeth was largely, if indirectly, responsible for Stuart excesses. "Determined never to have any heir of her own body," blithely unconcerned with the impact on future monarchs, and seeking to retain her independence and dignity, Elizabeth financed her government partly by selling the royal demesne lands. She thus managed to avoid "having frequent recourse to parliamentary supplies." Yet she also deprived future monarchs of an independent source of income.[120]

That lack of income sets the stage for a proper understanding of the Stuart monarchs. Repeatedly, the king has to go to Parliament to get money, and Parliament will grant it only if the king makes certain concessions. Grasping the political potential of this dynamic, the Commons left James I financially dependent by refusing to entail "the crown lands forever on the king's heirs and subjects." At the commencement of his reign, the Commons voted Charles I an absurdly low subsidy, "which discovers rather a cruel mockery of Charles than any serious design of supporting him." Despite their most dutiful submission, Parliament essentially bought royal prerogatives from Charles II when he took the throne.[121] The Stuarts, Hume argues, were caught in a temporal gap between two modes of financing the government. Up to Elizabeth, the crown enjoyed the demesne lands; the brief meetings of Parliament and popular ignorance ensured deference to royal authority. After the Stuarts, as a result of "many accidents," the crown enjoyed "the disposal of a large revenue," and it used patronage to entice "the private interest and ambition of the members [of Parliament], to restrain the public interest and

[119]*History* IV:196, also especially IV:30.
[120]*History* III:419; IV:201–202. Note here *History* VI:1–2.
[121]*History* IV:239, 380; V:446. See *History* IV:436–438 for an acute statement of the political difficulties in which the new financial situation placed Charles I.

ambition of the body." This gap provides the institutional context within which the machinations of the Stuart kings were played out. "It was the fate of the house of Stuart to govern England at a period when the former source of authority was already much diminished, and before the latter began to flow in any tolerable abundance."[122]

In demolishing the picture of the ancient constitution recaptured from Stuart tyranny, Hume does not want to whitewash the failings of the Stuart line. He writes that "his arbitrary disposition, and the bigotry of his principles [were the] two great characteristics of [James II's] reign, and bane of his administration"[123]—a sentiment amenable to the most vulgar Whig. He also levels specific points of criticism against the Stuarts. But their institutionally generated financial dilemma precludes casting them as scoundrels. If they insisted on prerogative, Hume is eager to point out, they insisted on no more than their predecessors had, even if their style was injudicious. James I, for example, had "direct precedents, some in the reign of Mary, some in the beginning of Elizabeth."[124]

Hume makes a more mischievous point about the vulgar Whig picture: "The English constitution, like all others, has been in a state of continual fluctuation." In 1688, did England recapture the Tudor constitution? Or was it the feudal constitution after Magna Carta? Perhaps it was "that before the signing of the charters, when neither the people nor the barons had any regular privileges"?[125] One need not be particularly sensitive to the vicissitudes of historical change to reject the mythical, unvarying ancient constitution. In Hume's view, the Whig use of the ancient constitution is not a properly historical argument at all.

Hume, then, cannot subscribe to the vulgar Whig interpretation of 1688. In his view, a satisfactory interpretation of 1688 need not commence any earlier than Charles I and the Long Par-

[122]*History* IV:542–543n.3A. See too *History* VI:141.
[123]*History* VI:232.
[124]*History* IV:259.
[125]*History* IV:185n. Note especially "Of the Coalition of Parties," in *Essays*, pp. 482–483.

liament, and the interpretation must center on "the never-failing pretence of religion" and the way "noble principles of liberty took root . . . under the shelter of Puritanical absurdities."[126] As a secular historian committed to discrediting talk of miracles,[127] Hume is in trouble, for he thinks that in the workings of religious faction, "effects correspond less to their known causes, than is found in any other circumstance of government."[128] Nonetheless, religious faction is at the heart of the story.

Hume starts by complicating the idea that a party of Puritans dreaming of liberty toppled Charles I: "The appellation *puritan* stood for three parties, which, though commonly united, were yet actuated by very different views and motives. There were the political puritans, who maintained the highest principles of civil liberty; the puritans in discipline, who were averse to the ceremonies and episcopal government of the church; and the doctrinal puritans, who rigidly defended the speculative system of the first reformers."[129] The "party," then, was hardly unified. Still, it swept the nation in waves of hysteria. After the Restoration, with the bloody experience of the Commonwealth fresh in mind, political actors could not employ religious rhetoric quite so freely. "The spirit of enthusiasm had occasioned so much mischief, and had been so successfully exploded, that it was not possible, by any artifice, again to revive and support it."[130] Yet here Hume writes too confidently. The rest of his account undercuts this claim. Hume is clear that, notwithstanding the discontinuities between 1640 and 1688, religious disputes still animated English politics after the Restoration. Obviously, Stuart Catholicism in Protestant England was not particularly endearing. Perhaps more important, though, the volatile combination of religion and politics persisted. If James II attended mass and sought reconciliation with the Pope, if he threatened Parliament to get his funding, then he was a Catholic tyrant, vi-

---

[126]*History* IV:118, 198.
[127]See *History* II:345, on Joan of Arc.
[128]*History* IV:285; also IV:43.
[129]*History* IV:439.
[130]*History* VI:153.

cious enough to stir a once-compliant Parliament and rekindle fears of Popery.[131] The struggle the second time around between king and Parliament was far more peaceful than the first. Instead of pitching the royal colors, James fled. Yet the reader of the *History* cannot but be struck by the continuities between the two struggles.

The History of England is thus itself an ironic tale. From a literary point of view, Hume's accomplishment is stunning. For, crudely, the joke is on him: instead of ironically indulging himself at the Puritans' expense, he cleverly crafts the tale so that his own aversion to religion is ironically impeached by an apparently impersonal stream of historical events. The outcome of the settlement of 1688 is Hume's coveted rule of law, "the most entire system of liberty that was ever known amongst mankind." Hume insists that this system of liberty was an innovation and chides the Whigs. Their claiming that the Stuart "administration was one continued encroachment on the *incontestable* rights of the people; is not giving due honor to that great event, which not only put a period to their hereditary succession, but made a new settlement of the whole constitution."[132] Yet the irony is threefold. First, the rule of law is largely an unintended outcome. Like his ancients, Hume's Puritans "were extremely fond of liberty, but seem not to have understood it very well."[133] Only one of the three parties we call Puritan had political liberty in mind, and throughout Hume's account even they are often interested more in gaining power than in establishing a rule of law. Second, the ongoing Parliamentary revolt against Charles's authority was unlikely to succeed in establishing a new constitution or even in resisting Charles, and so was irresponsibly imprudent. Contemporary royalists, Hume reports, might well have argued, "What madness, while everything is so happily settled under ancient forms and institutions, now more exactly poised and adjusted, to try the hazardous experiment of a new constitution, and renounce the mature wisdom of our ancestors for the crude

[131]*History* VI:232, 235–236, 251, 253.
[132]*History* VI:317.
[133]"Of the Populousness of Ancient Nations," in *Essays*, p. 406.

whimsies of turbulent innovators!"[134] Indeed, Charles's authority was so firm "that it is probable the patriots of that age would
have despaired of ever resisting it, had they not been stimulated
by religious motives, which inspire a courage unsurmountable
by any human obstacle."[135] Third, Hume owes his cherished
liberty to religious fanatics. The irony of English history, then,
is the consummate irony of Hume's career. Religious fanatics,
whom he detests, many of them intending the wildest excesses,
irresponsibly take on imposing odds (as only they would) and destroy the English constitution—and so give birth to the rule of
law.

I might pause for a note on consequentialism. Consequentialist views on morals and politics have struck many as invitations
to abominable behavior, to vicious means justified by shining
ends. Thus our conception of (and aversion to) consequentialism
has been shaped by artfully described hypothetical examples,
such as the one Ivan Karamazov poses with the possibility of
ushering in the new world by killing an innocent baby. Interesting as such examples may be, they distract our attention from
the central appeal of consequentialist doctrines of politics. We
face an all too frequent gap between intentions and outcomes,
and we have more pressing concerns in politics than rewarding
virtuous actors. Our typical problem is figuring out how to judge
in a world where we don't know the outcomes of our actions, not
considering vicious means guaranteed to purchase shining ends.
So even a pure consequentialist has a forceful rejoinder to Karamazov, or the bloody dictator of your choice: how do you know
the consequences? By emphasizing the sheer unlikeliness of Puritan rebellion yielding a rule of law, Hume reminds us of what
consequentialism once meant. It was, I suggest, a way of reintroducing moral standards in politics once the syrupy encomi-
ums to virtue touted by the likes of Shaftesbury were abandoned. For the point is not, "whatever they did is justified by the

[134]*History* V:77. Also *History* V:49; "Of the Coalition of Parties," in *Essays*, p.
480.
[135]*History* IV:536n.LL. On the imprudence of the religious, see *History* IV:
43, V:102; "Of the Coalition of Parties," in *Essays*, p. 485.

outcome"; instead, it is "how desperately lucky we are to have escaped so well from the nightmares they created!"

In any case, Hume's *History* is more than an ironic tale, more even than an interpretation of English history. The *History* yields a justification of a political theory that vindicates Hume's claim to be of no party. That political theory is above all one of moderation: "For my part, I shall always be more fond of promoting moderation than zeal; though perhaps the surest way of producing moderation in every party is to increase our zeal for the public."[136]

Recall that for Hume the rule of law is the guarantor of individual liberty. He thus punctures the idea that there is a necessary antagonism between authority and liberty. The rule of law bridges the two; only a regular government with authority can maintain the rule of law and so secure liberty. Here an innovation in the realm of descriptive theory, a deliberate break with contemporary understandings of sovereignty and the ancient constitution, opens up new and attractive normative possibilities. This innovation thus detaches Hume from the parties of his day. Tory and Whig, he believes, are "foolish terms of reproach" which have "sometimes without any material difference" divided England. They "confound and distract our government"; "to determine the nature of these parties is perhaps one of the most difficult problems that can be met with." The two are essentially court and country, but with an overlay of disagreement about succession. Tories prefer Stuarts; Whigs prefer Protestants.[137] Yet it is dangerous to argue over succession, where "there is no room for any compromise or accommodation, and where the controversy may appear so momentous as to justify even an opposition by arms to the pretensions of antagonists."[138] And after the Hanover succession, these quarrels are irrelevant and frivolous.

[136]"That Politics May Be Reduced to a Science," in *Essays*, p. 24; see too "Of the Coalition of Parties," in *Essays*, pp. 478–479; *History* VI:320. "Whigs" as staunch as Trenchard and Gordon had already taken much the same view: see *Cato's Letters*, 4 vols. (London, 1724), I:109–110; II:133, 170–171; III:88–90, 206–208.

[137]*History* VI:157; "Of the Parties of Great Britain," in *Essays*, pp. 68–70.

[138]"Of the Coalition of Parties," in *Essays*, p. 478.

Hume is willing and indeed eager to leave parties a place in English politics. He has little quarrel with court and country, "the genuine divisions in the British Government"; these parties, "while they oft threaten the total dissolution of the government, are the real cause of its permanent life and vigour."[139] Hume invites misunderstanding by telling us that court and country disagreed on the proper balance of liberty and monarchy; once again we find the vague *liberty* pressed into service. We can substitute *Parliament* for *liberty* here, however. The proper functioning of the English constitution—and so the rule of law—depends on a balance between Parliament and the crown, and the two parties dispute the proper balance. Hume is content to have them dispute, as long as they do not threaten to topple the government. Here is why zeal for the public will mean party moderation. Once the parties realize the public is best served by the rule of law, they will no longer overestimate the importance of their platforms, for both will agree on the end. In this respect, we can say that Hume's political theory is an early gesture toward the end of ideology.

The English constitution is the largely fortuitous outcome of decades of religious fanaticism. Hume does not downplay the nastiness of the genealogy of this scheme of liberty. Still, adherence to this constitution, even though it has no imposing pedigree, is justified. The rationale for obedience lies not in the constitution's longevity, but in its usefulness. The constitution provides the rule of law, which saves England from the perils of civil war and yet preserves liberty. It is thus a very good solution to a genuine historical problem; worlds without it are worse than the world with it. With this fittingly simple conclusion to Hume's analysis of English history, we see how justification works in a concrete social context. We need not escape the world and fly to language, or God, or mirages labeled the greatest happiness. Justification can proceed as an exploration and evaluation of possibilities in the world. Remembering the bleak possibilities of contemporary English politics, we will be hard pressed to

---

[139]"Of the Parties of Great Britain," in *Essays*, p. 72, also p. 64; *History* IV:534n.LL.

blame Hume for not developing a critique of the rule of law, or for not pushing on to see what the alternative possibilities are within that rule.

Points of Contact between Hume and Smith

Adam Smith is more than a friend of Hume, whom he labeled "by far the most illustrious philosopher and historian of the present age"; his theories are strikingly like Hume's.[140] Before turning to Smith's analysis of market society, I want briefly to establish some points of contact between Smith and Hume.

We can make some progress toward that end by cataloguing individual points of agreement and disagreement between the two. So we can note that Smith is as uninterested as Hume in enshrining ancient society as a model,[141] or that Smith shares Hume's belief that Elizabeth's sale of the demesne lands weakened the Stuarts.[142] A mere laundry list of individual similarities and differences, however, will not deepen our understanding of the relationship between their theories. Instead we want to locate structural similarities and differences.

In his *Theory of Moral Sentiments*, Smith appeals quite regularly to reason, God, and nature, apparently to do the critical work that Hume denies they can. Recall Hume's polemical pronouncement: "'Tis not contrary to reason to prefer the destruction of the whole world to the scratching of my finger." In a strikingly parallel passage, Smith wonders why "human nature startles with horror at the thought" of sacrificing millions of lives to preserve one's little finger. His candidate is "reason, principle, conscience, the inhabitant of the breast, the man within, the great judge and arbiter of our conduct."[143] The imprecision of

[140]*Wealth of Nations*, p. 970. Similarities between Hume and Smith have been expertly explored by Forbes, "Sceptical Whiggism, Commerce, and Liberty," in *Essays on Adam Smith*, ed. Andrew S. Skinner and Thomas Wilson (Oxford: Clarendon, 1975).
[141]Note Smith, *Lectures on Rhetoric and Belles Lettres*, ed. J. C. Bryce, Glasgow ed. (Oxford: Clarendon, 1983), pp. 178–181, on Athenian law.
[142]*Jurisprudence*, p. 266.
[143]*Moral Sentiments*, pp. 136–137. Compare p. 267, where reason "deter-

the list testifies not only to the discursive style of the book, but to the lack of a discriminating theoretical vocabulary I commented on earlier. Still, Smith does agree with the essentials of Hume's account: "It is altogether absurd and unintelligible to suppose that the first perceptions of right and wrong can be derived from reason"; instead, an "immediate sense and feeling" identifies virtue and vice.[144] Smith thought too that the general "rules of morality are the commands and laws of the Deity, who will finally reward the obedient, and punish the transgressors of their duty"; and he refused to publish Hume's *Dialogues concerning Natural Religion*.[145] It might, then, be tempting to recall Locke's full-blown attempt to center a moral theory on divine command. But Smith's references to God are fleeting and inconsequential. We can easily reconstruct his arguments without mention of divinity.

It will be less easy to make sense of Smith's use of nature as a critical standard. *The Theory of Moral Sentiments* abounds with references to "the intention of Nature," leaving us a far cry from Hume.[146] In the *Moral Sentiments*, Smith distinguishes final from efficient causes—but not to discard the former.[147] We do appeal to efficient causes in studying objects, but in studying the mind we use final causes, and "imagine that to be the wisdom of man, which in reality is the wisdom of God." Here Smith offici-

---

mines not only what are the proper means for attaining any end, but also what ends are to be pursued, and what degree of relative value we ought to put upon each." Nature and reason condemn primogeniture in *Jurisprudence*, pp. 49, 71; note too the place of reason in *Jurisprudence*, pp. 13, 31, 69, 126.

[144]*Moral Sentiments*, p. 320. Though the great feat of Smith's ethics lies in his exploring in detail the mechanisms of sympathy, in his refusing to treat approval as a brute fact of "immediate sense and feeling."

[145]*Moral Sentiments*, p. 163; for the publication of the *Dialogues*, see Price's introduction in Hume, *History and Dialogues*, pp. 107–128. Note too *Moral Sentiments*, p. 91 and p. 91n. (on Christian atonement), and the editors' very helpful app. II, pp. 383–401, reprinted with revisions from D. D. Raphael, "Adam Smith and 'The Infection of David Hume's Society,'" *Journal of the History of Ideas* 30 (April-June 1969): 225–248.

[146]*Moral Sentiments*, pp. 37, 47, 53, 71, 77, 78, 86, 93, 105, 116–117, 183, 212, 222, 226, 229, 335. Note too *Jurisprudence*, pp. 11, 26–27, 62, 126, and, on the "shocking and abominable" marriage of mother and son, pp. 163, 166–167, 446.

[147]*Moral Sentiments*, p. 87.

ates over an unhappy marriage of God and nature. I will not try
to decide here whether the *Moral Sentiments* can be rendered free
of appeal to vitalism or teleology.[148] *The Wealth of Nations*, on
which I will concentrate, is basically free of problematic appeals
to reason, God, and nature. (The question of why the two works
differ this way might profitably replace the old and bankrupt
"Adam Smith problem," that of resolving the alleged contradiction between the *Wealth of Nations'* callous egoism and the *Moral
Sentiments'* sympathetic benevolence.[149])

Smith sometimes reproduces Hume's hesitation between invariant human nature and shifting social context as modes of explanation. Illustrative here are Smith's comments on the division of
labor. It arises, he says, from "the propensity to truck, barter,
and exchange one thing for another."[150] Yet he has two different accounts of that propensity. In the *Lectures on Jurisprudence*,
Smith founds "this disposition of trucking" on "the naturall inclination every one has to persuade."[151] Yet in the *Wealth of Nations*, Smith declines to trace the propensity to "original principles in human nature." Instead, he takes up a social perspective:
"As it is the power of exchanging that gives occasion to the division of labour, so the extent of this division must always be limited by the extent of that power, or, in other words, by the extent of the market."[152] It may be that inside each of us is an
enthusiastic merchant striving to get out, but only in some social
settings—those with markets—will the merchant emerge. As in
Hume, we can make the use of human nature and social context
cohere. Men, we might say, are such that in a market they will
exchange. But it will then be fruitless to nominate human nature
as the explanation for trucking, bartering, and exchanging. Hu-

[148]Haakonssen, *Science of a Legislator*, pp. 55, 57, 59, 77–79, vigorously defends Smith, arguing that "however much teleological talk Smith allows himself" (p. 59), we can find efficient causes in his discussion.
[149]The "problem" is nicely disposed of in the editors' introduction to *Moral
Sentiments*, pp. 20–25.
[150]*Wealth of Nations*, p. 25. See too *Jurisprudence*, pp. 347, 351, 492; "Early
Draft of Part of *The Wealth of Nations*," in *Jurisprudence*, p. 570.
[151]*Jurisprudence*, p. 352, also p. 493.
[152]*Wealth of Nations*, pp. 25, 31. Note too *Jurisprudence*, pp. 355, 494, 529.

man nature is presumably more or less invariant. So it can hardly explain behaviors that sometimes appear, any more than the presence of oxygen can explain the explosion of an oil burner.

Illustrative too is Smith's famous comment: "Man is of all sorts of luggage the most difficult to be transported."[153] Large wage variations persist in the market, apparently because people just do not like to move. Here it might seem that Smith has uncovered a fundamental trait of human nature. Yet he subverts this innocent psychology by discussing the effects of corporation laws and especially poor laws. The obstacle posed by the latter is "the difficulty which a poor man finds in obtaining a settlement, or even in being allowed to exercise his industry in any parish but that to which he belongs."[154] The market in labor is distorted not by some inherent stubbornness people have about moving, but by state intervention. I emphasize this line of argument because of the frequently voiced suggestion that human nature is the key issue in political theory. All we need do, the idea is, is figure out just what people are like, and then all our political questions will be answered. Besides the equivocation here on nature—is the goal a descriptive psychology or a discovery of our final cause?—society somehow disappears, in a way guaranteed not to help answer our political questions. However long we rivet our gaze on human nature, we will not discover poor laws or their consequences.

Generally, we can say this: Smith improves on Hume in developing justification in a social context. Like any other generalization, this one admits exceptions. It is tempting, though, to take Smith's comment on travelers with fabulous tales as a deliberate rejoinder to Hume: "When a traveller gives an account of some distant country, he may impose upon our credulity the most groundless and absurd fictions as the most certain matters of fact."[155] Unlike Hume, Smith is not ready to dismiss certain

[153]*Wealth of Nations*, p. 93.
[154]*Wealth of Nations*, p. 152, generally 152–157.
[155]*Moral Sentiments*, p. 314, originally published eleven years after Hume's *Enquiry concerning Understanding*.

tales as beyond the repertoire of invariant human nature; much more seriously than Hume, Smith pursues variations in our moral beliefs traceable to social context.[156]

What distinguishes the *Wealth of Nations*, like Hume's *History*, is its singularly shrewd focus on social context. Like Hume's soldier and priest, Smith's philosopher and street porter derive their characters "from habit, custom, and education."[157] "A half-starved Highland woman frequently bears more than twenty children, while a pampered fine lady is often incapable of bearing any, and is generally exhausted by two or three." Luxury makes the difference.[158] Smith's awareness of the nuances and incentives of social context also yields him a magisterial detachment. His analysis of the East India Company, showing how "irresistible moral causes" make the company "perfectly indifferent about the happiness or misery of their subjects," stands in stark contrast to Edmund Burke's fiery indignation.[159] Instead of pointing an accusing finger at company officers, Smith explains why they act as they do; and his explanation does not represent an unconscionable neglect of morality. Precisely because of its descriptive force, it tells us how to stop the company's abuses.

Two Humean themes resounding frequently through Smith's works are the critique of the social contract, which Smith wholeheartedly accepts, and the obvious place of utility in morals and politics, which Smith rather doubts. Like Hume, Smith thinks that the social contract is parochial and that it rests on a strained understanding of consent: "It is in Britain alone that any consent of the people is required, and God knows it is but a very figurative metaphoricall consent which is given here."[160] Yet while

[156]*Moral Sentiments*, pp. 63, 100–101, 200–211.
[157]*Wealth of Nations*, p. 29, generally 28–30. Note too *Jurisprudence*, pp. 348, 493.
[158]*Wealth of Nations*, pp. 96–97. See *Jurisprudence*, pp. 451 (on superstition), 543 (on courage); *Moral Sentiments*, pp. 204–209.
[159]*Wealth of Nations*, p. 752, generally 746–755, also 635–641. On Burke and India, see Isaac Kramnick, *The Rage of Edmund Burke* (New York: Basic Books, 1977), especially pp. 126–134. Note the parallel suggestion on Alcibiades in *Jurisprudence*, p. 236.
[160]*Jurisprudence*, p. 323, generally pp. 315–316, 323–324, 402–404, 435.

Smith is glad to concede utility a place in morals and politics, he thinks Hume exaggerates both its importance and our realization of its role. Hence "a watch . . . that falls behind above two minutes in a day, is despised by one curious in watches," even though it works well enough; and "all men, even the most stupid and unthinking, abhor fraud, perfidy, and injustice, and delight to see them punished. But few men have reflected upon the necessity of justice to the existence of society, how obvious soever that necessity may appear to be."[161] From one point of view, Smith's acceptance of Hume's case against the social contract jars with his deflation of utility, since utility is the key to Hume's account of political obligation. From another point of view, though, the acceptance and deflation harmonize quite well. More than Hume, Smith sees society as an arena full of unintended consequences. Consent theories, suggesting that people design or control their institutions, do not fit in such a world. At the same time, utility is just too neat an explanation to be attractive. Smith takes particular satisfaction in showing not just how social arrangements are the product of no one's intentions, but how they fail to serve utility. These two ideas are prominent in Smith's *Wealth of Nations*, to which I now turn.

The Comparative Advantages of Market Society

Justification in the *Wealth of Nations* proceeds, as in Hume's *History*, as an exploration and evaluation of possibilities in the world. There is nothing surprising, then, about its combination of descriptive analysis and policy recommendations. Like Hume, Smith wants to sharpen the reader's understanding of the problems and possibilities of contemporary society. But perhaps because of an insensitivity to this approach to justification, the book has generated some very different interpretations. Joseph Cropsey casts Smith as "an architect of our present system of society."[162] Smith, though, rightly emphasizes the largely auton-

[161]*Moral Sentiments*, pp. 180, 89; see generally pp. 20, 71, 87–91, 179–193, 327; *Jurisprudence*, pp. 104–105, 475, 485.
[162]Joseph Cropsey, "Adam Smith," in *History of Political Philosophy*, ed. Leo

omous nature of social development. He may have been influential in many ways—most of them tangled and indirect—but he can hardly be said to have designed later society. Matters are only made worse by drafting Smith into twentieth-century debates.[163] Ernest Mossner, citing Smith's views on education, asserts "that one of the earliest philosophers of capitalism and free enterprise is at the same time one of the earliest philosophers of socialism and the welfare state." And Carl Becker finds in the *Wealth of Nations* a "principle of individual freedom in the economic realm" that is "scarcely more than pure rationalization of the business interests of capitalist employers."[164] Yet it is easy enough to show that Smith is not offering an ideological whitewash of capitalist employers.

Indeed, it is no wonder that some have made Smith a critic of capitalism. Consider the criticisms Smith levels at market society. Landlords "love to reap where they never sowed"; the rent they earn is a "monopoly price . . . not at all proportioned to what the landlord may have laid out upon the improvement of the land, or to what he can afford to take; but to what the former can afford to give."[165] Smith is unmistakably clear that the labor market is fundamentally coercive. Since masters can combine easily (workers' combinations were illegal in Smith's time) and "can hold out much longer" in labor disputes thanks to their savings, the masters "must generally have the advantage" in such disputes.[166] Fellow tradesmen "seldom meet together, even for

---

Strauss and Joseph Cropsey, 2d ed. (Chicago; Rand McNally College Publishing, 1972), p. 607; reprinted as "Adam Smith and Political Philosophy" in Skinner and Wilson, *Essays on Adam Smith*, p. 132. Compare the implausible formulation on the "inception" of societies in Cropsey, *Polity and Economy: An Interpretation of the Principles of Adam Smith* (Westport, Conn.: Greenwood, 1977), p. 56, and see p. 98.
[163]See Donald Winch, *Adam Smith's Politics* (Cambridge: Cambridge University Press, 1979), for a survey and spirited critique of this use of Smith. I cannot, though, assent to Winch's placing Smith in the republican tradition of civic virtue.
[164]Ernest Mossner, *Adam Smith: The Biographical Approach* (Glasgow: University of Glasgow Press, 1969), p. 19; Carl L. Becker, *Modern Democracy* (New Haven: Yale University Press, 1942), pp. 48–49.
[165]*Wealth of Nations*, pp. 67, 161. Compare on unearned income *Jurisprudence*, pp. 341, 490; "Early Draft," in *Jurisprudence*, p. 563.
[166]*Wealth of Nations*, pp. 83–85.

merriment and diversion, but the conversation ends in a conspir-
acy against the publick, or in some contrivance to raise
prices."[167] The struggle for riches is typically motivated by vanity; the rich want "to possess those decisive marks of opulence
which nobody can possess but themselves."[168] Market society is
inevitably inegalitarian: "For one very rich man, there must be at
least five hundred poor, and the affluence of the few supposes
the indigence of the many."[169] The government, "so far as it is
instituted for the security of property, is in reality instituted for
the defence of the rich against the poor, or of those who have
some property against those who have none at all."[170] Finally,
the division of labor dehumanizes the worker even as it showers
down wealth on society: "The man whose whole life is spent in
performing a few simple operations . . . generally becomes as
stupid and ignorant as it is possible for a human creature to become." He loses inventiveness and courage, becoming finally
"incapable of relishing or bearing a part in any rational conversation [or] of conceiving any generous, noble, or tender sentiment,
and consequently of forming any just judgment concerning
many even of the ordinary duties of private life."[171] This litany
is no "pure rationalization of the business interests of capitalist
employers."

The dehumanization of the worker leads to a key theme in
Smith's political economy, one which shows he is no Enlighten-
ment prophet of inevitable progress. At a crucial juncture of his
argument, Smith transforms the analytic distinction between
kinds of income (rent, wages, and profit) into a sociological typology of classes (landlords, workers, and merchants and manu-

[167] *Wealth of Nations*, p. 145.
[168] *Wealth of Nations*, p. 190. See too "Of the Imitative Arts," in Smith's *Essays on Philosophical Subjects*, ed. W. P. D. Wightman and J. C. Bryce, Glasgow ed. (Oxford: Clarendon, 1980), pp. 182–184; *Jurisprudence*, pp. 335–338; and the extraordinary passages in *Moral Sentiments*, pp. 50–66, 180–183. And note *Treatise*, pp. 310–311, 316–324, 357–365, 378; *Enquiry concerning Morals*, p. 246.
[169] *Wealth of Nations*, p. 710.
[170] *Wealth of Nations*, p. 715. See also *Jurisprudence*, pp. 208–209, 338; "Early Draft," in *Jurisprudence*, p. 563.
[171] *Wealth of Nations*, p. 782, generally 781–785. See too *Jurisprudence*, pp. 539–541; *Moral Sentiments*, p. 244. Compare *Wealth of Nations*, pp. 19, 20; *Jurisprudence*, pp. 345–347, 491–492.

facturers). The interests of both landlords and workers are "strictly and inseparably connected with the general interest of the society." But, Smith argues, drawing on his dynamic theory of profit, merchants and manufacturers flourish when society is badly off. There is a conflict of interest between them and the rest of society. And while their ways of life make landlords and workers "ignorant" and unable to understand "the consequences of any publick regulation," merchants and manufacturers cultivate a coolly penetrating understanding of their own interests.[172]

Merchants and manufacturers are, then, at once the only malevolent and the only intelligent actors in the political arena. They have taken full advantage of that status, inspiring some of Smith's most vehement language: "The cruellest of our revenue laws, I will venture to affirm, are mild and gentle, in comparison of some of those which the clamour of our merchants and manufacturers has extorted from the legislature, for the support of their own absurd and oppressive monopolies. Like the laws of Draco, these laws may be said to be written all in blood."[173] The mercantile system is not a mistake flowing from a misguided economic theory. It is the creation of "the producers whose interest has been so carefully attended to; and among this latter class our merchants and manufacturers have been by far the principal architects."[174] Some of the legislation "extorted" by merchants and manufacturers is "perfectly just and reasonable," Smith concedes.[175] Their proposals, however, "ought always to be listened to with great precaution," for they "have generally an interest to deceive and even to oppress the publick," and have done so.[176] Here, ironically, some intentions have been realized in society—but the consequences for the victims are distressing.

This context is most illuminating in considering Smith's defense of "the liberal plan of equality, liberty, and justice," "the

[172]*Wealth of Nations*, pp. 265–267.
[173]*Wealth of Nations*, p. 648; also *Jurisprudence*, pp. 82–83, 529.
[174]*Wealth of Nations*, p. 661. Compare p. 516, where "our country gentlemen" unsuccessfully try to imitate this manipulation of the legislature.
[175]*Wealth of Nations*, p. 643.
[176]*Wealth of Nations*, p. 267. Note p. 599, where merchants "complain of the extravagant gain of other people; but they say nothing of their own."

obvious and simple system of natural liberty" he sketches in the opening sections of the *Wealth of Nations*.[177] By starting with the clarity of his abstract model of the market, Smith can more easily cast the mercantile system as a clutter of absurdities. Self-interested economic man is not Smith's vision of "true" human nature or our "highest" possibilities. Nor are untrammeled market transactions some essence of perfection Smith invented in his armchair. Instead, economic man is part of Smith's abstract model, a prop helping to explain the workings of a free market; and that market is an available possibility, better than mercantilism is or the physiocratic system would be. Smith is not engaging in wholesale "advocacy of the system now called liberal capitalism";[178] he is merely suggesting a reform. The system of "natural" liberty is better than mercantilism. That is its justification. We can then dismiss the wholly ahistorical charge, pressed on the right and the left, that Smith is a chief culprit in the swallowing up of politics by economics.[179] Quite the contrary: Smith wants to break the stranglehold that merchants and manufacturers have on Great Britain's political system. (To add another Smithian rejoinder: the emergence of an independent economic realm is a fact of increasing social differentiation, not a catastrophic mistake.)

Smith is no Pangloss. Natural liberty will have its problems too, even with his proposed state intervention and public education. In the world of concrete political alternatives, no measures are flawless. Smith's noting the flaws of market society, then, is perfectly compatible with his choosing to endorse it. Justification is not, in his view, the identification of the perfect political order. So we need not be puzzled by his ambivalence, or tempted to credit him with two views of the division of labor or of economic plenty.[180] Indeed, Smith does not even expect complete victory for his imperfect alternative: "To expect, in-

[177] *Wealth of Nations*, pp. 664, 687.

[178] Cropsey, "Adam Smith," in Strauss and Cropsey, *History of Political Philosophy*, p. 607; in Skinner and Wilson, *Essays on Adam Smith*, p. 132.

[179] Cropsey, "Adam Smith," in Strauss and Cropsey, *History of Political Philosophy*, or Skinner and Wilson, *Essays on Adam Smith*; Sheldon Wolin, *Politics and Vision* (Boston: Little, Brown, 1960), pp. 292–305.

[180] Compare Cropsey, *Polity and Economy*, pp. 88–96; E. G. West, "Adam

deed, that the freedom of trade should ever be entirely restored in Great Britain, is as absurd as to expect that Oceana or Utopia should ever be established in it."[181] We can, however, expect a curtailment of mercantilism and a consequent easing of the poverty of the workers. There lie Smith's hopes for reform in publishing the *Wealth of Nations*, "the very violent attack I had made upon the whole commercial system of Great Britain."[182]

Feudalism's Collapse and the Fact/Value Gap

In book III of the *Wealth of Nations*, Smith outlines a natural history of economic progress.[183] The country gradually builds up a surplus, which enables the flourishing of the town, the growth of manufacturing, and finally foreign commerce. Yet, concludes Smith, "though this natural order of things must have taken place in some degree in every such society, it has, in all the modern states of Europe, been, in many respects, entirely inverted."[184] There follows a more richly detailed (real) history which combines descriptive and evaluative clout. I want now to suggest that there is nothing mysterious about the combination.

Commencing with the collapse of the Roman empire, land was broken up into large lots, the size of which was maintained by primogeniture and entails. "In those disorderly times, every great landlord was a sort of petty prince," serving as judge, legislator, and military commander. Had an estate been divided up,

---

Smith's Two Views of the Division of Labour," *Economica* 31 (February 1964): 23–32; Albert O. Hirschman, *Shifting Involvements* (Princeton, N.J.: Princeton University Press, 1982), pp. 46–50.

[181]*Wealth of Nations*, p. 476. See on Smith's recognition of the piecemeal nature of political change *Wealth of Nations*, pp. 435, 899.

[182]Smith to Andreas Holt, 26 oct 1780, in *The Correspondence of Adam Smith*, ed. Ernest Campbell Mossner and Ian Simpson Ross, Glasgow ed. (Oxford: Clarendon, 1977), p. 251.

[183]For a contemporary view of natural history, see Dugald Stewart, "Account of the Life and Writings of Adam Smith, LL.D.," in Smith, *Essays on Philosophical Subjects*, pp. 292–296; for a modern account, Andrew Skinner, "Natural History in the Age of Adam Smith," *Political Studies* 15 (February 1967): 32–48.

[184]*Wealth of Nations*, p. 380.

THEORY IN CONTEXT: HUME AND SMITH

it would have been exposed to being "oppressed and swallowed up by the incursions of its neighbours." Primogeniture thus solved the problem of ensuring security (though if the "neighbours" are other lords possessing their estates by primogeniture, the problem is also caused by primogeniture).

This modest beginning brings Smith to a critical point:

> Laws frequently continue in force long after the circumstances, which first gave occasion to them, and which could alone render them reasonable, are no more. In the present state of Europe, the proprietor of a single acre of land is as perfectly secure of his possession as the proprietor of a hundred thousand. The right of primogeniture, however, still continues to be respected, and as of all institutions it is the fittest to support the pride of family distinctions, it is still likely to endure for many centuries. In every other respect, nothing can be more contrary to the real interest of a numerous family, than a right which, in order to enrich one, beggars all the rest of the children.[185]

The argument beautifully exemplifies the genuinely critical force of historicism, a bugaboo conjured up by Leo Strauss. Focusing on the whirligig of history, argues Strauss, condemns us to whimsically subjective judgments; only natural right, he holds, can provide a truly critical standard.[186] But Smith needs no critical standard of nature to condemn primogeniture, an institution still supported by his contemporaries. He detaches himself from the received views of his day and critically evaluates them, not by asserting that they are contrary to nature but by showing they are useless and even harmful. There is, however, more here to say about the role of facts and values, is and ought, in history and political theory; so I will continue.

Surrounded by various tax schemes and other policies, primogeniture and feudalism persisted. For a variety of reasons, this tenure system precluded progress and development. But city dwellers, at first "a very poor, mean sett of people,"[187] gained

[185]*Wealth of Nations*, pp. 383–384.
[186]Leo Strauss, *Natural Right and History* (Chicago: University of Chicago Press, 1953), pp. 9–34, especially 17–18.
[187]*Wealth of Nations*, p. 397. Note *History* I:488.

their independence after some complex shifts in schemes of taxation and legal status. The emergence of cities as "a sort of independent republicks" and wealthy trading centers sets the stage for Smith to reveal some unintended consequences.[188] The conflicts of interest at this point are straightforward: "The lords despised the burghers, whom they considered . . . as a parcel of emancipated slaves"—and enviably wealthy slaves at that. The burghers, "plundered . . . upon every occasion without mercy or remorse[,] . . . naturally hated and feared the lords." The king, whose largely nominal authority over powerful lords was always open to forcible rebuttal, found himself joined by ties of interest to the burghers. "They were the enemies of his enemies, and it was his interest to render them as secure and independent of those enemies as he could."[189] The burghers took advantage of their security to continue economic advancement and thus escaped their mean poverty, eventually to become the bourgeoisie.

This inauspicious development was, Smith argues, of decisive political importance. Feudal law and order had been haphazard at best. Feudal lords "contrived to make war according to their own discretion, almost continually upon one another, and very frequently upon the king; and the open country still continued to be a scene of violence, rapine, and disorder." The lords had nothing better to do with their wealth than keep retainers, nothing better to do with retainers than send them into battle. But once the burghers offered their expensive goods for sale, the lords had a new way of consuming their wealth. "All for ourselves, and nothing for other people, seems, in every age of the world, to have been the vile maxim of the masters of mankind." So they dismissed their retainers to buy the proffered goods. "For a pair of diamond buckles perhaps, or for something as frivolous and useless, they exchanged the maintenance, or what is the same thing, the price of the maintenance of a thousand men for a year, and with it the whole weight and authority which it could give them. . . . Thus, for the gratification of the most childish, the meanest and the most sordid of all vanities, they

[188]*Wealth of Nations*, p. 401. The essentials of Smith's analysis are in Hume, *History* II:564–565, IV:215.
[189]*Wealth of Nations*, p. 402.

gradually bartered their whole power and authority."[190] Smith takes pleasure in dwelling on the irony of the situation. The nobles forfeited their power "for trinkets and baubles, fitter to be the play-things of children than the serious pursuits of men"; and neither the nobles nor the burghers ever intended to bring down the feudal order.[191]

But that is what they did. Smith notes two happy consequences of this historical outcome. First, quite simply, the death of feudalism meant the (quickly realized) possibility of "regular government," since there were no more nobles sporting private armies.[192] Second, the direct personal dependence marking feudalism was replaced by the interdependence of market society. That interdependence, Smith argues, is freedom. The expenditure of "a man of ten thousand a year" in market society contributes to the maintenance of many workers. "He generally contributes, however, but a very small proportion to that of each. . . . Though he contributes, therefore, to the maintenance of them all, they are all more or less independent of him, because generally they can all be maintained without him."[193]

Like any other good historian, Smith has of course done more than string brute facts together. His account includes social theory, allowing him to discuss interests and consequences, and a neat conceptual finesse in explaining how interdependence is independence. It is also shot through from start to finish with values of all kinds. The sort I am concerned with here are not those

[190]*Wealth of Nations*, pp. 418–419, and see 908–909 for a quick sketch of the argument. Compare the appearance of "jewels, trinkets, gewgaws" on p. 349. Smith carries through a parallel argument to explain the decline of the Church (pp. 802–804) and Roman and Athenian nobles (*Jurisprudence*, pp. 227, 410; *Lectures on Rhetoric and Belles Lettres*, pp. 150–151). See generally *Jurisprudence*, pp. 49–51, 188–191, 202–203, 417–420.

[191]*Wealth of Nations*, pp. 421, 422.

[192]*Wealth of Nations*, p. 421, also 412. See too, in no uncertain terms, *Jurisprudence*, pp. 262–264, especially 264 ("the nobility are the greatest opposers and oppressors of liberty that we can imagine"), and p. 333.

[193]*Wealth of Nations*, pp. 419–420. The point is in Hume, "Whether the British Government Inclines More to Absolute Monarchy or to a Republic," in *Essays*, p. 49. Arguably, for Smith a moral regard for all one's fellows, far from being wired into human nature, becomes possible only in a relatively egalitarian society: note *Moral Sentiments*, p. 55; *Lectures on Rhetoric and Belles Lettres*, p. 124. See too, on social structure and morality, *Wealth of Nations*, p. 794.

allowing him to frame a coherent discourse, but those identifying the burghers as mean, the nobles as childish, and the history as progress. What shall we say about this combination of facts and values?

Philosophers often write about the gap between is and ought, fact and value, in an oddly abstract way. Values, they tell us, are different from facts and cannot be derived from them, so there is something suspect about the introduction of values. It is as though we had been uttering purely descriptive propositions, and then someone offered a purely evaluative one. What would we say then? The situation would indeed be baffling. Fortunately, it never arises. There are social criteria for making "value judgments," criteria Smith draws on freely. These criteria shift over time. They are subverted by events and by arguments. But the process is a gradual one that never starts from scratch, and the piecemeal process of revision can be perfectly rational. Nothing suspect, then, is happening when Smith holds that the breakdown of the feudal order was a good thing. No alarms ring, no whistles screech, no umpires come rushing in from the sidelines to announce a foul.

To justify the claim that the breakdown of feudalism was a good thing, Smith need only show that people are better off after feudalism than they were under it. He does that by contrasting lawlessness with peace, dependence with interdependence, poverty with prosperity. Similarly, to justify his criticism of primogeniture, Smith need only show that it no longer serves any purpose better than family vanity. The burden of justification comes in exploring real and possible worlds. We need not think that justification means showing why peace, freedom, and prosperity are good, or why vanity is questionable. It is of course true that Smith never once derives ought from is, never once proves to the diligent skeptic that poverty is bad, never once finds immutable premises outside society and politics to ground his conclusions. But what would be the point of demanding that he do such things? If Smith's account is pretty much correct and complete—and no peculiarly philosophical issues arise in deciding whether it is—surely nothing more remains to be said.

The pattern of argument we find in Smith's *Wealth of Nations* and in Hume's writings, especially the *History*, is what I call contextual justification. Neither Smith nor Hume attempts the magician's trick of pulling values out of a world of disembodied facts. Instead, each focuses on a given social context to explore its problems and possibilities. That an institution is justified, in this view, is always a modest conclusion. It means not that it has been certified by some airtight philosophical theory as inherently correct, but that it is the best available option—or, with a pessimistic twist, that it is not so bad as the alternatives. Indeed, given our ignorance and the stickiness of political change, justification may identify an alternative that is just good enough. And that, once we leave our own philosophers' closets and recall our own politically bleak world, is the best we are going to get.

CONCLUSION

Like it or not, one fact about political argument is undeniable: it goes on interminably. Two interlocutors with passionate convictions may find that arguing into the wee hours of the morning will persuade each only that the other is dreadfully mistaken. I take it the experience of inconclusive and sometimes acrimonious political debate is common enough. But even meaningful and constructive debates, debates conducted by more thoughtful individuals, stretch on. Taken as a social phenomenon, our political debate is just the same. We learn some things (and forget others), so the debate changes; but it is never settled, never resolved. Certainly the same is true of that part of the debate conducted in academic journals.

What shall we make of this endlessness? Hobbesian skepticism beckons as a good explanatory theory. We dress up our particular appetites and aversions in the fancy wardrobe of moral language; our opponents do the same. Our debates, ringing with claims about justice, right, and the rest, may sound grandly objective. But, urges the skeptic, that appearance is illusory. The underlying reality is that we are brandishing mere personal preference. Some people simply like Medicaid funding for abortion; others dislike it. The subject in the end admits of no more reasoning than the choice between vanilla and chocolate ice cream.

There is another familiar route to skepticism here. A skeptic may agree that there is some political consensus in our society.

[218]

This skeptic, however, may be struck not by the idea that all the categories of political debate are epistemologically bankrupt, but by historical variation. Aristotle assigned politics a more essential role in the good life than liberals are willing to grant it. Perhaps, muses the skeptic, that sort of disagreement shows that political questions cannot have right answers. Nor would demonstrating the basic coherence of the Western tradition, assuming such a thing could be done, dissolve the skeptic's doubts. There are always cultural anthropologists ready and waiting to unveil exotic tribes and bizarre rituals. Their parade of astonishing societies will demolish any assurance that in the end we really can all agree. If Hobbes is moved by an epistemology leaving no room for objective values, this skeptic is moved by visions of cultural relativism and incommensurability. How can we rest content with our views, knowing as we do the extent of disagreement about them in other times and places, knowing even that they may be downright incoherent or incomprehensible to others?

These skeptics, then, react to political disagreement with two points: maybe it's all mere personal preference, and maybe political principles are inescapably culture-bound and therefore inadequate. If a justification must resolve these doubts, it seems, it must be more solid, more conclusive, than everyday political argument. Justification should supplant our fledgling and incompetent efforts; political theorists will boast expertise enabling them to succeed where we are doomed to fail.

We need not, then, think of foundationalism as motivated by an inordinate attachment to deduction and geometry. Instead we can cast it as a strategy to meet skeptical doubts. The foundationalist promises to find undeniable first premises and, adding only innocuous minor premises, deduce correct political conclusions. His justification should dispel doubts about the status of political arguments, for we have to grant both his premises and what follows deductively. His justification should also dispel doubts about cultural variation. He may take the high road and justify timeless political principles immune to social change. Then he can, with Hobbes, propose to teach his doctrine forever after in the universities, and so enable us to freeze our politics in eternal accord with some immutable rule of right. Or he may concede that political institutions ought to change in changing societies, but say that all the variation is worked in by the minor premises. If the first premises are true in all times and places, he will say, we can live with political variation.

Surely there are other routes to skepticism, other motivations for adopting a foundationalist strategy of justification. A full account would encompass much of the history of philosophy. Here I mean only to suggest that foundationalism is indeed the symbol of the quest for certainty. Again, it may be hard to find purely foundational arguments. Few if any political theorists today will claim that their arguments rest on undeniable premises safe from the ravages of historical change. Even in the history of political theory, that claim may well seem a deliberate piece of bragging, a conceit functioning as shameless self-advertising. Regardless, viewed as an ideal type, foundationalism should still be illuminating. Whatever their departures from the ideal type, many political theorists have indeed set out to achieve something very like a purely foundationalist justification. They have turned away from politics to such remote concerns as epistemology and theology. There they have hoped to find certainties that, suitably massaged, would yield firm political conclusions. Let me now quickly review the theories I've examined to emphasize my focus on justification.

It is safe to say—if only because he tells us so—that Hobbes was troubled by the political unrest and religious fanaticism of his time. Only an absolute state, he thought, could put an end to the wild excesses of Puritan radicalism. But Hobbes wanted to say something more than that: he wrote *Leviathan* as well as *Behemoth*. He tries to show that, given human nature, prudence dictates obedience to the sovereign in virtually all things, regardless of the social setting. He also tries to show that his conclusions have moral force, since they are built into the moral and political concepts. Yet, if the case for the Leviathan state is to be persuasive, Hobbes must focus on a social context specific enough to make his choice the real choice. And no amount of conceptual juggling, however magically executed, will provide responses to our substantive concerns about morals and politics. Nor, for that matter, will any amount of insistence on grim necessity.

Locke's *Second Treatise* simultaneously develops three social-contract arguments. As history, the social contract is one of the many weapons with which Locke assaults Filmer's political theory. As an ongoing and silent process that each individual takes part in on reaching majority, it provides a theory of political obligation. As a hypothetical agreement of rational agents, it provides a theory of political legitimacy. Yet the *Treatises* grind to an untimely halt. Locke fails to explain why consent obliges or why we should care for the choices of hypothetical agents. Through a host of other writings, ranging from epistemology to theology, Locke develops a moral theory centering on our knowledge of God's existence and will, the terrifying prospects of the afterlife, and the quintessentially rational pursuit of pleasure and avoidance of pain. That theory, I argued, neither works nor helps complete the argument of the *Treatises*.

In all its variants, utilitarianism presents a single principle supposed to make all our choices for us. All we need do is maximize utility, whether utility be conceived as a family of agreeable mental states or as a behaviorist's preference rankings. The procedure looks perfectly straightforward: name the alternatives, compute the utility each would produce, and choose the alternative yielding the highest utility score. Yet utilitarianism, I argued, unravels under closer inspection. Classical utilitarianism founders on incommensurability. And far from presenting a complete decision procedure, it leaves us helpless when confronted with questions about distributive considerations, risk and uncertainty, and time preference. Von Neumann–Morgenstern utilitarianism, while it avoids some of these difficulties, leaves us wholly unable to criticize preferences. More importantly, utilitarians of both stripes give us no good reasons to adopt their principle, and surely a principle nominated to do so much justificatory work itself stands in need of some justification.

I do not mean to underestimate the extraordinary dissimilarities among these theories. In other contexts—a study, say, of the role religion plays in political theory, or the use of rhetoric—the differences might prove decisive. Most remarkable for my purposes, however, is the basic strategy of justification they share. They may turn to an abstract account of human nature, to language, to God's will and rationality, to an immutable first (and last) principle of judgment. In each case, though, the project is to find undeniable premises outside society and politics to serve as foundations for building a theory. No one, Hobbes thinks, can deny that anarchy must always be a disaster worse than any state, or that whatever principles are embedded in our concepts are true. No one, Locke thinks, can deny his proof of God's existence and the resultant moral theory guaranteed to stand firm against all comers. No one, the utilitarians think, can deny the principle of utility and whatever judgments it yields. The quest for certainty drives these political theorists to dwell on extrapolitical concerns.

One result of investing theoretical energy in pursuing foundations is particularly noteworthy. For all their stature as political theorists, Hobbes and Locke spend little time writing about politics. And though utilitarians sometimes do focus quite intensively on politics—take Bentham's constitutional writings, concrete institutional analysis best measured out in reams—their political writings stand across a crucial gap from their utilitarianism. While they may assure us that this proposal is more felicific than that, they make no serious effort to perform the mandated calculations. Given the goal of constructing what Bentham calls a chain of proofs, a deductive argument stretching from epistemically secure first premises to politically controversial conclusions, it makes sense to shortchange politics. Detachment from controversy, thinks the foundationalist, requires leaving the realm of controversy behind for a while.

Now I can venture a suggestion—a suggestion and no more —on what is generally wrong with foundational theories. Suppose for a moment that someone succeeds, where so many have failed, in discovering the foundations of political theory. He arrives at some remote premises that we all concede are undeniable. Then he triumphantly unfolds the implications contained in the junction of the premises and the true minor premises he adds: the United States may sell grain to the Soviet Union, Medicaid should not fund abortions on demand for the poor, and secular liberal society is just fine, thank you very much. The outcome he counts on, of course, is agreement, the end of doubt—the best sign that he has developed a stunning justification. But contrast our political commitments to our commitment to his foundations. The political commitments are staunch, even fervent, carefully considered in vivid and concrete contexts; the foundational commitment is new, tentative, probably fuzzy because the foundations are so abstract. If it turns out they are incompatible, which are we more likely to abandon? What seemed undeniable on its own may seem controversial or false once its political implications are unveiled.

Our foundationalist may protest vociferously. We cannot just pick and choose our commitments this way. His premises are more than attractive; they are genuinely undeniable; the undeniability inheres in the premises, extorting our allegiance whether we like it or not. (Compare Kant's account of the tie between reason and the moral law or the rhapsodies to truth of William James's opponents.) Our procedure is whimsical, subjective, arbitrary, the death of reason. The protest, though, fails to come to terms with perfectly sensible features of the way our web of beliefs does evolve. We evaluate abstract views by examining their concrete implications. Perhaps the foundationalist will now urge that our putative knowledge is on an all too precarious footing to be secure. If we do evaluate beliefs by seeing how they cohere with our other beliefs, how they connect up with views we are reasonably confident of, still we should not. We are faulty epistemic engines, in need of radical overhaul.

Foundationalism and skepticism thus feed one another. The failure of each new attempt at creating a foundational justification makes skepticism more attractive. And skepticism makes foundationalism seem imperative; it confirms our intuitive view that only a foundational argument could count as a justification. A skeptic, we might say, is nothing but a disappointed foundationalist.

An illustration should help make the point. Suppose Carleton is given to philosophical doubts. Then he will rather indiscrimi-

nately appeal to Hume's is/ought gap to doubt all moral and political positions. If Hume's rule of law allows us to avoid tyranny, Carleton will urge that tyranny is merely monarchy
misliked. Reminded that there are good reasons for misliking
certain monarchs, reasons built into the criteria for tyranny,
Carleton will ask what makes them good reasons. Why not approve of Caligula? No values follow from the facts, so all values
are equally suspect. Carleton will then demand that Hume explain why people should not suffer and die under tyrants, that
Smith explain why peace, freedom, and prosperity are better
than their opposites. "Isn't it mere personal preference either
way?" he will ask.

A stance like Carleton's consigns us to a bleak choice: either
embrace skepticism or keep attempting to frame a foundationalist justification. There are plenty of other options, though. We
may find some alternative mode of argument that meets skeptical
doubts in some other way, or we may find an approach that ignores skeptical doubts. Those unhappy both with continuing attempts to create foundationalist justifications and with embracing skepticism have good reason to look for other options.

The option I want to endorse, of course, is what I call contextual justification, best exemplified by Hume, especially in the
History, and by Smith. Hume provides no deductive argument
from undeniable premises to defend the rule of law. Instead, he
appeals to a few senses of liberty to show that it is better than absolute sovereignty and civil war, two available alternatives. Similarly, Smith never seriously pursues his suggestion that a free
market is the system of natural liberty. Despite the foundationalist echoes of the label, he defends market society by showing
how it leaves people better off than mercantilism does or than the
physiocratic system would. I take it the viability of these arguments is clear enough. I want now to say something a bit more
schematic about their structure.

In a formula: one justifies something by showing that it is better than the alternatives. But how do we figure out what is better? Don't we first need a substantive moral and political theory
to rank outcomes? And wouldn't that theory be foundationally
derived? We need not think of two discrete steps, first framing

an evaluative theory and second canvassing possibilities. Instead the process is dialectical. We begin with the values we hold and the political world we inhabit. Our politics will fail to measure up to our expectations. It will yield bad outcomes in some contexts, pose problems in others, and be hard to make normative sense of still elsewhere. So our values will guide us to explore other possibilities. Just as a scientist is appropriately guided by existing theory in constructing alternative hypotheses, so we need not try to list all possibilities. And describing the possibilities as we normally do, with is and ought systematically interwoven, will force us to criticize and refine our values. To take an example, we may find that community in modern society would have to mean enforcing consensus, so it might come to seem less attractive. As the argument continues, we deepen our grasp of both our political options and what's attractive. So the reader of Hume's *History* gains a better understanding of liberty and finds the materials to scuttle the reigning notion of sovereignty. Likewise, the reader of Smith's *Wealth of Nations* gains a rich sense of the problems and possibilities of market society.

Nothing is certain, nothing is fixed, in such an argument. We have no incentive to find immutable premises, no reason to devote much energy to epistemology, theology, metaphysics, and the like. We cannot plausibly claim that our conclusions should be applied in all times and places. A contextual justification may then seem much weaker than a foundational justification. But successful foundational justifications are philosophers' pet unicorns; we have yet to see one. Contextual justifications provide a preponderance of good reasons, so they are good enough to qualify as justifications, even if they do not deliver the certainty that foundational arguments might.

A skeptic may want to deny that contextual justifications are good enough to count as justifications. Justification, she may urge, is supposed to meet doubt and disagreement. The sort of argument I am endorsing, however, doesn't begin to grapple with skeptical doubts. It evades all sorts of issues: What good is justice, or equality, or liberty? Why think our values are worth any weight in a political theory? They just happen to be ours, since we inherited them. Historical artifacts are the clutter we need to brush aside.

How should we interpret the skeptic's doubts? She may have in mind some theory of ideology. She may think, to take a crude version, that our deeply held values are nothing but epiphenomena, ideas tossed off by the material base of society that rationalize exploitation and so ensure the continued dominion of the ruling class. Now this suggestion a contextualist will be more than happy to entertain, for it is an intriguing way of using social facts and theory to criticize our values. We will then want to know if indeed that is the role our ideas play.

The skeptic may be pressing a rather different point, however. She may be once again urging the view that Carleton took: either our values are objective or they are mere personal preferences. In Robert Nozick's words, "In discussions of ethics one sometimes thinks, 'how could one convince some particular figure, say Stalin, Hitler, or Mao, that he is wrong; if there is no argument guaranteed to convince him, doesn't that show that ethics really is subjective, merely a matter of preference or opinion?'"[1] To press the force of the objection, the skeptic will ask her skeptical questions: What is wrong with killing innocent people for fun? Why treat people any differently from wrenches? Why not devote ourselves to maximizing the number of blue objects in the world? Why not take wearing a brown chamois shirt as an all-purpose excuse? Only a demonstration of objective moral and political truths will satisfy the skeptic.

I have no such demonstration to offer. (Has anyone else?) I do not believe, though, that we need to meet such doubts head on. Instead, provided we have an account of why they are not worth pursuing, we can ignore them. I am willing to concede that contextual justifications will not dislodge skeptical doubt and disagreement. My strategy is to fence them off, to explain what is different about them and why the differences entitle us to sidestep them. This strategy is hardly novel; indeed it seems a plau-

[1]Robert Nozick, *Philosophical Explanations* (Cambridge, Mass.: Harvard University Press, Belknap Press, 1981), p. 17.

sible extension of arguments from the history of ethics. I want now to canvass three accounts of what is odd about skeptical doubts and defend a fourth.

The first is from Samuel Clarke, that bitter foe of Thomas Hobbes. Moral principles, says Clarke, are "notoriously plain and self-evident," just like geometric axioms. Thus someone who advances the epistemological thesis that value is necessarily subjective is terribly confused. Similarly, someone who doubts our entrenched moral convictions is in as dubious a position as someone who wonders if the shortest distance between two points is a line. The bravery—or is it bravado?—of Clarke's account is charming, but it relies on an untenable moral epistemology. Critics and champions alike of the analytic/synthetic dichotomy will want to reject Clarke's account. The former will deny the existence of any statements privileged in the way Clarke supposed geometric axioms are. The latter will be hard pressed to assimilate moral judgments, oozing with import as they do, to geometry.

The second is from Prichard and Ross, twentieth-century intuitionists. Where Clarke casts our fundamental moral convictions as axioms, they think of them as unimpeachable sense-data. Someone who doubts a moral principle is to be treated just as someone who doubts a sensory experience in ideal observing conditions. Just as we cannot provide an independent line of argument proving the existence of the table we experience, we can say nothing more for our moral beliefs than that we experience them. Now, a diligent skeptic might embrace the suggestion that ethics is as solid as our knowledge of the external world. The skeptic might clutch a copy of Berkeley and say that neither is at all solid. But we need not retreat to such skeptical extremes to rebut this version of intuitionism. I have already noted that intuitionism relies on a full-blown moral reality as ontologically solid as the empirical world. I have noted too Bentham's crushing attack on such views: They make meaningful moral debate impossible once we reach the level of intuitive principles.

The third is from Hume, and it demands a bit more consideration:

Ask a man *why he uses exercise*; he will answer, *because he desires to keep his health.* If you then enquire, *why he desires health*, he will readily reply, *because sickness is painful.* If you push your enquiries farther, and desire a reason *why he hates pain*, it is impossible he can ever give any. This is an ultimate end, and is never referred to any other object. . . . It is impossible there can be a progress *in infinitum*; and that one thing can always be a reason why another is desired. Something must be desirable on its own account, and because of its immediate accord or agreement with human sentiment and affection.[2]

What makes this view plausible is the means/end scheme, which surprisingly Hume embraces with even more gusto than Aristotle does. If someone wonders why he ought not to kill his neighbor, there can be no answer; life is an ultimate end. If reason can pronounce only on means, never on ends, and skeptics propose different ultimate ends, then of course we cannot reason with the skeptic. This line gives away too much, however. In making constructive debate on ultimate ends impossible, it shares an embarrassing weakness with intuitionism. Nor will we get very far by embracing the means/end scheme and trying to show that reason can judge ends. Instead, we need to step outside the means/end scheme. It is a useful heuristic in some settings: it does a fair job capturing the deliberations of an agent aiming at a preappointed goal. But it hardly captures the full range of deliberation and human action. Again, witness Sidgwick's paradox of hedonism. We can defend one value not as a means to another, but as partly constitutive of another, or of a greater whole.[3] Even our most important values can be questioned, and defended by showing their place within the larger realm of our commitments.

[2]David Hume, *An Enquiry concerning the Principles of Morals*, in *Enquiries*, ed. L. A. Selby-Bigge, 3d ed. rev. by P. H. Nidditch (Oxford: Clarendon, 1978), p. 293. Hume's italics.

[3]These issues arise in interpreting Aristotle's *Ethics*. See J. L. Ackrill, "Aristotle on *Eudaimonia*," *Proceedings of the British Academy* 60 (1974): 339–359, reprinted in *Essays on Aristotle's Ethics*, ed. Amélie Oksenberg Rorty (Berkeley: University of California Press, 1980); John M. Cooper, *Reason and Human Good in Aristotle* (Cambridge, Mass.: Harvard University Press, 1975).

Talk of means and ends, however, does not offer the best starting point for working up a viable theory. Instead I wish to recall the controversy between descriptivists and prescriptivists. In particular, I have in mind Philippa Foot's "Moral Arguments" and "Moral Beliefs," and R. M. Hare's "Descriptivism."[4] Foot complains that, in the view of moral argument offered by Hare and others, one could offer completely eccentric moral views with impunity. Someone might say, for example, that no one should look at hedgehogs in the light of the moon. But this, Foot suggests, is nonsensical. Surely the eccentric has to tell some story about the point of this principle. Morality and goodness at the very least impose evidentiary rules on what plausible candidates are, rules buttressed in turn by human interests and the ordinary circumstances of human life. Responding, Hare defends the logical separability of evaluative and descriptive components of meaning. It may be, he says, that we take for granted certain criteria for good wines. It may even be that those criteria are now embedded in our vocabulary for discussing wines. Someone whose view differs, however, can always invent a new word, call it φ, to name the descriptive components of the words we use to commend wine. He could say that he saw why the wine was φ wine but still ask why it was good. Such a man, concludes Hare, would be making no logical error.

The conventional battle lines here have Foot opposing Hare down the line. But despite the prominence this debate has had, what I take to be the central thesis of Foot's view, even at this early date, is perfectly compatible with Hare's. Foot need not be read as defending the analytic implications of our current vocabulary. We can leave aside the issues involving the meaning of the moral concepts, and for that matter such related issues as whether illocutionary force exhausts the allegedly special commending role that evaluative discourse plays. We can grant Hare the is/ought gap once he deliberately retreats from conventional

[4]Both Foot essays, originally from the late 1950s, are reprinted in her *Virtues and Vices and Other Essays in Moral Philosophy* (Berkeley: University of California Press, 1978); Hare's essay is in his *Essays on the Moral Concepts* (Berkeley: University of California Press, 1973).

views to make what he insists is a purely logical point. Still, though, someone offering a quirky view needs to support it. There must be some account of why, for example, we should think killing innocent people for fun is permissible. Absent any such account—if for example the skeptic says, "Well, maybe it is; can you prove it's not?"—we are, I want to suggest, entitled to ignore the skeptic.

Suppose we challenge the skeptic, and she produces some account. Perhaps a special context, or some apparently strange beliefs about the consequences of murdering the innocent, will make sense of her suggestion. However strange the account, however far removed from our ordinary views, we can now launch an exploration into contextual justifications. We can compare and contrast the two views, and use the skeptic's views to deepen and refine our own. If incommensurability rears its ugly head, we need to try to find some theoretical ground capable of making both views comprehensible. A failure to find such a ground should be taken as a limitation of our current theoretical vocabulary, not a permanent tragedy. Incommensurability, if it exists, testifies to the narrowness of our current epistemic horizons, not any deep incoherence in the world.

But typically the skeptic will refuse to provide any account. She will offer just the one strange suggestion and deliberately leave it dangling, a lonely witness to the logical possibility of evaluative eccentricity. She may urge that her principle is good in itself, or an ultimate good, but that move simply declares that she will not support it. Far from offering an especially good reason, it offers no reason at all. Were we interested in ferreting out the skeptic's logical mistake, we would need some response. But why think our views are impeached by the mere logical availability of an alternative? The implicit standard motivating the attempt to refute skepticism must be that our current beliefs are worthless unless they have some unique logical status. Once identified, though, this standard seems decidedly odd. We can let the skeptic's point stand as a logical observation. But we seek substantively compelling views, not logically assured ones. Her views may be as logically conceivable as ours, but are they any more than that?

The view I am sketching is a pragmatist one.[5] My point is that we need consider only views advanced in a context making them intelligible. Nor is this some special requirement of evaluative discourse. There is no point debating the suggestion, offered on its own, that heat does not exist. But if the suggestion is advanced as part of a larger, theoretical story about the phenomena we now use heat to describe, we can sensibly discuss revising or even jettisoning our current views. Likewise, there is no point trying to make sense of the single utterance, "Horseflies are magical." But if that view is advanced along with (explicitly stated or implicitly understood) background views about magic, about the sacred and the profane, about the hierarchy of organic life, we can make sense of it. Finally, there is no point entertaining the suggestion, offered alone, that Hitler is the greatest figure in world history. The suggestion is perplexing not because it violates our "intuitions" on the matter, but because it comes with no accompanying account of greatness that plausibly applies to Hitler's deeds. In all these cases, the conceivability of views incredibly unlike our own does nothing to undercut our views.

This approach does not refute skeptical doubts, but it does, I believe, offer a principled account of which doubts we may ignore and why we may ignore them. Skeptical doubts are those offered with no supporting context, no reasons that make them intelligible.[6] To avoid misunderstanding, let me emphasize that

[5]I draw here, perhaps indiscriminately, on William James, *Pragmatism* (Cambridge, Mass.: Harvard University Press, 1975), and his *The Meaning of Truth* (Cambridge, Mass.: Harvard University Press, 1975); Ludwig Wittgenstein, *On Certainty*, ed. G. E. M. Anscombe and G. H. von Wright and trans. Denis Paul and G. E. M. Anscombe (New York: Harper & Row, 1972); and the now well-established antifoundationalist line in epistemology and philosophy of science. For an introduction, see Michael Williams, *Groundless Belief* (Oxford: Basil Blackwell, 1977), unfortunately missing any account of Paul Feyerabend; for a recent provocative exploration, Paul M. Churchland, *Scientific Realism and the Plasticity of Mind* (Cambridge: Cambridge University Press, 1979), which is useful as a challenge to Richard Rorty's *Philosophy and the Mirror of Nature* (Princeton, N.J.: Princeton University Press, 1979).

[6]It is tempting to adopt a theory of meaning in which the meaning of a concept lies in the way it connects up with other concepts, and the meaning of sentences is in turn bound up with a network of other sentences. Given such a theory, we could explore the possibility that the skeptic's suggestions are literally

skeptical doubts are not the same as politically radical doubts. The latter come complete with elaborate theories supporting them. Contextual justifications do bracket out skeptical doubts; yet they must evaluate radical alternatives when those are offered. There is then no reason to think that refusing to try our hands at the old game of refuting the skeptic means committing ourselves to any politically conservative outcomes. The method of argument I am endorsing has no commitments to incremental reform of the status quo. Reform might be better than where we stand, but so might revolution.

Some examples might help. Suppose Lizzie entertains political doubts. Hume's argument for the rule of law will make her wonder about shortcomings of the rule of law and possible benefits of tyranny. So she will ask about the social costs of legalistic rituals and the opportunity to enjoy moral rebirth under a freewheeling, dynamic leader. Or she may argue that the rule of law leaves us with a somnolent, pathetically mediocre society, whereas tyranny, with its unpredictability, makes for excitement and forges great leaders. These views we can take up and critically evaluate. Less hypothetically, consider Marx's attack on capitalism. Marx, I believe, offers no theory of justice condemning capitalism. Instead he attempts a justification at once radical and contextual of the claim that communism would be better than capitalism. Many of our moral convictions are transformed in the process (assuming we follow Marx). A profound theoretical reinterpretation of capitalism dictates revising our initial views, facts as well as values. Marxism, if right, gives us all sorts of good reasons to reject capitalism. Why demand a formal theory of justice in addition?

The contrast between Lizzie or Marx and the skeptic should further illuminate the difference between (philosophically) skeptical and (politically) radical doubts. The skeptic steps wholly outside our web of beliefs, or pretends to. She snatches up some belief, situates it in no alternative web, and demands an account of why it is not true. The radical may suspend her commitments

meaningless; they parasitically feed on our current views to seem meaningful, but since they deliberately depart from all of them, that appearance is illusory. I cannot here explore these issues.

to some part of our web. She may even over time spin a web very different from our own. But at any stage a supporting web is there to make sense of her stance. Piecemeal revision may take us to faraway destinations.

That radical opposition may be contextually framed, that it may sensibly lead us to a vision of politics wholly at odds with conventional views, should defuse the worry that our starting beliefs are mere historical artifacts. They are artifacts, from one point of view anyway, but that hardly shows they are arbitrary or irrational. In any case, they are all subject to criticism and revision, something that cannot be said of the first premises of a foundational view.

There is a tradition, growing out of Hume and Weber, of finding the activity of criticizing values mysterious. Granted, the argument goes, we can show that one value is an inappropriate means to realizing some greater value; or we can show that achieving the value is impossible, or too costly, given facts about society. But how can we mount frontal assaults on the value itself? Rationality can approach values only through discussions of means and ends.

I do not mean to underestimate the critical power of the means/end scheme. We can draw our opponent's attention to unsavory implications of his view and emphasize the attractiveness of our own. We can subvert his view, showing how it serves causes he reviles. But these moves are the beginning, not the end, of criticism. Again, all we need do is transfer our attention from the means/end scheme to the web of beliefs to notice other promising routes of attack. Taken together, our values have some point. There will be, say, some account of human interests that draws them together into a meaningful whole. In political theory, as in the social sciences, we want to be attentive to issues of meaning and interpretation as well as those of causation and consequences.[7] Such options mean that despite the plaintive la-

---

[7]This split goes back at least to Mill's "Coleridge" and "Bentham," and can be seen easily in Freud as interpreter of dreams and parapraxes against Freud as theorist of the causal primacy of childhood experience. For the best recent account and defense of an interpretive approach, see Clifford Geertz, "Thick De-

ments of neo-Aristotelians,[8] we need no highest good, no pyra-
midal ordering of our commitments, to sustain rational debate.

Reinterpreting our theoretical concepts is, then, one potent
tool of critical revision. Consider the claim that the right to sell
one's labor in the market is a precious hallmark of freedom. This
claim may be compelling as feudalism and apprenticeships stub-
bornly endure; it may be quite another matter in industrial capitalism. Or consider Sophocles's violent attack on heroic ethics:
Ajax, bloody with the slaughter of the sheep, is no advertisement
for the heroic life. His putative heroism is really butchery. Finally, consider Michael Walzer's reinterpretation of equality.[9]
Far from dictating a leveling world of relentless monotony,
equality can be cast as a celebration of human diversity, a refusal
to allow superiority in one context to have sway in other contexts. These cases are not arbitrary or magical feats of conceptual
legerdemain. Nor do they simply exploit a gap between means
and ends. Instead they weave together fact and value into a compelling vision of politics.

That means that we need not fear the failure of our everyday
concepts to conform to rigid, geometric standards of definition.
Our concepts are open-ended, fuzzy around the edges. Liberty,
equality, harm, coercion, self-interest, virtue, justice, human interests: all such concepts invite competing understandings.[10] Of
course we need to be clear in our use of them, but their pliancy is
precisely what allows us to embark on the process of piecemeal
revision. The endless re-sorting and shuffling that marks the ev-

---

scription" and "Deep Play: Notes on the Balinese Cockfight," both in his *The
Interpretation of Cultures* (New York: Basic Books, 1973), and "Blurred Genres,"
in his *Local Knowledge* (New York: Basic Books, 1983). Unhappily, no synthesis
is beckoning to reconcile these two traditions.

[8]See, for example, Alasdair MacIntyre, *After Virtue* (Notre Dame, Ind.:
University of Notre Dame Press, 1981); though note p. 201, where unaccount-
ably either "a *telos*—or . . . a variety of ends or goals" is needed. The latter candidate simply disappears.

[9]Michael Walzer, *Spheres of Justice* (New York: Basic Books, 1983).

[10]Along these lines, see Philippa Foot's reconceptualization of approval in
her "Approval and Disapproval," in *Law, Morality, and Society*, ed. P. M. S.
Hacker and J. Raz (Oxford: Clarendon, 1979), reprinted in her *Virtues and Vices*.
The point there is to transform approval from emotive yanking into a social
practice.

olution of our political theories, their progress as historical traditions, may be a sign of rationality. Social and political change, and pressures from all sorts of other contexts, strain our existing political views. Revision can be an ongoing creative attempt to solve the problems posed by change. Were our concepts fixed as firmly as Hobbes wished, we would not put a stop to civil war, and we would not finally enable someone to forge a scientific demonstration of our political principles. Instead we would be lost, unable to cope with a world of unending theoretical and institutional change.

For similar reasons, I want to suggest in all seriousness that we think of moral and political disagreement as a good thing, essential to continuing a constructive debate. Just as I argued that justification need not meet skeptical doubts, so I want to loosen the tie between justification and agreement. The point is familiar from Mill: a liberal democratic society can allow and even promote wide-ranging disagreement, and count on debate and experience to yield progress. A satisfactory justification need not put an end to all disagreements in politics; the drive to do so is drastically illiberal anyway. But our efforts at justification need not break down helplessly at the first mention of bitter, prolonged disagreement. Disagreement itself is only the beginning. We want to explore why people disagree, what reasons they offer to defend their views, how compelling in turn their reasons are. Some points of view may prove unjustifiable, the outcomes of ignorance, prejudice, political fancy. Others may prove finally less compelling than the alternatives. But not all views will necessarily fall to one shining alternative. Given our current theoretical development and the state of our politics, there may be really difficult choices, not just choices that seem difficult. Champions of different views may be able to marshal compelling arguments uniting far-flung considerations about politics, law, society, and morality. And we may be hard pressed at some point in time to offer a convincing judgment on which is most compelling. This facet of contextual justification is nothing but an acknowledgment of politics. Politics is not what we do in our lamentable ignorance, while waiting for philosophers finally to unveil the right view. A political theorist can pose issues profoundly, and we want a theory of justification that encourages us to break with received views by probing more deeply. It seems unreasonable, though, to require that political questions always have one right answer.

Given the rational ways our beliefs do change, the quest for timeless political principles is perverse. Contrast Athens, medieval Europe, Kwakiutl society, modern America, and some society of the future; think of both the extensive social, cultural, and political differences and the differences in knowledge. The former means that anything we can say now that holds in all times and places will be embarrassingly trivial. The latter means that anything we can say now may turn out to be wrong in the future. I take it political and epistemic change are enduring features of human life. Surely a theory of justification ought to acknowledge them.

A recognition of how different human societies can be should also defuse worries about relativism. Received moral and political views do indeed vary sharply across time and space, so sharply that no way of putting the point in our own language may adequately capture its ramifications. But it is premature to infer that whatever views a society holds must be right for them, or to hold that we are powerless to criticize other views. It is possible that others' views are right for them, and ours for us. Supporting that claim, though, will involve finding reasons to support their views in their context, as well as ours in our context. Disagreement here may run wider and deeper, even spectacularly so, but the argument seems basically the same as the argument within a society. Sometimes we can exploit existing common ground; sometimes we have to try to construct it or otherwise improvise; sometimes we start simply by trying to survey our own views from others' points of view. Instead of fearing deeply opposed views, we should welcome confronting them, as a chance to seriously scrutinize our own views.

In a contextual justification, is and ought, fact and value, are systematically interwoven. The alleged gap between is and ought becomes irrelevant. Instead of trying to hurdle the gap deductively, we can combine is and ought in theoretical accounts of where we stand. They may of course be disentangled, and that exercise will be important if someone claims to have indissolubly wedded them. But the is/ought gap is a useful skeptical weapon only against those trying to deduce ought from is. For those making no attempts to bridge the gap, a reminder that they have not deduced ought from is will come as no surprise—and no objection. To take a single example of welding the two: At the end of the *Protestant Ethic*, Weber turns from his officially scientific account of rationalization to bitterly decrying the iron cage we are caught in. Weber's own gloss on the move—"this brings us to the world of judgments of value and of faith, with which this purely historical discussion need not be burdened"[11]—unhappily summons up his misleading account of the way values are arbitrarily tacked on to facts. Should his analysis of rationalization be accurate, despair is the right tone to strike. No doubt the logical possibility of differing remains, as with Hare's eccentric wine taster. Again, though, it would take an interesting account actually to celebrate rationalization, instead of pointing out the conceivability of celebrating it.

I have no moral epistemology to offer here.[12] But morality, in a contextual view, is neither objective in the traditional sense nor mere personal preference. Moral principles are not lying out there like rocks, waiting for us to observe them, but that hardly makes them mere personal preference. Unlike preferences, our moral principles can be defended with reasons. (Compare the awkwardness of trying to explain why chocolate ice cream is better than vanilla.) And the reasons are not irreducibly arbitrary. The criteria here are contingent and historically shaped, and there will (appropriately) be debate over the best way to characterize morality. But such concepts as human interests must come up, and not just anything can count as a human interest. Criteria make reason-giving a rule-governed activity, and provided the

[11]Max Weber, *The Protestant Ethic and the Spirit of Capitalism*, trans. Talcott Parsons (New York: Scribner's, 1956), p. 182.
[12]Though I should note that I am wholly in sympathy with Morton White's attempt, in his *What Is and What Ought to Be Done* (New York: Oxford University Press, 1981), to extend the Duhem/Quine web-of-belief account to ethics. But White comes perilously close to embracing empirical and moral sense-data; note particularly pp. 27–28 on patches of color and the like, and pp. 40–47 on "the feeling of obligation." Here I would dissent.

rules make sense, our moral principles are more than mere personal preferences.

This last point should defuse a powerful motivation for supporting foundational views. As long as we think our only alternatives are foundationalism and mere personal preference, we will champion the former to make room for real arguments. But again this choice is a fallacy of false alternatives. The more interesting distinction—does the view allow for arguments or not?—actually crosscuts the distinction between foundations and preferences. For some variants of foundationalism, like intuitionism, do not allow for debate. Such variants are troubling in just the same way brute preferences are. To evaluate different views and see which are justified, we need debate; and we can have debate without either foundations or mere personal preference.

Nor do we need objective principles to rank one alternative as better than another. Aristotle's sentiments are on the mark: a carpenter can tell the difference between a well-made joint and a shabby one without any knowledge of the good. Likewise, moral and political debate need not rely on such lofty knowledge. Defensible criteria for evaluation are caught up in specific contexts. My by now tiresome point holds once again: these criteria too are subject to critical revision as we go. It helps, however, to keep things anchored in concrete contexts. We should be wary of an abstract approach to finding priority rules. We never have to ask such sweepingly abstract questions as, "Is equality more important than liberty?" Concepts like equality and liberty are enormous balloons containing all sorts of implications. More than a childish glee is gained by popping the balloons to see what is at stake in particular contexts. For example, we might hesitate to say anything about the relative worth of family pride and family prosperity as such. Yet given Smith's account of the workings of primogeniture, there pride properly gives way.

Similarly, many of the questions traditionally at the center of foundational theories are best approached indirectly. I doubt, for example, that anything illuminating can be said about deontology and teleology at an abstract level. The debates from ethics of this century have shown that we have commitments in both directions, but no one has shown which ones are correct. Nor is it clear how such a showing could be produced—or recognized.

Again, though, there is no need for despair. We need never ask such oddly abstract questions. In exploring concrete choices, we can deepen our understanding of deontology and teleology and see what is at stake in adopting each approach. The decisions we can make in concrete cases can be defensible without our first producing some overarching theory of the good and the right. We can develop priority rules out of the concrete cases, rules sensitive to the vicissitudes of context. Those rules can guide our reflections in new cases and ensure consistency. They are then useful, but they are not magic wands to wave at conflicting commitments.

All this talk about piecemeal revision of an interconnected web of beliefs points in a perfectly familiar direction. Contextual justification is a coherence view, of the sort championed by the pragmatists. Unless we are intent on making logical points, and so inviting charges of scholasticism, there is no good reason to dwell on the is/ought gap or other such philosophical divides. Instead we need to spin a compelling web, one that makes far-flung considerations cohere. We have and need no epistemically privileged starting point.

Why, then, call it contextual justification? Is this an attempt to avoid catching all the flak directed at coherence views by just changing the name? No; rather it is the beginning of a more detailed typology than foundational/coherence offers. Once we decide that justification can be a matter of coherence, we still need an account of what elements must cohere. One option, for example, is that our moral beliefs are justified once they are given a coherent structure. But this option confuses justification and explication. At the other extreme, the general thrust of a coherence view may well be to maximal coherence: the more elements, the merrier. Here justifying a political theory would involve situating it in a view that weaves it together with molecular physics, etymology, theories of tribal rituals, and so on. But this demand is surely excessive. No one can be conversant in all areas of human knowledge; and at any rate different realms of our beliefs have partial autonomy from others. Moving from teleology to mechanism affected political theory dramatically. Moving from contemporary physics to a unified field theory probably will not.

Again, we need an account of what elements must cohere. I

have chosen *contextual justification* to emphasize the central place of social and political facts. We can situate our discussion of these matters in a concrete social context. Hume's comment is perfect: "The question is not concerning any fine imaginary republic, of which a man forms a plan in his closet." Godwin's anarchism, Fourier's socialism, Morris's neighborly countryside: political theory has often been a freewheeling exploration of the realm of value, quite deliberately a departure from actuality. It is almost as if the more irrelevant the theory, the better. I do not mean to belittle the utopian mentality; nor do I wish to minimize the political possibilities of rebuking a grim present with delicious vistas of a dreamy future (or past, to take an elegiac approach). But the approach to political theory I am pursuing here is different. Like it or not, we are caught in the present, and we want to know what we ought to do. Our normative concerns thus redirect our attention to the descriptive project of understanding our society and its politics. What sort of world do we live in? What possibilities does it pose?

Contextual justifications draw, then, on a panoply of fields devoted to understanding the world: history, sociology, political science, economics, anthropology, and so on. But identifying possibilities is no cut-and-dried business. We have no social theory resembling classical mechanics, no way of ascertaining the outcomes of various policies. For that matter, identifying the relevant context is tricky and controversial business. Here again, our values play into our descriptions of the world—quite properly so. Is the welfare state best seen as an institutionalized commitment to equality? or a way of suppressing the contradictions of mass production and mass poverty, so enabling a newly flexible capitalism to survive? or a commendable but misguided step down the road to serfdom? or an unwarrantable intrusion on private property rights? or a bureaucratic nightmare demanding decentralization and participation?

In a contextualist view, these are appropriate terms of debate. But I can provide no neutral procedure for identifying "the right context." The question is already a political one, fraught with questions of fact and value, is and ought—hinging especially on theoretical issues in such descriptive fields as political sociology. The arguments go on and on, round and round. Provided progress is made, provided we move in a spiral instead of a circle, we have nothing to complain about.

Much the same view of these matters was taken by T. D. Weldon. His *Vocabulary of Politics* enjoyed some prestige during the 1950s but was vehemently criticized and then forgotten. Since I may seem to be dusting off the philosophical curios of yesteryear, it is incumbent on me either to defend Weldon or to distinguish my position from his. I mean to take both tacks, but first let me rehearse the apparent similarities.

Weldon argued, as I have, that political theories do not need foundations, that philosophical skepticism is what makes finding foundations seem important, that we can have meaningful arguments about what ought to be done without finding objective standards, that our political judgments are always open to criticism and revision, that the means/end scheme creates unnecessary worries about justifying ultimate ends, and that political theorists should wholeheartedly take up empirically oriented questions. Most strikingly, Weldon occasionally sounded a purely pragmatist tone in explaining how to handle skeptical doubts:

> I do not, therefore, mind saying that some political behaviour is obviously right, or wicked, or silly. "Obviously" is used here in the way in which it is correctly used of observations made by people with normal eyesight in a good light. In these conditions it is pointless to ask "How do you know that this pillar-box is red?" It seems to me equally pointless to ask "How do you know that it is wicked to torture human beings or animals?" But I think it is a mistake to use words like "intuition" or "self-evident" in describing such statements since these suggest that there is something odd about them which needs explanation. There is nothing odd about them at all. They are perfectly clear.[13]

All these views I am quite happy to endorse. Unfortunately,

[13]T. D. Weldon, *The Vocabulary of Politics* (Baltimore: Penguin, 1960), p. 16. Given his other views, Weldon could not here be embracing an intuitionist epistemology.

they were the proverbial baby thrown out with the bath water, for Weldon also treated the political theories he examined in an extraordinarily cavalier way; and his argument came in the wrappings of logical positivism and Wittgenstein's *Investigations*.[14] He wanted for instance to say that Marx and Engels advanced only a definition when they wrote that the state is a committee for managing the affairs of the bourgeoisie. (Not quite, indicatively, what they said.) But that claim is not empty word play; it is an answer to a substantial theoretical question—What is the state?—that I see no reason to discard. Nor need we think, as Weldon mischievously held, that words have real essences in order to think that the question is worth answering. Weldon suggested too that the question of whether one should obey the law is exhausted by a reminder that it is the law.[15] But doubt there seems not at all the skeptical kind, as we can verify by noting the people who have entertained it. Antigone, the Puritans, and Thoreau, for example, were hardly philosophical skeptics pursuing an academic exercise. And though Weldon bravely resisted the deflation of moral language to emotive gibbering, he did, I think, succumb to a more or less crass verificationism; he brandished the claim that our judgments must be empirically grounded to fight off all sorts of abstract normative questions as meaningless rubbish. Again, though, I do not want to say that such questions are meaningless. Rather I want to say that they are a waste of time. Political theorists need not spend their time constructing ideal utopias or refuting diligent skeptics.

Weldon's case has been buried under heaps of criticism and scorn. He sounded to many as though he wanted to say that political theory is a colossally absurd enterprise. We can, however; extract from Weldon a more subtle and I think powerful case that political theorists should redeploy their efforts. More historical and empirical work too can count as political theory. What else could we call works like Hume's *History*?

Doubtless there is much more to be said on all these issues and

[14]The influence of the latter is especially clear in Weldon, "Political Principles," in *Philosophy, Politics and Society*, ed. Peter Laslett, 1st ser. (Oxford: Basil Blackwell, 1967).
[15]See on both counts Weldon, *Vocabulary*, pp. 11–12, 18, 36–41, 57.

on scads of other issues I have left wholly untouched. But a conclusion is, after all, just that; I hope only to have sketched the basic structure of a theory of justification. Let me close by briefly considering two questions.

How is this a theory of justification at all? It tells us only to unite our moral and political views with social and political facts in a coherent theoretical structure. It doesn't begin to tell us how to do that; it leaves so very much wholly indeterminate. In discussing Hume and Smith, I have offered some examples and examined their particular structure. But my basic response is, quite so! Providing more of a general theory would be like trying to provide a recipe or algorithm for creativity. Political theory is like other fields: we must be opportunistic and grab progress where we can find it. It is reasonable to ask what a justification might look like. It is unreasonable to ask for detailed instructions on how to generate one. Is a foundationalist theory of justification any less a theory if it doesn't tell us where to find the first premises?

Next, why take contextual justification as a superior alternative to foundationalism? That is, what justifies adopting contextual justification? If the alternative being considered is foundationalism, the answer is easy. Contextual justifications may lack the appeal of foundational ones. They cannot promise to put an end to our political disagreements; nor can they demonstrate the objective rightness of our political commitments. But they sometimes succeed; and even when they fail, we learn much about society and politics in the process. Justifications of the sort Hume and Smith offer are addressed to political opponents, not philosophical skeptics. They deepen our understanding of our opponents' views, instead of simply ignoring them, or suggesting that they don't stand on secure foundations and so are too shaky to bother with. Hume's and Smith's work suggests forcefully that there is something eerily apolitical about foundational political theories. These considerations make it easy to justify the recommendation that we adopt a contextual strategy of justification. It's better than the foundational alternative.

BIBLIOGRAPHY OF
WORKS CITED

Ackrill, J. L. "Aristotle on *Eudaimonia*." *Proceedings of the British Academy* 60 (1974): 339–359.

Acton, H. B., ed. *The Philosophy of Punishment*. New York: St. Martin's Press, 1969.

Anscombe, G. E. M. "Modern Moral Philosophy." *Philosophy* 33 (January 1958): 1–19.

Austin, J. L. *How to Do Things with Words*. Ed. J. O. Urmson and Marina Sbisà. 2d ed. Cambridge, Mass.: Harvard University Press, 1977.

Axelrod, Robert. "The Emergence of Cooperation among Egoists." *American Political Science Review* 75 (June 1981): 306–318.

Axtell, James L., ed. *The Educational Writings of John Locke*. Cambridge: Cambridge University Press, 1968.

Ayers, M. R. "Mechanism, Superaddition, and the Proof of God's Existence in Locke's Essay." *Philosophical Review* 90 (April 1981): 208–251.

Barry, Brian. "Warrender and His Critics." *Philosophy* 43 (April 1968): 117–137.

Baumgardt, David. *Bentham and the Ethics of Today*. Princeton, N.J.: Princeton University Press, 1952.

Becker, Carl L. *Modern Democracy*. New Haven, Conn.: Yale University Press, 1942.

Bentham, Jeremy. *Deontology*. Ed. John Bowring. 2 vols. London, 1834.

————. *An Introduction to the Principles of Morals and Legislation.* Ed. J. H. Burns and H. L. A. Hart. London: Athlone Press, 1970.

————. *Works of Jeremy Bentham.* Ed. John Bowring. 11 vols. New York: Russell & Russell, 1962.

Borges, Jorge Luis, and Adolfo Bioy-Casares. *Chronicles of Bustos Domecq.* Trans. Norman Thomas di Giovanni. New York: Dutton, 1976.

Botwinick, Aryeh. "A Case for Hume's Nonutilitarianism." *Journal of the History of Philosophy* 15 (October 1977): 423–435.

Bradley, F. H. *Ethical Studies.* 2d ed. Oxford: Clarendon, 1967.

Brandt, Richard B. *Ethical Theory.* Englewood Cliffs, N.J.: Prentice-Hall, 1959.

————. *A Theory of the Good and the Right.* Oxford: Clarendon, 1979.

Brown, K. C., ed. *Hobbes Studies.* Oxford: Basil Blackwell, 1965.

Brown, Stuart M., Jr. "Hobbes: The Taylor Thesis." *Philosophical Review* 68 (July 1959): 303–323.

[Burnet, Thomas.] *Remarks upon an Essay concerning humane understanding.* London, 1697.

Campbell, Blair. "Prescription and Description in Political Thought: The Case for Hobbes." *American Political Science Review* 65 (June 1971): 376–388.

Catlin, George. *Thomas Hobbes as Philosopher, Publicist, and Man of Letters.* Oxford: Basil Blackwell, 1922.

Churchland, Paul M. *Scientific Realism and the Plasticity of Mind.* Cambridge: Cambridge University Press, 1979.

Cohen, Marshall, Thomas Nagel, and Thomas Scanlon, eds. *War and Moral Responsibility.* Princeton, N.J.: Princeton University Press, 1974.

Conniff, James. "Hume on Political Parties: The Case for Hume as a Whig." *Eighteenth-Century Studies* 12 (Winter 1978–79): 150–173.

Cooper, John M. *Reason and Human Good in Aristotle.* Cambridge, Mass.: Harvard University Press, 1975.

Cropsey, Joseph. *Polity and Economy: An Interpretation of the Principles of Adam Smith.* Westport, Conn.: Greenwood, 1977.

Daniels, Norman, ed. *Reading Rawls.* New York: Basic Books, n.d.

Davidson, Donald, J. C. C. McKinsey, and Patrick Suppes. "Outlines of a Formal Theory of Value, I." *Philosophy of Science* 22 (April 1955): 140–160.

Day, J. P. "Locke on Property." *Philosophical Quarterly* 16 (July 1966): 207–220.

Dick, Oliver Lawson, ed. *Aubrey's Brief Lives.* London: Secker and Warburg, 1950.

Dunn, John. "Consent in the Political Theory of John Locke." *Historical Journal* 10 (1967): 153–182.

———. "Justice and the Interpretation of Locke's Political Theory." *Political Studies* 18 (February 1968): 68–87.

———. *The Political Thought of John Locke.* Cambridge: Cambridge University Press, 1969.

Dworkin, Ronald. *Taking Rights Seriously.* Cambridge, Mass.: Harvard University Press, 1980.

Foot, Philippa. *Virtues and Vices and Other Essays in Moral Philosophy.* Berkeley: University of California Press, 1978.

Forbes, Duncan. *Hume's Philosophical Politics.* Cambridge: Cambridge University Press, 1975.

Fullinwider, Robert K. "Fanaticism and Hare's Moral Theory." *Ethics* 87 (January 1977): 165–173.

Gauthier, David. "David Hume, Contractarian." *Philosophical Review* 88 (January 1979): 3–38.

———. *The Logic of Leviathan.* Oxford: Clarendon, 1969.

———. "Thomas Hobbes: Moral Theorist." *Journal of Philosophy* 76 (October 1979): 547–559.

———. "Why Ought One Obey God? Reflections on Hobbes and Locke." *Canadian Journal of Philosophy* 7 (September 1977): 425–446.

Geertz, Clifford. *The Interpretation of Cultures.* New York: Basic Books, 1973.

———. *Local Knowledge.* New York: Basic Books, 1983.

Gettner, Alan. "Hare and Fanaticism." *Ethics* 87 (January 1977): 160–164.

Gutmann, Amy. *Liberal Equality.* Cambridge: Cambridge University Press, 1980.

Haakonssen, Knud. *The Science of a Legislator: The Natural Jurisprudence of David Hume and Adam Smith.* Cambridge: Cambridge University Press, 1981.

Hacker, P. M. S., and J. Raz, eds. *Law, Morality, and Society.* Oxford: Clarendon, 1979.

Hall, Everett W. "The 'Proof' of Utility in Bentham and Mill." *Ethics* 60 (October 1949): 1–18.

Hare, R. M. *Applications of Moral Philosophy.* Berkeley: University of California Press, 1973.

———. *Essays on the Moral Concepts.* Berkeley: University of California Press, 1973.

———. *Essays on Philosophical Method.* Berkeley: University of California Press, 1972.

————. *Freedom and Reason.* Oxford: Clarendon, 1963.

————. *The Language of Morals.* Oxford: Clarendon, 1952.

————. *Moral Thinking.* Oxford: Clarendon, 1981.

————. "The Promising Game." *Revue internationale de philosophie* 18 (1964): 398–412.

————. "Rawls' Theory of Justice." *Philosophical Quarterly* 23 (April 1973): 144–155; 23 (July 1973): 241–252.

————. "Rules of War and Moral Reasoning." *Philosophy & Public Affairs* 1 (Winter 1972): 166–181.

————. "What Is Wrong with Slavery." *Philosophy & Public Affairs* 8 (Winter 1979): 103–121.

————. "What Makes Choices Rational?" *Review of Metaphysics* 32 (June 1979): 623–637.

Harrison, Jonathan. *Hume's Moral Epistemology.* Oxford: Clarendon, 1976.

————. *Hume's Theory of Justice.* Oxford: Clarendon, 1981.

Harrod, R. F. "Utilitarianism Revised." *Mind* 45 (April 1936): 137–156.

Harsanyi, John C. "Cardinal Welfare, Individualistic Ethics, and Interpersonal Comparisons of Utility." *Journal of Political Economy* 63 (August 1955): 309–321.

————. *Essays on Ethics, Social Behavior, and Scientific Explanation.* Dordrecht, Holland: D. Reidel, 1976.

————. "Ethics in Terms of Hypothetical Imperatives." *Mind* 67 (July 1958): 305–316.

————. "Morality and the Theory of Rational Behavior." *Social Research* 44 (Winter 1977): 623–656.

————. "Nonlinear Social Welfare Functions: Do Welfare Economists Have a Special Exemption from Bayesian Rationality?" *Theory and Decision* 6 (August 1975): 311–332.

————. *Rational Behavior and Bargaining Equilibrium in Games and Social Situations.* Cambridge: Cambridge University Press, 1977.

Hart, H. L. A. *The Concept of Law.* Oxford: Clarendon, 1975.

Hirschman, Albert O. *Shifting Involvements.* Princeton, N.J.: Princeton University Press, 1982.

Hobbes, Thomas. *A Dialogue between a Philosopher and a Student of the Common Laws of England.* Ed. Joseph Cropsey. Chicago: University of Chicago Press, 1971.

————. *The Elements of Law Natural and Politic.* Ed. Ferdinand Tönnies. 2d ed. New York: Barnes & Noble, 1969.

————. *The English Works of Thomas Hobbes.* Ed. William Molesworth. 11 vols. London, 1839–1845.

————. *Hobbes's Leviathan*. With an essay by the late W. G. Pogson Smith. Oxford: Clarendon, 1967.

————. *Leviathan*. Ed. C. B. Macpherson. Harmondsworth: Penguin, 1968.

————. "The Life of Thomas Hobbes of Malmesbury." Trans. J. E. Parsons, Jr., and Whitney Blair. *Interpretation* 10 (January 1982): 1–7.

————. *Man and Citizen*. Ed. Bernard Gert. New York: Doubleday, 1972.

Hubin, D. Clayton. "The Scope of Justice." *Philosophy & Public Affairs* 9 (Fall 1979): 3–24.

Hudson, W. D., ed. *The Is-Ought Question*. New York: St. Martin's Press, 1969.

Hume, David. *Enquiries concerning Human Understanding and concerning the Principles of Morals*. Ed. L. A. Selby-Bigge. 3rd ed. rev. by P. H. Nidditch. Oxford: Clarendon, 1978.

————. *Essays: Moral, Political, and Literary*. Great Britain: Oxford University Press, 1974.

————. *History of England*. New ed. 6 vols. Boston: Little, Brown, 1872.

————. *The Letters of David Hume*. Ed. J. Y. T. Grieg. 2 vols. Oxford: Clarendon, 1969.

————. *The Natural History of Religion and Dialogues concerning Natural Religion*. Ed. A. Wayne Colver and John Valdimir Price. Oxford: Clarendon, 1976.

————. *A Treatise of Human Nature*. Ed. L. A. Selby-Bigge. 2d ed. rev. by P. H. Nidditch. Oxford: Clarendon, 1980.

Irwin, Terence. *Plato's Moral Theory*. Oxford: Clarendon, 1977.

James, William. *The Meaning of Truth*. Cambridge, Mass.: Harvard University Press, 1975.

————. *Pragmatism*. Cambridge, Mass.: Harvard University Press, 1975.

Jeffrey, Richard C. "On Interpersonal Utility Theory." *Journal of Philosophy* 68 (October 21, 1971): 647–656.

Jervis, Robert. "Cooperation under the Security Dilemma." *World Politics* 30 (January 1978): 167–214.

King, Lord. *The Life of John Locke*. London, 1829.

Kramnick, Isaac. *Bolingbroke and His Circle*. Cambridge, Mass.: Harvard University Press, 1968.

————. *The Rage of Edmund Burke*. New York: Basic Books, 1977.

Kretzmann, Norman. "Desire as Proof of Desirability." *Philosophical Quarterly* 8 (July 1958): 246–258.

Krook, Dorothea. "Thomas Hobbes's Doctrine of Meaning and Truth." *Philosophy* 31 (January 1956): 3–32.

Laslett, Peter, ed. *Philosophy, Politics and Society.* 1st ser. Oxford: Basil Blackwell, 1967.

Laslett, Peter, W. G. Runciman, and Quentin Skinner, eds. *Philosophy, Politics and Society.* 4th ser. London: Basil Blackwell, 1972.

Lewis, H. D., ed. *Contemporary British Philosophy.* 4th ser. London: Allen & Unwin, 1976.

Lively, Jack, and John Rees, eds. *Utilitarian Logic and Politics.* Oxford: Clarendon, 1978.

Locke, Don. "The Trivializability of Universalizability." *Philosophical Review* 77 (January 1968): 25–44.

Locke, John. *Epistola de Tolerantia: A Letter on Toleration.* Ed. Raymond Klibansky. Trans. J. W. Gough. Oxford: Clarendon, 1968.

———. *An Essay concerning Human Understanding.* Ed. Peter H. Nidditch. Clarendon ed. Oxford: Clarendon, 1979.

———. *Essays on the Law of Nature.* Ed. and trans. W. von Leyden. Oxford: Clarendon, 1954.

———. *Two Tracts on Government.* Ed. Philip Abrams. Cambridge: Cambridge University Press, 1967.

———. *Two Treatises of Government.* Ed. Peter Laslett. 2d ed. Cambridge: Cambridge University Press, 1970.

———. *The Works of John Locke.* 10 vols. London, 1823.

Luce, R. Duncan, and Howard Raiffa. *Games and Decisions.* New York: Wiley, 1957.

Lyons, David. *Forms and Limits of Utilitarianism.* Oxford: Clarendon, 1965.

———. *In the Interest of the Governed: A Study in Bentham's Philosophy of Utility and Law.* Oxford: Clarendon, 1973.

Lyons, William. "Against an Orthodox Interpretation of Hobbes." *Philosophical Quarterly* 27 (October 1977): 302–312.

MacIntyre, Alasdair. *After Virtue.* Notre Dame, Ind.: University of Notre Dame Press, 1981.

MacKay, Alfred F. "Interpersonal Comparisons." *Journal of Philosophy* 72 (October 2, 1975): 535–549.

Mackie, J. L. *The Cement of the Universe.* Oxford: Clarendon, 1980.

———. *Ethics: Inventing Right and Wrong.* Harmondsworth: Penguin, 1977.

———. *Hume's Moral Theory.* London: Routledge & Kegan Paul, 1980.

———. *The Miracle of Theism.* Oxford: Clarendon, 1982.

———. *Problems from Locke.* Oxford: Clarendon, 1976.

————. "Sidgwick's Pessimism." *Philosophical Quarterly* 26 (October 1976): 317–327.

McNeilly, F. S. *The Anatomy of Leviathan*. London: Macmillan, 1968.

Macpherson, C. B. *The Political Theory of Possessive Individualism*. Oxford: Clarendon, 1962.

————. "The Social Bearing of Locke's Political Theory." *Western Political Quarterly* 7 (March 1954): 1–22.

Mansfield, Harvey C., Jr. "Hobbes and the Science of Indirect Government." *American Political Science Review* 65 (March 1971): 97–110.

Martin, Rex. "A Defence of Mill's Qualitative Hedonism." *Philosophy* 47 (April 1972): 140–151.

Mill, John Stuart. *Autobiography and Literary Essays*. Ed. John M. Robson and Jack Stillinger. *Collected Works*. Vol. 1. Toronto: University of Toronto Press, 1981.

————. *Essays on Ethics, Religion, and Society*. Ed. J. M. Robson. *Collected Works*. Vol. 10. Toronto: University of Toronto Press, 1969.

————. *Essays on Politics and Society*. Ed. J. M. Robson. *Collected Works*. Vols. 18–19. Toronto: University of Toronto Press, 1977.

————. *A System of Logic*. Ed. J. M. Robson. *Collected Works*. Vols. 7–8. Toronto: University of Toronto Press, 1973.

Miller, David. *Philosophy and Ideology in Hume's Political Thought*. Oxford: Clarendon, 1981.

Mintz, Samuel. *The Hunting of Leviathan*. Cambridge: Cambridge University Press, 1962.

Moore, G. E. *Ethics*. New York: Oxford University Press, 1965.

————. *Principia Ethica*. Cambridge: Cambridge University Press, 1980.

Mossner, Ernest Campbell. *Adam Smith: The Biographical Approach*. Glasgow: University of Glasgow Press, 1969.

————. "Was Hume a Tory Historian? Facts and Reconsiderations." *Journal of the History of Ideas* 2 (April 1941): 225–236.

Nagel, Thomas. "Hobbes's Concept of Obligation." *Philosophical Review* 68 (January 1959): 68–83.

Narveson, Jan. "Liberalism, Utilitarianism, and Fanaticism: R. M. Hare Defended." *Ethics* 88 (April 1978): 250–259.

Nell, Onora. *Acting on Principle*. New York: Columbia University Press, 1975.

Nozick, Robert. *Anarchy, State, and Utopia*. New York: Basic Books, 1974.

————. *Philosophical Explanations*. Cambridge, Mass.: Harvard University Press, Belknap Press, 1981.

Oakeshott, Michael. *Hobbes on Civil Association*. Berkeley: University of California Press, 1975.

O'Meara, Dominic J., ed. *Studies in Aristotle*. Washington, D.C.: Catholic University of America Press, 1981.

Patrides, C. A., ed. *The Cambridge Platonists*. Cambridge, Mass.: Harvard University Press, 1970.

Pennock, J. Roland. "Hobbes's Confusing 'Clarity'—The Case of Liberty." *American Political Science Review* 54 (June 1960): 428–436.

Peters, Richard. *Hobbes*. Harmondsworth: Penguin, 1956.

Pitkin, Hanna. "Obligation and Consent." *American Political Science Review* 59 (December 1965): 990–999; 60 (March 1966): 39–56.

Plamenatz, John. "Mr. Warrender's Hobbes." *Political Studies* 5 (October 1957): 295–308.

Pocock, J. G. A. *The Ancient Constitution and the Feudal Law*. New York: Norton, 1967.

Popkin, Richard H. "A Note on the 'Proof' of Utility in J. S. Mill." *Ethics* 61 (October 1950): 66–68.

Price, John Valdimir. *The Ironic Hume*. Austin: University of Texas Press, 1965.

Price, Richard. *A Review of the Principal Questions in Morals*. Ed. D. D. Raphael. Oxford: Clarendon, 1974.

Prichard, H. A. "Does Moral Philosophy Rest on a Mistake?" *Mind* 21 (January 1912): 21–37.

———. *Moral Obligation*. Oxford: Clarendon, 1971.

Quinton, Anthony. "On Punishment." *Analysis* 14 (June 1954): 133–142.

Raphael, D. D. "Adam Smith and 'The Infection of David Hume's Society.'" *Journal of the History of Ideas* 30 (April–June 1969): 225–248.

———, ed. *British Moralists*. 2 vols. Oxford: Clarendon, 1969.

Rawls, John. *A Theory of Justice*. Cambridge, Mass.: Harvard University Press, Belknap Press, 1971.

———. "Two Concepts of Rules." *Philosophical Review* 64 (January 1955): 3–32.

Read, Herbert. *Anarchy and Order*. Boston: Beacon Press, 1971.

Riley, Patrick. *Will and Political Legitimacy*. Cambridge, Mass.: Harvard University Press, 1982.

Rorty, Amélie Oksenberg, ed. *Essays on Aristotle's Ethics*. Berkeley: University of California Press, 1980.

Rorty, Richard. *Philosophy and the Mirror of Nature*. Princeton, N.J.: Princeton University Press, 1979.

Rosenblum, Nancy. *Bentham's Theory of the Modern State*. Cambridge, Mass.: Harvard University Press, 1978.

Ross, W. D. *The Right and the Good*. Oxford: Clarendon, 1973.

Ryan, Alan, ed. *The Idea of Freedom*. Oxford: Oxford University Press, 1979.

Schelling, Thomas C. *Micromotives and Macrobehavior*. New York: Norton, 1978.

Schochet, Gordon J., ed. *Life, Liberty, and Property: Essays on Locke's Political Ideas*. Belmont, Calif.: Wadsworth, 1971.

Searle, John R. "How to Derive Ought from Is." *Philosophical Review* 73 (January 1964): 43–58.

Selby-Bigge, L. A., ed. *British Moralists*. 2 vols. Oxford, 1897.

Sidgwick, Henry. *Elements of Politics*. 4th ed. London: Macmillan, 1919.

———. "The Establishment of Ethical First Principles." *Mind* 4 (January 1879): 106–111.

———. *The Methods of Ethics*. 7th ed. Chicago: University of Chicago Press, 1962.

Simmons, A. John. *Moral Principles and Political Obligations*. Princeton, N.J.: Princeton University Press, 1979.

———. "The Principle of Fair Play." *Philosophy & Public Affairs* 8 (Summer 1979): 307–337.

———. "Tacit Consent and Political Obligation." *Philosophy & Public Affairs* 5 (Spring 1976): 274–291.

Singer, Peter. "Is Act-Utilitarianism Self-Defeating?" *Philosophical Review* 81 (January 1972): 94–104.

———. "Sidgwick and Reflective Equilibrium." *Monist* 58 (July 1974): 490–517.

Skinner, Andrew. "Natural History in the Age of Adam Smith." *Political Studies* 15 (February 1967): 32–48.

Skinner, Andrew, and Thomas Wilson, eds. *Essays on Adam Smith*. Oxford: Clarendon, 1975.

Smart, J. J. C., and Bernard Williams. *Utilitarianism: For and Against*. Cambridge: Cambridge University Press, 1973.

Smith, Adam. *The Correspondence of Adam Smith*. Ed. Ernest Campbell Mossner and Ian Simpson Ross. Glasgow ed. Oxford: Clarendon, 1977.

———. *Essays on Philosophical Subjects*. Ed. W. P. D. Wightman and J. C. Bryce. Glasgow ed. Oxford: Clarendon, 1980.

———. *An Inquiry into the Nature and Causes of the Wealth of Nations*. Ed. R. H. Campbell, A. S. Skinner, and W. B. Todd. Glasgow ed. 2 vols. Oxford: Clarendon, 1979.

———. *Lectures on Jurisprudence*. Ed. R. L. Meek, D. D. Raphael, and P. G. Stein. Glasgow ed. Oxford: Clarendon, 1978.

———. *Lectures on Rhetoric and Belles Lettres*. Ed. J. C. Bryce. Glasgow ed. Oxford: Clarendon, 1983.

———. *The Theory of Moral Sentiments*. Ed. D. D. Raphael and A. L. Macfie. Glasgow ed. Oxford: Clarendon, 1976.

Smith, Norman Kemp. *The Philosophy of David Hume*. London: Macmillan, 1941.

Spencer, Herbert. *Social Statics*. New York: Schalkenbach, 1970.

Spooner, Lysander. *No Treason*. Colorado Springs: Ralph Myles, 1973.

Spragens, Thomas A., Jr. *The Politics of Motion: The World of Thomas Hobbes*. Great Britain: University Press of Kentucky, 1973.

Strauss, Leo. *Natural Right and History*. Chicago: University of Chicago Press, 1953.

———. *The Political Philosophy of Hobbes*. Trans. Elsa M. Sinclair. Oxford: Clarendon, 1936.

Strauss, Leo, and Joseph Cropsey, eds. *History of Political Philosophy*. 2d ed. Chicago: Rand McNally College Publishing, 1972.

Taylor, A. E. "The Ethical Doctrine of Hobbes." *Philosophy* 13 (October 1938): 406–424.

[Trenchard, John, and Thomas Gordon.] *Cato's Letters*. 4 vols. London, 1724.

Tucker, Josiah. *A Treatise concerning Civil Government*. New York: Augustus M. Kelley, 1967.

Ullmann, Walter. *Medieval Political Thought*. Harmondsworth: Penguin, 1975.

von Leyden, W. "John Locke and Natural Law." *Philosophy* 31 (January 1956): 23–35.

Waldman, Theodore. "A Note on John Locke's Concept of Consent." *Ethics* 68 (October 1957): 45–50.

Waldner, Ilmar. "The Empirical Meaningfulness of Interpersonal Utility Comparisons." *Journal of Philosophy* 69 (February 24, 1972): 87–103.

Walzer, Michael. *Spheres of Justice*. New York: Basic Books, 1983.

Warrender, Howard. *The Political Philosophy of Hobbes*. Oxford: Clarendon, 1957.

Watkins, J. W. N. *Hobbes's System of Ideas*. London: Hutchinson University Library, 1965.

———. "Philosophy and Politics in Hobbes." *Philosophical Quarterly* 5 (April 1955): 125–146.

Weber, Max. *From Max Weber*. Trans. H. H. Gerth and C. Wright Mills. New York: Oxford University Press, 1980.

————. *The Protestant Ethic and the Spirit of Capitalism*. Trans. Talcott Parsons. New York: Scribner's, 1956.

Weinberger, J. "Hobbes's Doctrine of Method." *American Political Science Review* 69 (December 1975): 1336–1353.

Weldon, T. D. *The Vocabulary of Politics*. Baltimore: Penguin, 1960.

West, E. G. "Adam Smith's Two Views of the Division of Labour." *Economica* 31 (February 1964): 23–32.

West, Henry R. "Mill's Qualitative Hedonism." *Philosophy* 51 (January 1976): 97–101.

White, Morton. *What Is and What Ought to Be Done*. New York: Oxford University Press, 1981.

Williams, Michael. *Groundless Belief*. Oxford: Basil Blackwell, 1977.

Wills, Garry. *Explaining America*. Garden City, N.Y.: Doubleday, 1981.

Winch, Donald. *Adam Smith's Politics*. Cambridge: Cambridge University Press, 1979.

Wittgenstein, Ludwig. *On Certainty*. Ed. G. E. M. Anscombe and G. H. von Wright and trans. Denis Paul and G. E. M. Anscombe. New York: Harper & Row, 1976.

Wolff, Robert Paul. "A Critique and Reinterpretation of Marx's Labor Theory of Value." *Philosophy & Public Affairs* 10 (Spring 1981): 89–120.

————. *In Defense of Anarchism*. New York: Harper & Row, 1976.

Wolin, Sheldon. *Hobbes and the Epic Tradition of Political Theory*. Los Angeles: University of California Press, 1970.

————. "Hume and Conservatism." *American Political Science Review* 48 (December 1954): 999–1016.

————. *Politics and Vision*. Boston: Little, Brown, 1960.

Yolton, John W., ed. *John Locke: Problems and Perspectives*. Cambridge: Cambridge University Press, 1969.

INDEX

Library of Congress Cataloging in Publication Data

Herzog, Don, 1956–
  Without foundations.

  Bibliography: p.
  Includes index.
  1. Political science—History. 2. Justification (Theory of knowledge) I. Title.
JA83.H46   1985   320'.01   84-21492
ISBN 0-8014-1723-6 (alk. paper)